This We Believe *in Action*

Implementing Successful Middle Level Schools

National Middle School Association is dedicated to improving the educational experiences of young adolescents by providing vision, knowledge, and resources to all who serve them in order to develop healthy, productive, and ethical citizens.

This We Believe *in Action*

Implementing Successful Middle Level Schools

Thomas O. Erb, Editor

National Middle School Association

Westerville, Ohio

National Middle School Association
4151 Executive Parkway, Suite 300
Westerville, Ohio 43081
Telephone: (800) 528-NMSA
www.nmsa.org

Printed in the United States of America. Second Printing, October 2006

ISBN 10: 1-56090-190-X

ISBN 13: 978-1-56090-190-7

Library of Congress Cataloging-in-Publication Data

This we believe in action: implementing successful middle level schools/
Thomas O. Erb, editor
p. cm.
Includes bibliographical references.
ISBN 1-56090-190-X (pbk.)
1. Middle schools--United States. 2. Middle school education--United States. I. Erb, Thomas Owen

LB1623.5.T45 2005
373.23--dc22 2005054401

Contents

Foreword

Since its publication in 2001, *This We Believe . . . And Now We Must Act* has been a best seller for National Middle School Association. Based on the 1995 version of *This We Believe: Developmentally Responsive Middle Level Schools*, each chapter provided an in-depth analysis of one of the 12 characteristics that collectively comprise the middle school concept. Thousands of schools have used this book to help develop and improve their programs.

In 2003 *This We Believe: Successful Schools for Young Adolescents* extended and updated our understanding of this age group and appropriate schools for them. Now *This We Believe in Action* builds on this more complete vision. In addition, a DVD accompanies the book illustrating in dramatic fashion examples of each of the 14 characteristics in *This We Believe* (2003). This resource provides the best elaboration of what schools that are fully implementing the middle school concept are like. The authors deserve thanks for producing a resource relevant to the challenges middle level education faces in an age of accountability and school reform. After a preface and a foundational chapter, chapters 2-15 correspond in order to the characteristics outlined in *This We Believe*. The concluding chapter draws generalizations from efforts to implement the middle school concept over the last three decades while it challenges educators to renew their commitment for young adolescents.

The DVD is also organized according to the 14 characteristics described in *This We Believe*. The richness of each characteristic is illustrated through five or six video clips, each showing a cultural characteristic or middle grades practice in one of the schools. Every video clip weaves scenes, interviews, and narrative to highlight how that school implements practices to exploit its strengths and best meet its students' needs. Because schools are tapestries of culture and practices, some video clips appear in more than one place in the DVD.

We encourage you to carefully consider the complexity of each characteristic as described in *This We Believe* as you watch each video clip. Be prepared to look at each cultural characteristic or each practice from your own vantage and experience as well as from the different contexts of the schools presented in the DVD. While no short video clip can fully demonstrate the richness with which a school implements middle school practices and nurtures a healthy culture, it is our hope that each clip will unveil new perspectives to assist you in your work.

NMSA would like to especially thank students, parents, teachers, and administrators from the eight schools featured in the DVD. Being identified as models for everyone else is a large task, but one that these schools handle well.

- Central Middle School, Kansas City, Missouri
- Chapel Hill Middle School, Douglasville, Georgia
- Jefferson Middle School, Champaign, Illinois
- Maranacook Community Middle School, Readfield, Maine
- Scuola Vita Nuova, Kansas City, Missouri
- Thurgood Marshall Middle School, Chicago, Illinois
- Warsaw Middle School, Pittsfield, Maine
- William Thomas Middle School, American Falls, Idaho

As before, thanks to Tom Erb, editor of *Middle School Journal*, for his excellent work in editing *This We Believe in Action*. Thanks also to Mary Henton, NMSA's director of research and development, who saw this DVD project through from beginning to end. Eric Johnson of Educational Video Publishing in Yellow Springs, Ohio, was the director and oversaw the technical aspects of producing the DVD. His skill in capturing both the students and the educators as they were engaged in their ongoing—and unrehearsed—activities is very evident.

Since this resource, which combines text with a DVD is unique, a special section "How To Use This Resource" follows. You will want to read it so you will understand how the DVD and the text are related and how to get maximum benefit from both.

This We Believe in Action, the book and the DVD, will be useful to schools, parent groups, community organizations, and others who seek to understand and see successful middle level schools in action.

Sue Swaim
Executive Director
National Middle School Association

Preface

Educators, patrons, and policymakers continue the search for the best way to educate young adolescents. In the first decade of the 21st century, the federally-mandated No Child Left Behind (NCLB) initiative entered the scene and narrowed the focus of the curriculum to reading, writing and basic math, relegating core subjects such as social studies and science, not to mention electives and exploratory classes, to insignificant, or even nonexistent, roles in the curriculum. At the same time, many urban districts have confirmed that large middle schools, ones that have not implemented the middle school concept, are failing to provide a quality education to their young adolescents. Adding fuel to the debate about effective middle schools, these districts are often deciding to move their sixth, seventh, and eighth graders from separate middle grades schools into K-8 settings in an attempt to solve an educational problem by administrative action—and perhaps save money as well. The popular press is full of rhetoric focusing on one aspect of middle grades schooling or another, primarily on student achievement as determined by standardized tests.

Educators, patrons, and policymakers, therefore, would benefit from a comprehensive overview of what effective middle grades education ought to be like. Such a description can be found in this volume. In *This We Believe in Action*, 25 of the foremost authorities on the education of young adolescents describe those policies, programs, and practices that have shown themselves to be effective in developing the talents, skills, knowledge, and character of young adolescents. *This We Believe in Action* does not focus on just one or two aspects of education, but rather on the elements and educational objectives that make up a complete educational program for youngsters who are coming of age.

Along with reading and reflecting on these descriptions, readers can view examples of these programs and practices on the accompanying DVD. Shot on location in middle grades classrooms throughout the country, it provides vivid scenes showing the middle school concept in action. Marginal notes and photographs in the text relate to DVD segments. Viewing these scenes and listening to the commentary of practitioners can provide dramatic images of the types of educational experiences used daily to promote academic learning and personal growth among our youth in successful middle schools.

Leading the fight to improve the education of young adolescents in North America and throughout the world has been National Middle School Association (NMSA). Since its founding in 1973, the then fledgling association did much to promote middle grades education. However, just what constituted an effective middle school had not yet been clearly defined. Concerned about this situation, John Swaim, 1980 president of NMSA, appointed a committee to prepare a position paper that would consolidate in one concise statement a consensus view of the essential elements of middle school education as understood at that time.

After much deliberation and numerous drafts, a paper was submitted to the NMSA Board of Trustees for approval, and *This We Believe* was published in 1982. That first edition featuring ten essential elements of a "true" middle school became an influential standard.

Though NMSA has led the battle to provide for young adolescents the type of education they need, the association has not been without allies over the years. In the mid-1980s, the National Association of Secondary School Principals (NASSP) issued its succinct *An Agenda for Excellence at the Middle Level,* which outlined twelve dimensions of schooling necessary for excellence at the middle level. NASSP has continued its efforts to improve middle grades education over the past two decades and will publish *Breaking Ranks in the Middle: Strategies for Leading Middle Level Reform* in 2006.

The decade of the '80s also saw the publication of numerous tracts calling for educational reform in the United States. Prominent among these were John Goodlad's *A Place Called School* (1984), Ernest Boyer's *High School* (1983), Theodore Sizer's *Horace's Compromise* (1984), and the U.S. Department of Education's *A Nation at Risk* (1983). The focus of these reports, however, was primarily on secondary schools.

In the late 1980s, officials at the Carnegie Corporation in New York turned their attention to the plight of young adolescents in the United States. In 1987 the Carnegie Council on Adolescent Development, which counted among its members representatives from the fields of medicine, academia, public school education, state and national government, and the private sector, appointed a Task Force on the Education of Young Adolescents. In June 1989, after two years of studying the developmental needs of young adolescents and the conditions in the schools established to educate them, the task force issued its report, *Turning Points: Preparing American Youth for the 21st Century.* Decrying the fact that middle grades schools had been virtually ignored in the discussions of educational reform in the decade of the '80s, the task force found "a volatile mismatch . . . between the organization and curriculum of middle grades schools, and the intellectual, emotional, and interpersonal needs of young adolescents"

(p. 8). *Turning Points* set forth eight recommendations for transforming the education of young adolescents. This widely circulated volume was instrumental in putting middle level education on the national agenda.

As we entered the 1990s, increased attention continued to be placed on the education of young adolescents, with NMSA remaining at the forefront of this movement. Realizing that a decade had passed since the initial publication of *This We Believe,* NMSA reissued this seminal document in 1992 with very minor changes. However, as the knowledge base of middle grades education burgeoned in the '90s, it became clear that a more thorough reexamination of the vision of middle grades education was needed. In 1994, Sue Swaim, executive director of NMSA, appointed a committee to take a thorough look at middle grades education and revisit its position paper. In 1995 the committee issued a completely new document on the education of young adolescents under the expanded title of *This We Believe: Developmentally Responsive Middle Level Schools*. This time NMSA's statement defined six foundational characteristics of these developmentally responsive schools and six major elements or program components that together create the kind of schools young adolescents need and deserve.

In an attempt to expand on its recommendations and make them even more accessible and meaningful to citizens, educators, and policymakers around the world, NMSA published *This We Believe . . . And Now We Must Act* in 2001. Some writers of the 1995 version of *This We Believe* were joined by others to further elaborate on those 12 characteristics of effective middle grades schooling and how they might be made operative.

As NMSA revised *This We Believe* in the mid-1990s, a new group formed out of the work of a number of private foundations that had been advocating for whole-school reforms at the middle level. In 1997 the National Forum to Accelerate Middle-Grades Reform was created to stimulate this reform. The Forum is an alliance of more than 60 educators, researchers, national associations, and officers of professional organizations and foundations committed to promoting the academic performance and healthy development of young adolescents.

As the forces that affect middle grades education continued to press forth around the turn of the century, NMSA once again found the need to reexamine its position paper. The result was the 2003 publication of *This We Believe: Successful Schools for Young Adolescents*. Eight middle grades experts refined the 12 characteristics in the 1995 version of *This We Believe* and added two more. This current volume of *This We Believe in Action*, along with the accompanying DVD, is an effort to bring the ideas in *This We Believe* (2003) to life.

In preparation during the late 1990s was a follow-up document to *Turning Points*. Written by Anthony Jackson, who was the lead author of the

1989 report, and Gayle Davis, who had been actively involved in national middle grades reform efforts, *Turning Points 2000: Educating Adolescents in the 21st Century* (2000) refined and elaborated on the earlier Carnegie Corporation report. The two documents, *This We Believe in Action* and *Turning Points 2000,* provide thought-provoking guidance for those who are not satisfied with the state of education for young adolescents. Unlike standards documents issued by various groups in the '90s or the No Child Left Behind legislation, which focuses on a narrow curricular spectrum, *Turning Points 2000* and *This We Believe in Action* examine the entire school experience of young adolescents.

In addition to these two publications, one based on the work of the Carnegie Corporation and one from NMSA, readers will find *Breaking Ranks in the Middle* from NASSP to be released in early 2006, the National Forum's Comprehensive School Reform project, its Schools To Watch criteria, and its Vision Statement valuable guides to whole-school reform for middle grades education. These organizations and their publications "speak with one voice" to provide a vision, a conceptualization of schooling, descriptions of practice, and evidences of success to guide those who desire to improve the education of young adolescents. By so doing, these publications, alone among the mass of reports and mandates, will help educators sort out the conflicting recommendations in order to create a total-school program that is concurrently academically sound, developmentally responsive, and socially equitable.

Thomas O. Erb
September 2005
Westerville, Ohio

How To Use This Resource

This We Believe: Successful Schools for Young Adolescents identifies 14 characteristics that work in concert to create successful middle level schools. Eight of the characteristics are facets of the culture of such schools, and six are practices that thrive in positive school cultures. This classification helps us to understand the interconnectedness of all 14 characteristics, recognizing the influence each has on every other. In the dynamic atmosphere of successful schools, culture and practice work together; change one and every other aspect of a school is also changed.

The graphic that follows shows how the DVD is organized and illustrates the intricate and dynamic nature of the characteristics by spreading them across the design. Each characteristic is color-coded—blue for school practices, green for cultural characteristics.

The DVD and book are complementary and interdependent. The eight schools that have been filmed are different from those referenced by any chapter authors. Pictures and quotes from the DVD are placed in appropriate places with identifying information to assist the reader in reviewing the related video clip(s). Our goal is to offer many examples, in the hopes that you will find yourself and your students in these pages and images, and consider new possibilities.

There is no one right way to use this book and DVD. Use them in whatever way best fits your needs or interests. You may want to just explore the text and the DVD at first to get a feel for the materials, to view several segments on the DVD, or to see how pictures and quotes from the DVD relate to the text. You may want to choose a starting point based on

- Personal interest or known collective interest of the staff
- Priorities, highlighted in the school improvement plan
- Reaffirming and building on known strengths.

Following are some general suggestions for how to use *This We Believe in Action* for professional development:

- Staff members read a particular chapter prior to a meeting and together view and discuss one or more segments from the DVD on that characteristic. Over the course of future meetings, faculty reviews other segments.
- Use one or two segments from the DVD and then follow up by reading the appropriate chapter before gathering for discussion, either at the next meeting or in teams.
- Small teams meet for preliminary discussion around a specific characteristic, then view the DVD segments as a larger staff.
- Study the opening chapter on curriculum foundations and the concluding chapter on lessons learned; both warrant study and discussion, individually and by teams or faculty.
- To further enrich learning, use complementary material from *This We Believe: Successful Schools for Young Adolescents*. For example, staff members come to a session having read a chapter from *This We Believe in Action*. Staff views video segments as a group, then follows up by examining the corresponding material from *This We Believe: Successful Schools for Young Adolescents,* with subsequent discussion.

Readers should quickly recognize that *This We Believe in Action* is not just another good book worth reading; it is rather a unique and rich resource like no other, a very functional tool that can assist in implementing more fully the research-supported middle school concept. Exploit its manifold possibilities—for the sake of our young adolescents.

SUCCESSFUL MIDDLE SCHOOLS FOR YOUNG ADOLESCENTS

NMSA has identified 14 school practices and cultural characteristics that, when consistently integrated and fully implemented, create successful schools for young adolescents.

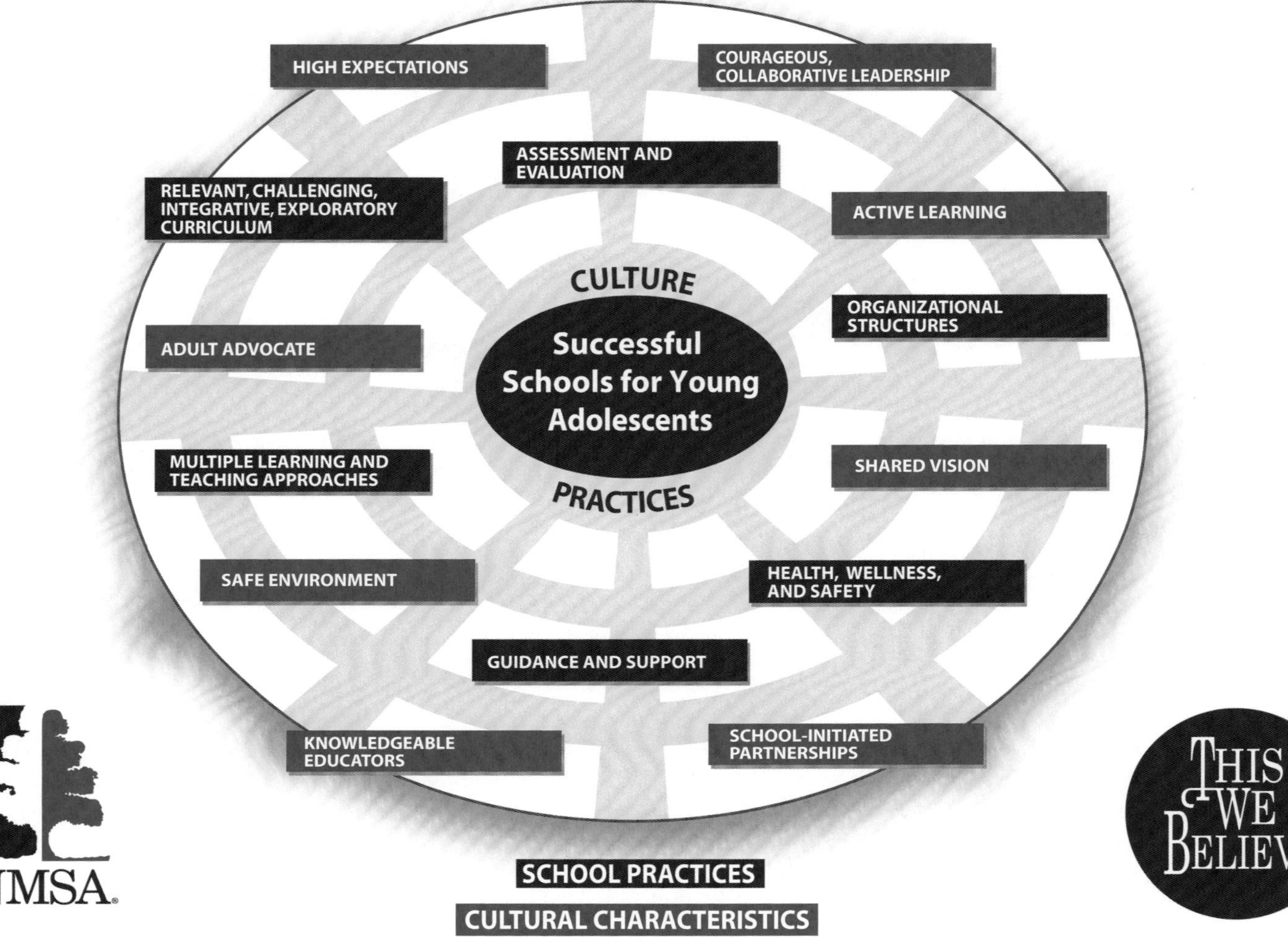

NMSA®

SCHOOL PRACTICES

CULTURAL CHARACTERISTICS

THIS WE BELIEVE

1

Enacting Comprehensive Middle Grades Reform

Thomas O. Erb

> ***Who is looking after the whole?*** *. . . Few sources were available that examined or related the several content areas to each other in relation to the whole child. . . . I would ask here that others think with me about why so few people seem to be thinking, studying, and writing about the nature of the whole curriculum at any level much less K-12. Is it because it has just grown too big for any one person or team of people to grasp? Are scholars and educators so specialized by training and interests that they do not wish to look beyond their specialty? Is there no demand from any quarter for consideration of the whole curriculum?*
>
> *Whatever the explanation for the current specialized subjects inquiry and standards-setting arrangements, I am not convinced that the learning experiences of children and youth are best served by this division of labor and the seeming lack of conversation about coherent curriculum models. Neither are the teachers and administrators well served who must negotiate alone among the subject areas' demands.* (Gehrke, 1997, p. 74)

At about the same time that Natalie Gehrke put her concerns into print, National Middle School Association (NMSA) responded with the publication of a new vision of what the middle level schooling of many diverse young adolescents should be like—*This We Believe: Developmentally Responsive Middle Level Schools* (1995). This position paper was a completely new version of the association's vision (NMSA, 1982, 1992). However, by the early 2000s, research on middle school reform coupled with changing conditions surrounding the education of young adolescents prompted NMSA (2003) to substantially revise its position paper, resulting in the publication of *This We Believe: Successful Schools for Young Adolescents*. This most recent version of *This We Believe* described eight general characteristics of successful schools for young adolescents and then delineated six practices or program components necessary to achieve schools that display the characteristics of successful middle grades schools.

The entire school—the total learning environment—was envisioned. Indeed, the learning experiences of students are not confined to their exposure to separate subject specialists. Students learn from the total experience of a school. As important as the standards movement has been over the past decade, this movement has really consisted of a series of parallel movements each operating in isolation from the others. The work of the math standards writers was not coordinated with the work of the English standards writers, nor that of the science standards writers, nor the social studies writers, who themselves competed with the separate standards writers in history, civics, and geography. As Gehrke lamented, who was looking at the whole picture of middle grades education—or the whole picture of education at any level for that matter?

There are now four sources that provide a comprehensive vision of schooling for the middle level. One is *Turning Points 2000: Educating Adolescents in the 21st Century* (Jackson & Davis, 2000) which follows up on a decade's research and practice subsequent to the original publication of *Turning Points: Preparing American Youth for the 21st Century* (Carnegie Council on Adolescent Development, 1989). *Turning Points 2000* was an attempt to not only refine the elements of an excellent and equitable education for young adolescents, but also to provide more concrete guidance for educators intent on improving their middle schools. Unlike the original *Turning Points,* which was more of a concept piece, *Turning Points 2000* built on a decade's worth of empirical research on middle grades reform to describe what works. In a similar manner, *This We Believe in Action*, a second source, makes more practical and accessible the basic concepts identified in the 2003 version of *This We Believe*.

In addition, following two decades of work stretching from *An Agenda for Excellence at the Middle Level* (NASSP, n.d. [1985]), the National Association of Secondary School Principals will publish *Breaking Ranks in the Middle* in 2006. Finally, the National Forum to Accelerate Middle-Grades Reform (www.mgforum.org) provides guidelines for total-school reform in the middle grades in its Vision

Statement, Criteria for Schools to Watch, and descriptions of seven Comprehensive School Reform initiatives (National Forum to Accelerate Middle-Grades Reform, 1998; 1994-2003a, 1994-2003b).

There are remarkable parallels between the design elements in *Turning Points 2000* and NMSA's characteristics of successful middle level schools as presented in *This We Believe* (NMSA, 2003). Though the wording varies, three of the *This We Believe* characteristics match three of the *Turning Points* design elements. In addition, whereas *Turning Points* combines curriculum and assessment into one element, *This We Believe* separates these into two characteristics. Next, *Turning Points* addresses instruction as one element, but *This We Believe* separates instruction into active engagement and multiple approaches. Then, *Turning Points* emphasizes the overarching need to organize human relationships for learning while *This We Believe* breaks this aspect of schooling into three separate parts: organizational structures (e. g., teaming), an adult advocate for every student, and multifaceted guidance and support services. Finally, while *Turning Points* describes the need for schools to be democratically governed, *This We Believe* focuses on four of the important characteristics of such governance: courageous, collaborative leadership; a shared vision; high expectations for all; and a supportive, safe school climate.

Figure 1 (p. 4) illustrates the points of agreement about the important elements that are required to ensure success for every student, but it is misleading when displayed as parallel lists. In fact, the design elements outlined in *Turning Points 2000* and the aspects of successful middle level schools from *This We Believe* would best be displayed as webs. Much as the human body consists of several separate systems working together (circulatory, reproductive, muscular, skeletal, nervous, digestive); these elements constitute a system of interrelated parts that function to support each other, ensuring success for every student.

One of the most powerful lessons of the past decade is how important it is to implement multiple elements of middle grades reform and maintain those elements over time in order to see positive outcomes for students. Which of the systems of the human body could you eliminate that would not be debilitating if not fatal? Amputations and organ removals may leave a body living, but they leave a body with diminished capacity. So it is with middle grades reform. Flexible structures and a shared vision are important, but without a challenging curriculum, varied learning approaches, and programs for health and wellness, the middle grades school will function with diminished capacity.

Without a challenging curriculum, varied learning approaches, and programs for health and wellness, the middle grades school will function with diminished capacity

FIGURE 1

Turning Points 2000 Compared to *This We Believe*

Turning Points Design Elements	*This We Believe* Characteristics
1. Teach a curriculum grounded in standards, relevant to adolescents' concerns, and based on how students learn best; and use a mix of assessment methods.	1. Curriculum that is relevant, challenging, integrative, and exploratory. 2. Assessment and evaluation that promote quality learning.
2. Use instructional methods that prepare all students to achieve high standards.	3. Multiple learning and teaching approaches that respond to their diversity. 4. Students and teachers engaged in active learning.
3. Organize relationships for learning.	5. Organizational structures that support meaningful relationships and learning. 6. An adult advocate for every student. 7. Multifaceted guidance and support services.
4. Govern democratically, involving all school staff members.	8. A shared vision that guides decisions. 9. Courageous, collaborative leadership. 10. High expectations for every member of the learning community. 11. An inviting, supportive, and safe environment.
5. Staff middle grades schools with teachers who are expert at teaching young adolescents and engage teachers in ongoing professional development.	12. Educators who value working with this age group and are prepared to do so.
6. Provide a safe and healthy school environment.	13. School-wide efforts that foster health, wellness, and safety.
7. Involve parents and communities in supporting student learning and healthy development.	14. School-initiated family and community partnerships.

A learning environment is very complex. Even attempting to understand just one element—curriculum—from the *Turning Points 2000-This We Believe* perspective is more complicated than it seems at first look. Curriculum for many is the set of standards or goals for student performance. However, this only describes what might be called the "planned" curriculum. Most of the standards statements issued in the 1990s are limited to this narrow view of curriculum. However, what educational planners and standards writers prescribe as the curriculum is not the same thing as what teachers actually teach. The taught or "enacted" curriculum is influenced by several factors. Furthermore, the curriculum teachers enact hardly represents the curriculum that students experience daily. If the goal is to ensure success for every student, we must be concerned about this "experienced" curriculum.

The curriculum experienced by students is a function of many factors, not all of which are under the control of teachers. Official goals and standards are just a part, and perhaps a small part, of the curricular experience of students. Schwab (1973), who believed that the school itself ought to be the center of practical inquiry, has provided perhaps the best model for understanding curriculum as experienced by students. In his model, subject matter is only one of four major components of curriculum. Students' learning is a social activity that takes place in a setting involving a lot more than a source of information such as a textbook. In addition to subject matter, Schwab includes the students themselves as well as teachers as elements in curriculum. Finally, he included what he called milieu, since learning always takes place in a larger societal context. For example, learning to achieve science standards in a multi-million-dollar physics lab tied to Web resources in Silicon Valley is not the same as it is in a converted gymnasium where there are not enough textbooks, no lab, and no computers in sight. Figure 2 makes evident the complexity associated with just one of the design elements in *Turning Points 2000* and *This We Believe*—the curriculum.

The curriculum that teachers enact hardly represents the curriculum that students experience daily. If the goal is to ensure success for every student, we must be concerned about this "experienced" curriculum.

These four elements, each with multiple characteristics, interact to produce the learning environment. Evertson, Weeks, and Randolph (1996) have expanded on this notion of curriculum to define a learning community as involving an interweaving of social and academic aspects. The social aspects include such things as students understanding how to respect and rely on others, how to listen, share, and be constructive partners and team members. Academic aspects include engaging students in problem solving, using multiple sources of information, and using computers effectively.

Figure 2

The Four Elements of Curriculum*

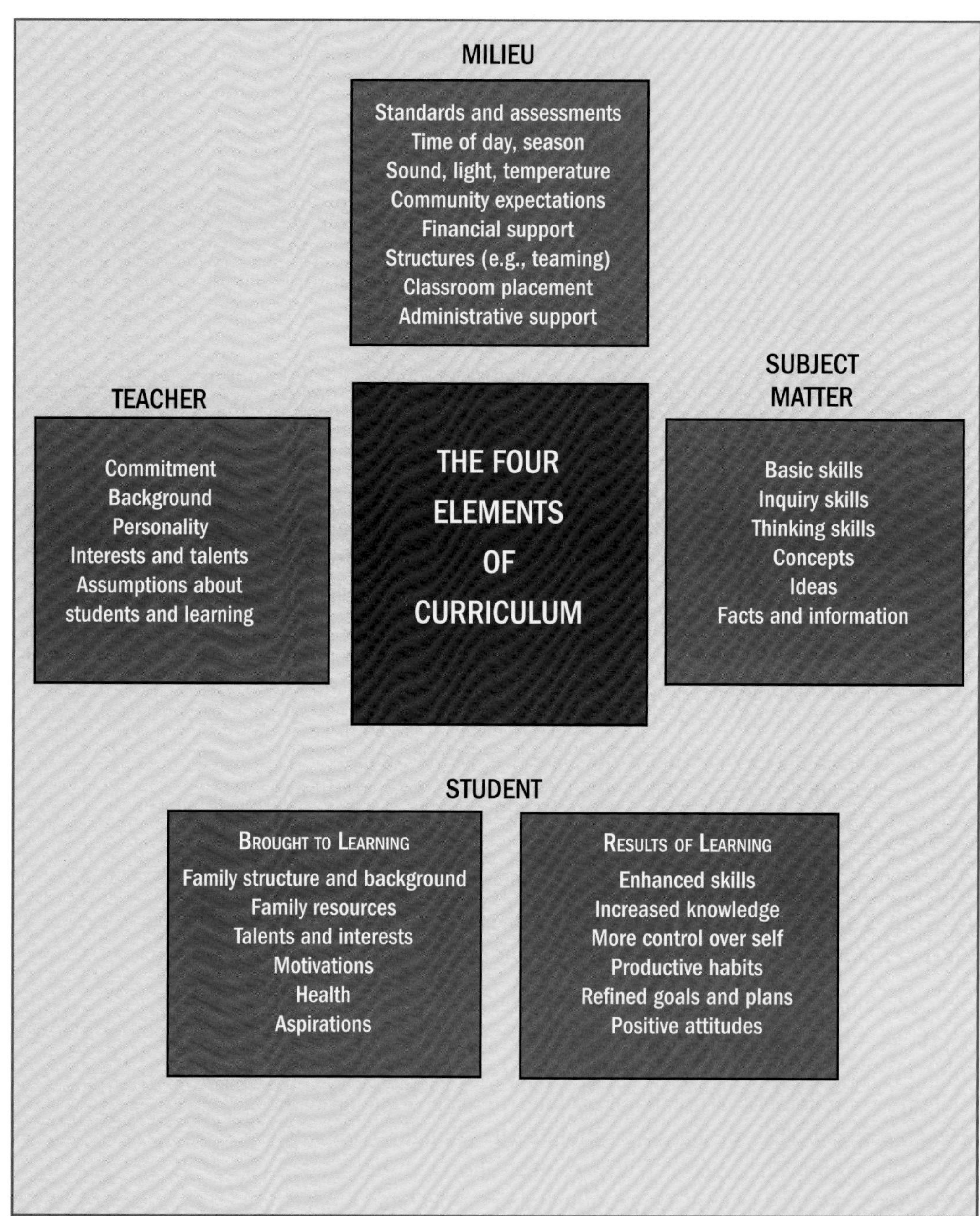

*Based on Schwab (1973)

The complex interplay of social and academic aspects or the interactions of the four elements posited by Schwab offer a caution to those who would reduce schooling to setting standards and assessing them with tests. Though it is tempting to say that standardized test scores are "the bottom line" in evaluating educational outcomes as profits are in evaluating corporate success, we must not forget that a child is not a "line item." While corporations might be able to fix profit margins by eliminating jobs, we should not fix test scores by eliminating children! Quite the opposite, schools cannot be fixed until every student is successful.

In 1994, a distinguished group of people concerned about the education of young adolescents, with support from several foundations, began meeting under the aegis of the National Forum to Accelerate Middle-Grades Reform. The forum developed a statement that envisioned high-performing middle grades schools as ones that are (1) academically excellent, (2) developmentally responsive, and (3) socially equitable. The forum's manifesto for middle grades reform was articulated in the article "Speaking with One Voice" (Lipsitz, Mizell, Jackson, & Austin, 1997). The essence of the ideas contained in *This We Believe* have the support of not only National Middle School Association, but this broader group concerned about the fate of young adolescents.

This We Believe in Action is designed to help middle level educators better understand the characteristics of successful middle level schools and faithfully implement them. Each of the 14 characteristics is fully described in its own chapter. In addition, DVD scenes with practitioner commentary help clarify these characteristics. The DVD shows how successful practices look, sound, and feel. Both the book and DVD chapters flesh out the vision embodied in the 2003 version of *This We Believe* and can be used as guides or examples to assist middle level educators in assessing the current state of their own reform, be that in K-8, 6-8, 7-12, or any other school configuration populated with young adolescents.

The National Forum to Accelerate Middle-Grades Reform has envisioned high-performing middle grades schools that are

- **academically excellent**
- **developmentally responsive**
- **socially equitable.**

Regardless of where a school may find itself, the explanations and descriptions in *This We Believe in Action* can help a faculty take the next steps toward a fuller implementation of a successful and truly developmentally responsive middle school. We know from research done on middle grades reform in the past decade (Anfara & Lipka, 2003; Backes, Ralston, & Ingwalson, 1999; Brown, Roney, & Anfara, 2003; Davis & Thompson, 2004; Erb & Stevenson, 1999a, 1999b; Felner, Jackson, Kasak, Mulhall, Brand, & Flowers, 1997; Flowers, Mertens, & Mulhall, 1999, 2000, 2003; Mertens & Flowers, 2003; Picucci, Brownson, Kahlert, & Sobel, 2004; Stevenson & Erb, 1998) that implementing more elements for longer periods of time does, with certainty, lead to improved student outcomes in all three major goal areas—academic, behavioral, and attitudinal. Yet most schools that are trying to systematically improve have only completed the first part of the journey.

In *Turning Points 2000: Educating Adolescents in the 21st Century* Jackson and Davis (2000) described the situation this way:

> However, as we have learned over the past ten years, it can be difficult for schools to maintain their momentum for improvement as they get closer to the heart of schooling —classroom practice. Some schools change structures but go no further. In a study of middle schools with excellent reputations, Jeannie Oakes found that, beneath an attractive surface of structural changes, classroom practices and climates had scarcely changed at all (Slavin, 1999, p. 3). Lipsitz, Mizell, Jackson, and Austin (1997, p. 535) recognized middle grades schools' success in making crucial structural changes, but also argued that it is time for schools to stop being merely "poised" for curricular and instructional change and to get on with the job. Without improvements in classroom practice, the goal of ensuring success for every student will remain out of reach. (pp. 28-29)

Jackson and Davis (2000), in the concluding chapter of *Turning Points 2000*, then, challenged educators with these words:

> This book should also stand as an affirmation of the enormous progress in improving middle grades education that has been made not only in the past decade but also since the "movement" began many years earlier. It is also a statement—not *to* the community of middle grades educators, but *from* that community—that we are not satisfied with the quality of middle grades education today and we know there is a great deal of difficult work ahead. And that we accept and are capable of meeting the challenges we face. (p. 219)

In *Breaking Ranks in the Middle,* NASSP's recommendations are clustered into three core areas:
- **collaborative leadership**
- **curriculum, instruction, and assessment**
- **personalization.**

This We Believe (NMSA, 2003) along with *Turning Points 2000* (Jackson & Davis, 2000), *Breaking Ranks in the Middle* (NASSP, in press), and the Web site of the National Forum to Accelerate Middle-Grades Reform (www.mgforum.org) are the sources currently available that address for educators and policymakers the whole picture regarding middle grades school improvement. The standards promulgated by the separate disciplinary associations—useful as they are—and the assessments produced by the several states—politically necessary as they are—provide only fragmented frameworks for reform. Neither provides specifics on how to construct learning environments that truly lead to student growth and development. *This We Believe in Action* joins this limited group of resources to provide a fleshed-out vision of middle grades reform. Keep in mind as you review this resource, while it is important to understand the dimensions of each characteristic of reform, it is also important to realize that these characteristics are not just additive; they are interactive. When these characteristics are implemented over long periods of time, you will be able to demonstrate to your school board, patrons, and politicians that your school has been able to positively influence student outcomes.

References

Anfara, V. A., Jr., & Lipka, R. P. (2003). Relating the middle school concept to student achievement. *Middle School Journal, 35*(1), 24-32.

Backes, J., Ralston, A., & Ingwalson, G. (1999). Middle level reform: The impact on student achievement. *Research in Middle Level Education Quarterly, 22*(3), 43-57.

Brown, K. M., Roney, K., & Anfara, V. A., Jr. (2003). Organizational health directly influences student performance at the middle level. *Middle School Journal, 34*(5), 5-15.

Carnegie Council on Adolescent Development. (1989). *Turning points: Preparing American youth for the 21st century*. New York: The Carnegie Corporation.

Davis, D. M., & Thompson, S. C. (2004). Creating high-performing middle schools in segregated settings: 50 years after Brown. *Middle School Journal, 36*(2), 4-12.

Erb, T. O., & Stevenson, C. (1999a). What difference does teaming make? *Middle School Journal, 30*(3), 47-50.

Erb, T. O., & Stevenson, C. (1999b). Fostering growth inducing environments for student success. *Middle School Journal, 30*(4), 63-67.

Evertson, C. M., Weeks, K. W., & Randolph, C. H. (1996, August). *Creating learning-centered classrooms: Implications for classroom management.* Paper written for the Blue Ribbon Schools. Washington, DC.: U.S. Office of Research and Education.

Felner, R. D., Jackson, A. W., Kasak, D., Mulhall, P., Brand, S., & Flowers, N. (1997). The impact of school reform for the middle years: A longitudinal study of a network engaged in Turning Points-based comprehensive school transformation. *Phi Delta Kappan, 78*, 528-532, 541-550.

Flowers, N., Mertens, S. B., & Mulhall, P. F. (1999). The impact of teaming: Five research-based outcomes. *Middle School Journal, 31*(2), 57-60.

Flowers, N., Mertens, S. B., & Mulhall, P. F. (2000). What makes interdisciplinary teams effective? *Middle School Journal, 31*(4), 53-56.

Flowers, H., Mertens, S. B., & Mulhall, P. F. (2003). Lessons learned from more than a decade of middle grades research. *Middle School Journal, 35*(2), 55-59.

Gehrke, N. J. (1997, August). *In search of the better school curriculum.* Paper written for the Blue Ribbon Schools. Washington, DC: U.S. Office of Research and Education.

Jackson, A. W., & Davis, G. A. (2000). *Turning points 2000: Educating adolescents in the 21st century.* New York & Westerville, OH: Teachers College Press & National Middle School Association.

Lipsitz, J., Mizell, M. H., Jackson, A. W., & Austin, L. M. (1997). Speaking with one voice: A manifesto for middle-grades reform. *Phi Delta Kappan, 78,* 533-540.

Mertens, S. B., & Flowers, N. (2003). Middle school practices improve student achievement in high poverty schools. *Middle School Journal, 35*(1), 33-45.

National Association of Secondary School Principals (n.d. [1985]). *An agenda for excellence at the middle level.* Reston, VA: Author.

National Association of Secondary School Principals. (in press). *Breaking ranks in the middle: Strategies for leading middle level reform.* Reston, VA: Author.

National Forum to Accelerate Middle-Grades Reform. (1998). *Vision Statement.* Retrieved July 23, 2005, from http://www.mgforum.org/about/vision.asp

National Forum to Accelerate Middle-Grades Reform. (1994-2003a). *Criteria for Schools to Watch.* Retrieved July 23, 2005 from http://www.mgforum.org/Improvingschools/STW/STWcriteria.asp

National Forum to Accelerate Middle-Grades Reform. (1994-2003b). *Comprehensive School Reform Models.* Retrieved July 23, 2005, from http://www.mgforum.org/Improvingschools/CSR/csr_intro.htm

National Middle School Association. (1982). *This we believe.* Columbus, OH: Author.

National Middle School Association. (1992). *This we believe.* Columbus, OH: Author.

National Middle School Association. (1995). *This we believe: Developmentally responsive middle level schools.* Columbus, OH: Author.

National Middle School Association. (2003). *This we believe: Successful schools for young adolescents.* Westerville, OH: Author.

Picucci, A. C., Brownson, A., Kahlert, R., & Sobel, A. (2004). Middle school concept helps high-poverty schools become high-performing schools. *Middle School Journal, 36*(1), 4-11.

Schwab, J. J. (1973). The practical 3: Translation into curriculum. *School Review, 81,* 501-522.

Slavin, R. E. (1999). *Technical proposal: Design, development, and testing of comprehensive school reform models.* Baltimore: Success for All Foundation.

Stevenson, C., & Erb, T. O. (1998). How implementing Turning Points improves student outcomes. *Middle School Journal, 30*(1), 49-52.

2

Educators Who Value Working With This Age Group and Are Prepared To Do So

C. Kenneth McEwin
Thomas S. Dickinson

The most successful middle level teachers value working with young adolescents and make conscious choices to teach them. One of the most important qualities middle level teachers bring to their classrooms is their commitment to the young adolescents they teach. Without this commitment there is little substantive progress for either party, and teaching and learning is reduced to some lifeless and mechanical act, the consequences of which fall most heavily on the young adolescents, their families, and ultimately the nation. Teachers who are committed to working with young adolescents, however, breathe life and opportunity into their classrooms and into the future of the youth with whom they work.

The Duality of Commitment

"Educators who value working with this age group" (National Middle School Association, 2003, p. 9) are characterized by two equally important aspects of their commitment:

1. The provision of "significant academic learning experiences" (p. 9) for young adolescent students, learning experiences that are characterized by rigorous content and high expectations for all learners.

2. The provision of developmentally appropriate classrooms, schools, programs, and practices for all young adolescent students within the learning community.

The presence of significant learning experiences (rigorous content and high expectations) within a developmentally appropriate, safe, and supportive school context is an identifiable characteristic of developmentally responsive middle level schools. And while *This We Believe: Successful Schools for Young Adolescents* (NMSA, 2003) is a policy document that establishes broad goals for the profession, these twin aspects of commitment are attainable, regardless of the specific characteristics of individual school communities, or the overall grade configuration of the building.

This duality of commitment (significant academic learning and developmentally appropriate context) has numerous implications for the roles of middle level teachers. Teachers of young adolescents committed to the students they teach perform at least five specific roles: (a) student advocate, (b) role model, (c) supporter of diversity, (d) collaborator, and (e) lifelong learner. As well, the duality of commitment has implications for the professional preparation of middle level teachers and for their continuing professional development focusing on refining and extending their knowledge, dispositions, and skills to perform these and related roles successfully.

The role of advocate

Being a student advocate is a complex, but essential, responsibility at the middle level. This advocacy has two fundamental audiences—a readily recognizable external audience (e.g., parents, colleagues, administrators, and the wider community) and a less-well acknowledged internal audience made up of the young adolescents themselves. The role of student advocate revolves around the dual aspects of commitment: advocating for developmentally appropriate programs and practices within classrooms and schools and advocating for learning experiences that are "rich" (Arnold, 1993) in all their curricular and instructional aspects.

Committed middle level educators help educate family members and others about the developmental realities of early adolescence while exploding some of the negative myths frequently associated with the age group.

To advocate for young adolescents to external audiences calls for depth of knowledge about "the developmental uniqueness of young adolescents" (NMSA, 2003, p. 9). Committed middle level educators use their position to help educate family members and others about the developmental realities of early adolescence while exploding some of the negative myths frequently associated with the age group.

Middle level teachers who are committed to working with young adolescents advocate for realistic assessments of where individuals are and where they are going. These teachers value teaching the age group as their students learn new skills, chart new avenues of growth, and confront the challenges and promises of life.

Role model

Teaching under relentless scrutiny is a fact of life for middle level teachers. Acting as a positive role model for youth during such examinations brings with it moral obligations. Being an appropriate role model takes several complementary avenues at the middle level. The most visible is to model behaviors for young adolescent students.

The second aspect of being a role model for young adolescents involves modeling relationships. Young adolescents learn how to affiliate with others by observing both peers and adults. The ways teachers cooperate with colleagues, their appreciation of differences, and their dispositions towards others speak volumes, often more powerfully than the planned curriculum.

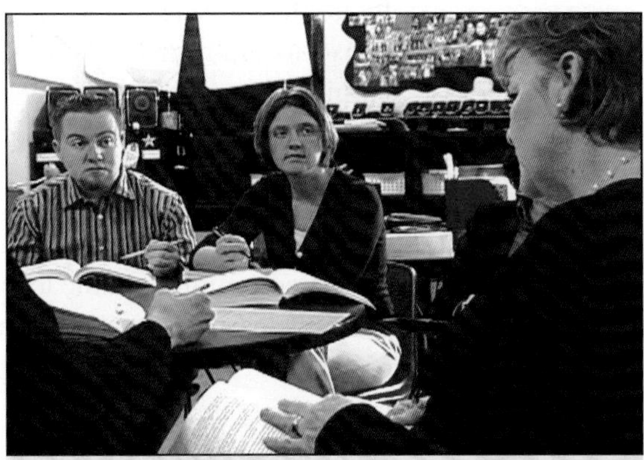

Meeting in weekly study groups, teachers model lifelong learning and cooperation.
— DVD, Scuola Vita Nuova, "Book Studies"

The third aspect of modeling for young adolescents involves a relatively new phase of teacher responsibility—modeling healthy development. In an age when risk factors abound for youth, the approach that teachers take to their own health and safety has acquired increased significance.

Supporter of diversity

Teachers who value working with young adolescents are marked by their dedication and respect for the diversity inherent in middle level classrooms. This implies both the traditional definitions of diversity (e.g., race, ethnicity, gender) and other facets such as developmental differences, learning styles, and exceptionalities. By being supporters of diversity in the classroom, committed middle level teachers embrace rather than overlook the needs, interests, and special abilities of their students.

Collaborator

Being a committed middle level teacher means that professionally one is connected to members of the interdisciplinary team, to other teachers and teams throughout the building, and to administrators and support staff. Being a successful middle level teacher is a role that is characterized by a series of nested relationships.

Within individual classrooms there are connections to the team. These connections are about the students the team has in common, the intersections that characterize the team's curriculum, and the instructional practices that support and sustain learning among students. Collaborating with colleagues calls for cooperation for student purposes—high achievement for all. But collaboration goes beyond the team because middle level teachers who value working with their students have an obligation to be part of programs at the grade and school level, whether or not these programs involve advisories, intramurals, clubs, or other aspects of the middle level learning environment.

Lifelong learner

A committed middle level teacher is a model of lifelong learning. This learning is widespread and continuous: new teaching materials and teaching techniques, new and emerging technologies that have impact in the classroom, and new subject matter knowledge. As the knowledge explosion continues, committed middle level teachers, rather than complaining and acting like Luddites, read, experiment, travel, and study. Their lifelong learning stance takes them to seminars, formal coursework, travel, focused training and apprenticeships, adventures in individual study, and other learning opportunities.

Lifelong learners know that moving beyond their own immediate comfort zones as learners is important for themselves and their students.

Lifelong learners know that moving beyond their own immediate comfort zones as learners is important for themselves and their students. They also know that one does not just learn "things" but also develops an appreciation of the what and how behind the learning. They develop an understanding of how truly difficult some aspects of learning are and what it means to try and fail as well as to try and succeed.

Specialized Middle Level Teacher Preparation

Making conscious decisions to teach at the middle level and being dedicated to teaching young adolescents are very important beginning points for those entering the profession. It seems logical that these dedicated professionals would begin their careers well-equipped with the specialized knowledge, skills, and dispositions needed to be successful in the challenging and rewarding world of teaching young adolescents. However, many prospective teachers who make decisions to teach young adolescents find that specialized professional preparation programs that focus on teaching 10- to 15-year-olds are unavailable in their states. Further, they frequently learn that if they wish to have a career in middle level education, they must major in elementary education or in a content area in secondary education. Those who are not discouraged and select one of these options typically spend the vast majority of their professional preparation learning about teaching young children or focusing on teaching one or two subjects in senior high schools. Upon completion of these programs, they are awarded licensure to teach in the elementary and middle grades (K-8) or the middle and senior high school grades (6-12) after receiving little or no specialized professional preparation for teaching young adolescents.

The fact that these preparation programs can be completed and licensure awarded without candidates' receiving specific preparation for teaching young adolescents or completing middle level field experiences serves as an example of the malpractice in which many teacher preparation programs and licensure agencies or professional practice boards are currently engaged. They are not promoting and protecting the rights of young adolescents by guaranteeing that middle level teachers have demonstrated the specialized knowledge, skills, and dispositions needed to teach effectively. In many states, the message from teacher preparation institutions, licensure agencies and boards, and even the profession itself seems to be, "Anyone with any kind of professional teacher preparation can teach at the middle level. There is no specialization needed." As has been the case historically, the education and welfare of young adolescents and their teachers have been largely

All teachers at William Thomas Middle School receive instruction and coaching in reading and writing across the curriculum.
— DVD, William Thomas MS, "School-Wide Literacy"

ignored and forgotten in the name of politics and administrative convenience (McEwin, Dickinson, & Smith, 2003; 2004).

One major result of the unfortunate situation just discussed is that many middle level teachers, and other educators, work intensely in well-intentioned ways that damage rather than enhance the quality of learning opportunities provided for young adolescents. This lack of match between intentions and appropriate behaviors rarely results from malice or a lack of caring, but rather is virtually always the result of a lack of knowledge that should have been a crucial part of professional preparation programs that focused directly and exclusively on teaching young adolescents.

Consensus on the need for specialized programs

There is a growing consensus regarding the importance of and need for specialized middle level teacher preparation.

There is a growing consensus regarding the importance of and need for specialized middle level teacher preparation. Advocacy for comprehensive, specialized middle level courses, field experiences, and other program components that are considered essential for effective middle level teacher preparation is increasingly emerging from teacher educators, foundations, professional organizations, and other sources. There is also increasing support from middle level teachers for comprehensive, specialized middle level teacher preparation (Arth, Lounsbury, McEwin, & Swaim, 1995; Jackson & Davis, 2000; Jackson, Andrews, Holland, & Pardini, 2004; McEwin, Dickinson, Erb, & Scales, 1995; McEwin, Dickinson, & Hamilton, 2000; McEwin, Dickinson, & Smith, 2003, 2004; National Forum to Accelerate Middle-Grades Reform, 2002; NMSA, n.d.; NMSA, 2003; Scales & McEwin, 1994).

Essential program components

A solid consensus about the essential programmatic components that should be included in specialized middle level teacher preparation has also emerged (Cooney, 2000; Jackson & Davis, 2000; Ference & McDowell, 2005; McEwin, Dickinson, & Smith, 2003, 2004; National Forum to Accelerate to Middle-Grades Reform, 2002; National Middle School Association, n.d.). Furthermore, middle level teacher preparation standards, written by National Middle School Association and approved by the National Council for Accreditation of Teacher Education (NCATE), that reflect these essential components are widely used throughout the nation (NMSA, 2001).

The following components represent those that are unique to the middle level program and do not include other elements that are essential to all teacher preparation programs (e.g., diversity, instructional technology). These components are: (a) a comprehensive study of young adolescent development, middle level philosophy and organization, and middle level curriculum; (b) an intensive focus on planning, teaching, and assessment using developmentally and culturally responsive practices; (c) early and continuing field experiences in a variety of good middle level settings; (d) study and practice in the collaborative role of middle level teachers in working with colleagues, families, and community members; (e) preparation in two broad teaching fields; and, (f) a collaborative teacher preparation partnership between faculty at middle level schools and university-based middle level teacher educators.

Looking to the future

In large measure, the future success of young adolescents depends greatly upon the dedication and hard work of teachers and other educators who choose to teach them and serve them in other important ways. Deliberate career choices and dedicated work alone, however, are not sufficient to guarantee that all young adolescents will have opportunities to achieve their full potential. Teachers and other educators need access to professional preparation programs that provide them with the specialized knowledge, skills, and dispositions needed to be highly accomplished in their practice.

Teachers and other educators need access to preparation programs that provide them with specialized knowledge, skills, and dispositions needed to be highly accomplished in their practice.

Agreeing that the specialized professional preparation of middle level educators is an important idea is not enough. Courageous steps need to be taken by middle level educators, professional associations, accreditation agencies, and other stakeholders to develop and support specialized middle level professional preparation programs and the middle level licensure that support and sustain them. Only when action is taken to significantly improve the professional preparation of all who teach and work with young adolescents will middle level schooling universally provide the high quality educational opportunities needed to assure successful futures for our nation's youth.

References

Arnold, J. (1993). A curriculum to empower young adolescents. *Midpoints Occasional Paper 4*(1). Columbus, OH: National Middle School Association.

Arth, A. A., Lounsbury, J. H., McEwin, C. K., & Swaim, J. H. (1995). *Middle level teachers: Portraits of excellence*. Columbus, OH: National Middle School Association and Reston VA: National Association of Secondary School Principals.

Cooney, S. (2000). *A middle grades message: A well-qualified teacher in every classroom matters*. Atlanta, GA: Southern Regional Education Board.

Ference, R., & McDowell, J. (2005). Essential elements of specialized middle level teacher preparation programs. *Middle School Journal, 36*(3), 4-10.

Jackson, A. W., Andrews, P. G, Holland, H., & Pardini, P. (2004). *Making the most of middle school: A field guide for parents and others*. New York: Teachers College Press.

Jackson, A. W., & Davis, G. (2000). *Turning points 2000: Educating adolescents in the 21st century.* New York: Teachers College Press and Westerville, OH: National Middle School Association.

McEwin, C. K., Dickinson, T. S., Erb, T. O., & Scales, P. C. (1995). *A vision of excellence: Organizing principles for middle grades teacher preparation*. Columbus, OH: National Middle School Association.

McEwin, C. K., Dickinson, T. S., & Hamilton, H. (2000). National board certified teachers' views regarding specialized middle level teacher preparation. *The Clearing House, 73*(4), 211-213.

McEwin, C. K., Dickinson, T. S., & Smith, T. W. (2003). Middle level teacher preparation: Status, progress, and challenges. In P. G. Andrews and V. A. Anfara (Eds.), *Leaders for a movement: Professional preparation and development of middle level teachers and administrators* (pp. 3-26). Greenwich, CT: Information Age Publishing.

McEwin, C. K., Dickinson, T. S., & Smith, T. W. (2004). The role of teacher preparation, licensure, and retention in creating high performing middle schools. In S. Thompson (Ed.), *Creating high performing middle schools: A focus on policy issues* (pp. 109-129). Greenwich, CT: Information Age Publishing.

National Forum to Accelerate Middle-Grades Reform. (2004). *Policy statement: Teacher preparation, licensure, and recruitment*. Newton, MA: Education Development Center. Retrieved February 12, 2005, from http://www.mgforum.org

National Middle School Association (n.d.). *National Middle School Association's position statement on professional preparation of middle level teachers*. Westerville, OH: Author. Retrieved February 12, 2005, from http://www.nmsa.org

National Middle School Association. (2003). *This we believe: Successful schools for young adolescents*. Westerville, OH: Author.

National Middle School Association/National Council for Accreditation of Teacher Education-Approved middle level teacher preparation standards. (2001). Westerville, OH: Author. Retrieved February 14, 2005, from http://www.nmsa.org

Scales, P. C., & McEwin, C. K. (1994). *Growing pains: The making of America's middle school teachers*. Columbus, OH: National Middle School Association.

Courageous, Collaborative Leadership

Patti Kinney
Linda Robinson

It is fitting that the word courage is derived from the French word *coeur,* meaning heart; for at the very center of every successful school for young adolescents beats the heart of a courageous, collaborative leader. And while courageous, collaborative leadership is but one of the characteristics described in *This We Believe: Successful Schools for Young Adolescents* (National Middle School Association, 2003), it is pivotal as a school weaves together all fourteen characteristics into the tapestry of a high-performing middle school.

Being an effective middle school leader is not for the fainthearted. One must be a master juggler with the ability to work with people, solve problems, listen, communicate, organize, laugh at oneself, and be patient—just to name a few essential qualities. It also requires being an instructional leader with the best interests of students at heart; establishing a culture where teachers, parents, community members, and students work together to turn a shared vision of high expectations into reality; and thinking outside the box to continually challenge the status quo in the name of school improvement. And all this in addition to dealing with the never-ending responsibilities of school management, budgeting, staff supervision, student discipline, district office requirements, and on and on and on.

Not surprisingly, research also recognizes the critical nature of leadership in transforming schools. *Research and Resources in Support of This We Believe* (Anfara et al., 2003) summarizes, "High-performing middle schools have high-performing, learning-centered leaders—principals and teachers—working collaboratively to enhance student learning" (p. 61). In *Turning Points 2000,*

An effective principal such as Mr. Barillas nurtures a school climate that promotes teamwork, encourages debate, and values democratic participation.
— DVD, Thurgood Marshall MS, "School Climate"

Jackson and Davis (2000) concur: "One of the most consistent findings in educational research is that high-achieving schools have strong, competent leaders" (p. 156). They further state, "No single individual is more important to initiating and sustaining improvement in middle grades school students' performance than the school principal" (p. 157). These conclusions are confirmed in a study published by the Wallace Foundation (Leithwood, Louis, Anderson, & Wahlstrom, 2004), which reports school leadership is "Second only to teaching among school-related factors in its impact on student learning" (p. 3). Their findings further indicate that effective leadership is the result of three practices: setting directions, developing people, and redesigning the organization (p. 8).

Given the crucial nature of leadership to the success of a middle school, it is disturbing to note that very few middle level principals have had formal coursework in middle level education (Valentine, Clark, Hackmann, & Petzko, 2002, p. 63) or have received training in shared leadership and decision making (Jackson & Davis, 2000, p. 157). So then, what characteristics combine to create a courageous, collaborative leader at the middle level?

It Begins with a Vision

The road to a successful school for young adolescents begins with a vision. While this vision must be developed, nurtured, and shared with others before it can become a full-fledged reality, it begins in the mind and heart of the school leader. It must be based on a set of sound educational beliefs that speak to the dignity, equality, and uniqueness of the young adolescents served by the school. The leader must be able to clearly articulate these beliefs and demonstrate by both actions and words that he or she holds firm to them. This is not always an easy or comfortable undertaking, as it requires courage to challenge practices that are detrimental to students or to deal with issues or situations that are out of alignment with the school's vision.

Drawing on this vision to set direction for the school then becomes a significant component of a leader's job; for as Warren Bennis had stated, "Leadership is the capacity to translate vision into reality." Using the 14 tenets found in *This We Believe: Successful Schools for Young Adolescents* (NMSA, 2003) as guiding principles will help develop a firm foundation for school decision making and put feet to the vision. Yogi Berra once said, "If you don't know where you are going, you will end up somewhere else." A courageous, collaborative leader with a vision always knows where he or she is going.

A Culture of Collaboration and Shared Decision Making

A story is told of a young administrator in China who was completing his final oral exams. The old Zen master asked him how he would best apply what he had learned. The eager student replied, "I will lead fairly, with compassion, and with knowledge of what is best for all." The Zen master replied, "Then every last person will suffer under your leadership!"

A courageous, collaborative leader clearly understands that school improvement is a joint effort; a single individual simply cannot know what is best for all. The young man in the above example would be well advised to heed the words of former president Woodrow Wilson—"I not only use all of the brains I have, but all I can borrow."

A courageous, collaborative leader understands that school improvement is a joint effort; a single individual simply cannot know what is best for all.

The nature of leadership has changed significantly over the past few decades and the traditional role of the principal as the manager of all aspects of the school is no longer effective in building and maintaining a successful middle school program. To sustain ongoing and enduring change, a principal must nurture a school culture that promotes teamwork, encourages debate on effective middle level practices, and values input from all members of the school community. Whenever appropriate, he or she must relinquish the role as sole decision maker and, instead, cultivate leadership skills in others, empowering them to make decisions and enact changes. The job of today's principal is to ask questions rather than provide answers, to facilitate the process of school improvement rather than prescribe how it should be done, and to suggest alternatives to former policies and practices rather than mandate the ones that will be used. Only when this climate of collaboration and shared decision making is in place can a school create the shared vision necessary for student success and turn it into a reality.

Just as the role of the principal has evolved into more than the manager of school business, the roles and influence of teachers have also grown beyond the classroom. In truly successful schools for young adolescents, teachers are no longer isolated individuals behind closed doors, but active collaborators in the school learning community. These teacher-leaders participate in spirited discussions regarding their professional practices as a way to ensure success for all students. They are involved members of their teams eagerly seeking ways to make their curriculum integrative, relevant, and challenging for their students; and they collectively share their expertise to help the school solve problems, make decisions, and set policy.

It is a memorable experience to visit a school for young adolescents where the leader understands the power of collaboration and has encouraged it to permeate the school culture. By involving others in sharing responsibilities and letting them take credit for accomplishments, the leader has tapped into the magic of synergy and created a school that is far greater than the sum of its parts.

A Passion for Young Adolescents

Leaders at the middle level must possess a deep understanding of the students that have been entrusted to their care. They must recognize students' strengths, appreciate their mercurial nature, and celebrate their uniqueness. They must demonstrate a deep love for their students by being around them, talking with them, and building genuine connections; middle school students can spot a phony in a minute. It is this unwavering devotion to the education of young adolescents that moves a leader beyond competent to exemplary.

Middle level leaders must possess a deep understanding of the students entrusted to their care. — DVD, Thurgood Marshall MS, "School Climate"; Central MS, "Smart Teachers"; Warsaw MS, "Common Language"

This passion for middle level students and their educational needs must also play out in the decisions that a leader makes daily. To effectively make decisions in the best interests of the students, a leader needs a firm foundation in the elements of middle level education such as teaming, student advocacy, and flexible scheduling as well as a sound understanding of curriculum, pedagogy, and assessment practices as applied to the middle level. This knowledge, combined with a passion for middle level students, ensures a leader can be confident that decisions held up to the standard of "Is it best for all students?" can be answered with a resounding *yes*.

A leader's zeal for young adolescents must also extend beyond the schoolhouse door. We are past the time when advocacy was an option—it is now an imperative and a leader desiring to sustain school improvement must build support for middle level education at all levels. This can start by simply keeping the superintendent and school board informed of research on effective middle level practices. For they can be key allies only if they know and understand what one is trying to accomplish at the middle level. But advocacy efforts also need to be directed at other stakeholders—parents, key community members, policymakers, state and federal officials in the education process. It takes courage to step forward and be a passionate advocate, but it is a vital component of successful middle level leadership.

A Role Model for Risk Taking and Reflective Learning

Being a courageous, collaborative leader means putting yourself in the line of fire; for as Albert Schweitzer said, "Example is not the main thing in influencing others. It is the only thing." Your actions will speak much louder than your words and those around you will watch closely to see if you hold true to your convictions. This type of leader recognizes that risks are embedded in the very nature of teaching and learning. Middle school students take a risk every time they ask a question, venture an answer, or attempt a new task. Teachers face a risk every time they walk into the classroom; they do not magically know what they will need to do in order to help a struggling student be successful, and they do not automatically know how to handle every situation that arises during a day.

Being a courageous, collaborative leader means putting yourself in the line of fire.

Leaders often encourage others to try something new, take a chance, or stretch their comfort zone. But is the leader modeling this behavior? Do students and staff see their leaders trying new things or admitting they do not have the solution for every problem that comes their way? Do they see them making mistakes and learning from them? Do their actions send the message that it is okay not to know something, but it's not okay to not seek out the answer? A courageous, collaborative leader understands and appreciates that it is the very action of taking the risk, rather than its result, that creates the opportunity for personal growth. And since the very definition of risk implies a chance of harm or loss, the leader must always be prepared to model how best to handle the consequences of a failed endeavor.

Reflective leaders are risk takers. These leaders are willing to try something new in order to learn something new. They regularly reexamine and challenge their professional practices because they understand that education at its best is ongoing and dynamic, changing and adapting to the needs of the learners. They take charge of their own learning and lead the way in establishing the school as a learning community for both adults and students.

School leadership sometimes requires standing strong for effective middle grades practice in the face of conflicting policies.
— DVD, Central MS, "Professional Development"

A courageous, collaborative leader's modeling of risk taking and reflective learning is a key element in the process of school improvement. At its heart, school improvement is about people improvement—challenging, changing, refining, and strengthening the pedagogy, beliefs, and values of those who work together in a school. An effective leader infuses professional development into the school routine as evidenced by the sharing and discussion of professional articles, the existence of study groups, the exchange of new ideas learned at a workshop, and participation in professional organizations. Additional evidence includes staff members who engage in action research, the constant presence of formal and informal discussions regarding best practices for young adolescents, and most of all, the school's utter commitment to student success.

Accepting Responsibility for Student Achievement

While at first glance it may seem at odds with a culture of shared-decision making, a courageous, collaborative leader must assume the ultimate responsibility for the well-being of the school or the classroom. There can be no pointing of fingers or pushing the blame on to others. These leaders must be mindful of the sign that President Harry Truman kept on his desk—"The buck stops here."

For the teacher it means accepting full responsibility for the success of students in his or her classroom. Stricken from the vocabulary are statements such as *My students don't want to learn; I teach them, they just don't do the work; My students don't speak English;* or *If only the parents were more supportive*. While some of these reasons may indeed make the challenge of teaching more difficult, they cannot be used as excuses for students not learning. The effective teacher accepts that he or she is the key to student success and therefore uses formal and informal assessment data to drive both individualized planning and instruction, learns all he or she can about the special needs of the population of students in the classroom, seeks out information on up-to-date effective professional practices, and never gives up on students. Most important, he or she realizes that ultimately it is his or her skills and attitude coupled with the setting of high expectations for all students that makes the difference between student success and failure.

The principal must accept an even broader range of responsibility for school success. Just as the teacher is responsible for the growth and development of students within the classroom, so is the principal accountable for the growth and development of the school staff—and this responsibility begins with hiring teachers who are highly effective at working with middle level students. This requires the principal and the hiring team to employ only teachers who understand the development of young adolescents, who are competent in multiple content areas, and who are skilled in instructing middle schoolers. A principal focused on student achievement must also accept the responsibility to ensure that these new teachers are effectively inducted into the school culture through mentorship and professional development. In addition to hiring and developing effective teachers, the leader must also address retention concerns through a systematic plan that provides new teachers with the support and nourishment needed for long-term success.

Accepting responsibility for the instructional leadership of a school is another sign of a courageous, collaborative leader. This role does not require the principal to be an expert in every area of instruction but rather to make certain that the school's teachers "have the skills, knowledge, and resources necessary to make effective learning-based decisions" (NMSA, 2003, p. 63). Leaders of this caliber will regularly be found encouraging quality teaching by providing feedback that promotes effective instruction, by analyzing and using data to drive school achievement, and by keeping the school focused on maintaining high expectations for every student.

A story is told of a chicken and a pig discussing the preparation of a special breakfast for the farmer. The chicken suggested bacon and eggs to which the pig replied, "That's easy for you to say. For you to provide eggs is only a contribution, for me it's a total commitment!" Many stakeholders in the educational process today contribute to school reform efforts, but it is the total commitment to the education of young adolescents that distinguishes the courageous, collaborative leader.

Getting to the Heart of the Matter

Being a leader in a school for young adolescents is a daunting task; add courageous and collaborative to the description and the bar is raised even higher. But it can be done. The recipe? Take good people and organizational skills, add in liberal doses of intelligence and common sense, throw in hard work, mix in a love of young adolescents with a commitment to stay the course, and stir with a passionate heart. Author and speaker Robert Cooper may well have had a middle school leader in mind when he said, "Leadership is doing all you can to have the heart of a lion, the skin of a rhino, and the soul of an angel." Measuring one's self against this standard of leadership may cause one to feel more like the cowardly lion than the king of the jungle, but take heart and begin the journey. There are many, many fine courageous, collaborative leaders found in middle level schools around the world. Some indicators that reveal the presence of such a leader include

Leadership is doing all you can to have the heart of a lion, the skin of a rhino, and the soul of an angel.

- Consistent, frequent interaction with adults and students both inside and outside the classroom.
- Regular interaction with parents and the community that informs them of issues pertaining to the education of young adolescents and involves them in school affairs.
- An empowered leadership team focused on school improvement.
- Shared governance that allows input from all stakeholders.
- A clearly articulated vision driving a well-developed improvement plan that adapts to the shifting needs of the school.
- Effective use of data that ties the curriculum to effective instruction and assessment practices.
- Ongoing, embedded professional development designed to further student achievement.
- Promoting and modeling best practices for young adolescents.
- The active development of leadership skills in others.
- Employing effective adult learning practices.
- A sense of humor that allows one to laugh at oneself —and with others.
- The ability to listen well and know when and who to ask for help.
- A finger on the pulse of the school and the knowledge and ability to respond accordingly.

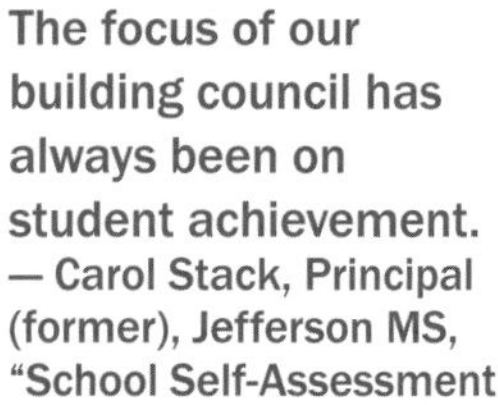

The focus of our building council has always been on student achievement.
— Carol Stack, Principal (former), Jefferson MS, "School Self-Assessment"

But what should an aspiring leader do if a critical look in the mirror indicates one does not quite merit the description of courageous and collaborative? Put your heart into it and take action with the following measures:

- Educate yourself on the middle school concept. Begin with *This We Believe: Successful Schools for Young Adolescents* (NMSA, 2003).
- Find a mentor—someone you can observe, question, and learn from.
- Join local, state, and national professional organizations and take advantage of their offerings.
- Participate in professional development activities—attend workshops, conferences, lectures, and classes.
- Visit successful middle level schools.
- Stay current in the field by reading monthly journals and recently published resources.
- Freely admit you need to learn more and invite others to join you on the journey.

The human body is comprised of many systems working together in harmony and so is a successful school for young adolescents. The 14 characteristics of effective middle level schools described in *This We Believe: Successful Schools for Young Adolescents* (NMSA, 2003) must not be looked at individually, but rather as an integrated system functioning as a whole. But just as the heart gives life to the body, a courageous, collaborative leader gives life to the school. This leader is the heartbeat of the school and the goal is clear—every middle level school deserves to be led by a courageous, collaborative leader with a heart that beats loud and strong for young adolescents.

References

Anfara, V., Jr. (Ed.), Andrews, P. G., Hough, D., Mertens, S., Mizelle, N., & White. G. (2003). *Research and resources in support of* This We Believe. Westerville, OH: National Middle School Association.

Jackson, A. W., & Davis, G. (2000). *Turning points 2000: Educating adolescents in the 21st century.* New York: Teachers College Press and Westerville, OH: National Middle School Association.

Leithwood, K., Louis, K., Anderson, S., & Wahlstrom, K. (2004). *How leadership influences student learning*. New York: The Wallace Foundation.

National Middle School Association. (2003). *This we believe: Successful schools for young adolescents*. Westerville, OH: Author.

Valentine, J., Clark, D., Hackmann, D., & Petzko, V. (2002). *A national study of leadership in middle level schools*. Reston, VA:

National Association of Secondary School Principals.

A Shared Vision that Guides Decisions

Sue Swaim

How do you begin the journey of implementing a successful middle school? It starts with a vision . . . *a shared vision* developed and implemented under the guidance and nurturing of school leaders in collaboration with all the various stakeholders: students, teachers, parents, administrators, board of education members, central office personnel, and community members. The importance of a shared vision should not be underestimated. Idealistic and uplifting, the vision "reflects the very best we know and lights the way toward achieving a truly successful middle level school. It reveals how research and practice can work in harmony to provide the foundation for building a school in which every student can succeed" (National Middle School Association, 2003, p. 11).

Without a shared vision that is understood and supported by its stakeholders, middle level school improvement efforts will be seriously flawed from the onset and potentially short-lived because "ownership" rests more with a single leader rather than the school community as a whole. Instead, the school community should collaboratively build a strong and enduring vision—one that reflects the very best we can imagine about all the elements of schooling, including student achievement, student-teacher relationships, and community participation. The "heart" of the shared vision must focus on the nature and needs of young adolescent learners. We have learned that when middle school educators implement practices based on their knowledge of learning and human development, students make measurable gains in academic achievement while moving forward in becoming healthy, ethical, and productive citizens.

Developing and Implementing a Shared Vision

A shared vision must evolve out of the lives and philosophies of the educators involved, not just out of a committee consensus.

In order to develop a shared vision, many districts begin with the formation of a task force. Actually, the development of a school-wide shared vision can also begin with a school-based task force. However, it is important to note that the resulting shared vision and its accompanying mission statement must evolve out of the lives and philosophies of the educators involved, not just out of a committee consensus that is then announced to the larger community for its acceptance.

The task force is usually comprised of representatives from all stakeholder groups who need to work together if schools are to grow and change. The task force process needs to be collaborative to help develop educational partnerships among the stakeholders that are crucial to the long-term success of any school's program. As young adolescent learners have many different learning styles, so do the members of a task force. Therefore, extensive opportunities are provided to enable task force members to build a common knowledge base and philosophy. This involves both individual study and give-and-take dialogue among members of the group.

In addition to NMSA's (2003) *This We Believe: Successful Schools for Young Adolescents* and *Research and Resources in Support of This We Believe*, there are several other resources that should be considered as foundational reading. They include *Turning Points 2000: Educating Adolescents in the 21st Century* (Jackson & Davis, 2000), the National Forum to Accelerate Middle-Grades Reform's Vision Statement and Schools to Watch Criteria (1998), and National Association of Secondary School Principals' *Breaking Ranks In the Middle* (in press). Collectively, these documents, based upon research and practice, "speak with one voice" regarding the characteristics of successful middle schools. Additional resources such as Thompson's (2004), *Reforming Middle Level Education: Considerations for Policymakers,* Doda and Thompson's (2002) *Transforming Ourselves, Transforming Schools: Middle School Change,* and Dickinson's (2001) *Reinventing the Middle School* should be examined. Shared literature study must allow ample discussion time and be a part of the information-gathering and digesting process.

Shared literature study plus ample discussion and question and answer sessions must be a part of the information-gathering and digesting process.

Seeing something in action is also an important part of the process. Visiting schools with strong middle level programs in place is especially valuable. However, before embarking on school visits, it is important to be clear about what the team needs to see. Consider using the 14 characteristics in *This We Believe* (NMSA, 2003) as a framework for the visits. How are these recommended characteristics implemented in the school being visited? Are the characteristics being implemented in concert with one another, or has the school chosen to deal with a few while ignoring others? How does the school's professional development initiative focus on these issues? Are people working together in study groups focused on learning results and analyzing student work with the goal of improving student achievement? These are examples of questions that can be addressed by using *This We Believe* to help guide the visit and follow-up discussions.

Effective schools involve all stakeholders in creating vision, defining mission, and establishing consistent expectations and common language for the learning community. — DVD, Thurgood Marshall MS, "School Climate"; Chapel Hill MS, "Shared Vision"; Warsaw MS, "Common Language"

Visitors observe various programs in action and confer with teachers, administrators, parents, and students about what is happening in that school. Team members should include representatives of all stakeholder groups. This enables members to see things from different viewpoints, continue discussions upon return, and be responsive to the constituency each person represents.

Likewise, attending middle level conferences and workshops provides opportunities for people to confer with others in the field and to directly benefit from others' experiences and ideas. It is best for teams of stakeholders to attend these events so several representatives can hear the same message at the same time, ask questions of the presenters, and return to school to continue discussion. These activities give the task force an opportunity to develop a common knowledge and set of questions that must be addressed within its own community to help middle schools become all they should and can be.

The middle level task force reaches out to involve the community during the development process. Members identify key people in the community who have a direct interest in early adolescence such as pediatricians or other health professionals, youth club leaders, social workers, juvenile law enforcement personnel, or religious leaders. As leaders they become resource people in addressing the community's expectations for the middle school, and they can help articulate the vision throughout the community.

Ongoing communication is vitally important. The developmental characteristics of young adolescents, how developmentally appropriate middle schools lead to improved academic achievement, and financial considerations of implementing the middle school concept are among topics that need to be addressed and shared with the community.

It is important to have a plan for sharing and disseminating information regarding the mission and resources needed to implement a successful middle school. A variety of formats may be used such as guest speakers at highly publicized public meetings, special briefings for reporters and editors, school district policy sessions, pamphlets disseminated to parents, coffees hosted by principals, and open forums for community input. Teachers, parents, and students should be directly involved in these events, for they are the ones who will implement the shared vision.

Developing and Implementing an Operational Mission Statement

Once the vision for middle level education has been developed and articulated at the district and the school level, each school community needs to create its own mission statement. When the shared vision and mission statement work in concert, they provide the foundation (a) for setting a clear course for school growth and improvement; (b) for supporting and developing the skills, talents, and academic growth of all members of the learning community; and (c) for creating a school organization that supports rather than inhibits teaching and learning.

While the middle school mission statement takes into account the district's philosophy and goals as well as relevant state guidelines, it should be "personalized" and unique to its own situation. Too often mission statements are quickly developed by relatively few, approved routinely by a faculty, and consequently remain merely rhetoric. All stakeholders must actively participate in the process of formulating a mission statement if it is to guide the school's course.

One of the challenges is developing a mission statement that is succinct while reflecting the top priorities and beliefs of each school. Long, wordy mission statements soon disappear from consciousness, while a succinct mission statement is remembered and used as a guidepost when making specific decisions about programs and practices.

An operational mission statement is revisited as the school community grows and learns through doing and as new research and practices emerge. One responsibility of a school leader is to keep listening to all members of the school's community and regularly ask for input on the school's vision and mission statement.

An operational mission statement constantly raises the question, *Is what we are doing best for our students based on what we know about the human growth and development of youngsters ages 10 to 15?* When contradictory policies coexist, school supporters will be able to effectively advocate for what is best for their school and its students. For example, a middle school comprehensive health committee might question the presence of soda machines in the school as being a direct contradiction to the school's commitment to the health and well-being of its students. The mission statement as a guide for the school's policies, goals, and operational procedures is an important tool for addressing policy inconsistencies.

Fidelity to a school-wide shared vision has ensured that student achievement continues to improve even as students move into the district and new teachers join the staff.

— Chapel Hill MS, "Shared Vision"

Without a shared vision and operational mission statement that is understood and supported by all the stakeholders, a sense of aimlessness may prevail and limited harmony may exist. Uninformed and uninvolved people can easily open the door to criticism of the school, especially if a change takes place without adequate understanding or advance communication. Ultimately, the sincere efforts and hard work of those involved can be undermined if a shared vision and mission statement do not exist or are underused.

Communicating the Shared Vision and Operational Mission Statement

One of the most important aspects of developing and implementing a shared vision and the related mission statement is how to communicate these to the wider audiences who need to hear and understand the message. Three important audiences are (a) elementary and high school staffs, including support personnel; (b) all parents; and (c) the community at large, including its news media, business leaders, civic organizations, and religious leaders. Building understanding and support for your middle school is an ongoing process that does not end once a shared vision and mission statement have been developed. If they are expected to support the school and help sustain its commitment to young adolescents, *new* middle level parents, teachers, policymakers, community members, and others need to understand the foundational pieces of your middle school's policies and practices. Therefore, developing a planned, ongoing communication program is important. This communication program helps a variety of audiences understand the rationale for middle level education as set forth in *This We Believe: Successful Schools for Young Adolescents* (NMSA, 2003) as well as become familiar with the characteristics of this age group. They need to see how putting the shared vision and mission statement into action will increase student achievement and better meet the developmental needs of 10- to 15-year-olds.

Educating young adolescents is a complex undertaking. National Middle School Association's (2003) *This We Believe: Successful Schools for Young Adolescents* succinctly delineates the multifaceted issues that should be addressed if we are to implement schools that truly focus on the academic growth and well-being of all our students. Implementing the 14 characteristics in harmony with one another, consistently over time, must become our collaborative commitment. The journey starts by developing a shared vision and a related operational mission statement to guide the way.

References

Dickinson, T. S. (Ed.). (2001). *Reinventing the middle school*. New York: RoutledgeFalmer.

Doda, N. M., & Thompson, S. C. (Eds.) (2002). *Transforming ourselves, transforming school: Middle school change*. Westerville, OH: National Middle School Association.

Jackson, A. W., & Davis, G. (2000). *Turning points 2000: Educating adolescents in the 21st century*. New York: Teachers College Press and Westerville, OH: National Middle School Association.

National Association of Secondary School Principals. (in press). *Breaking ranks in the middle*. Reston, VA: Author.

National Forum to Accelerate Middle-Grades Reform. (1998). *Vision Statement*. Retrieved April 11, 2005, from www.mgforum.org/about/vision.asp

National Forum to Accelerate Middle-Grades Reform. (1994-2003). *Criteria for Schools to Watch*. Retrieved April 11, 2005, from www.mgforum.org/ImprovedSchools/STW/STWCriteria.asp

National Middle School Association. (2003) *This we believe: Successful schools for young adolescents*. Westerville, OH: Author.

Thompson, S. C. (Vol. Ed.). (2004). *Reforming middle level education: Considerations for policymakers*. In V. A. Anfara, Jr. (Series Ed.), *Handbook of Research in Middle Level Education*. Greenwich, CT: Information Age Publishing and Westerville, OH: National Middle School Association.

5

An Inviting, Supportive, and Safe Environment

Marion Johnson Payne

Successful schools for young adolescents are universally characterized by a culture that is inviting, supportive, and safe. The social and educational atmosphere, the ambience of a school, can make or break the school program. A positive school atmosphere is rooted in a vision that all stakeholding groups were involved in from its birth.

As schools get larger and as youth spend less time under the supervision of adults in their out-of-school lives, it becomes increasingly important that schools provide a stable atmosphere characterized by positive and long-term relationships. And middle schools have a special responsibility to provide protective custody, or what might be likened to a cocoon, as these fragile and vulnerable young people move beyond their limited lives as children and experience the option-oriented and even precarious life of young adolescents. When their school is viewed as a safe haven, students are more willing to ask questions, take risks, and try out unfamiliar things, which their new exploratory nature urges them to do.

What To Look For

What does an inviting, supportive, and safe environment feel like? In inviting, safe, and supportive buildings, one senses a feeling of warmth. The decor in such a school also makes an immediately visible statement about the caring commitment of its faculty and staff. The physical plant is attractive and welcoming with visual messages and stimuli that reflect a sense of pride. Students, staff, and even visitors feel that they belong. Their sense of safety and security is strong as measures are in place to ensure that students and adults are indeed safe and secure. Visitors observe staff members who are cordial to each other, teachers and administrators who speak to students by name, and students who interact comfortably and respectfully with adults and with one another. Attendance is typically quite high in such schools.

National Middle School Association (2003) describes such an atmosphere in these words:

> Statements of encouragement and positive feedback outnumber disciplinary or correctional comments. Interactions among staff members and between students reflect democracy, fairness, and mutual respect. Teachers, staff, and students learn and put into practice the skills of direct feedback, mediation, healthy and appropriate confrontation, positive risk taking, and personal and collaborative goal setting. Students and adults have a shared language to discuss issues of diversity and equity. The essence of a happy, healthy school lies in the talk one hears. (p. 13)

Van Hoose, Strahan, and L'Esperance (2001) employed a musical metaphor to depict a school: "A successful school is much like a symphony. As the harmonizing of many parts results in powerful music, so too the appropriate blending of many factors in school results in powerful experiences for students" (p. 2). Having an inviting, supportive, and safe environment is not just desirable, it is a prerequisite for maximizing student achievement. Schools with such environments encourage students and teachers to take risks, to explore, and to create. Consequently, critical thinking is refined and productivity increases. Students and teachers take pride in the school as problems are identified and solutions pursued.

Lily Hope Wilkinson, an eighth grader at Frank Strong Middle School in Durham-Middlefield, Connecticut, spoke convincingly about the importance of relationships at the 2005 New England League of Middle Schools conference. She said, in part

> I will never as long as I live forget my experience at middle school. It is the most vital part of any person's development, and I feel personally that . . . Strong Middle School shaped me as a person. It's at middle school where you are first faced with adult responsibility, and for the first time we form adult relationships outside our family. Whether it is the coach that pushed you to improve your jump shot, the teacher that opened your eyes and made you want to

make a difference, or the friend who was always there for you, the relationships made in the middle school have an impact on you forever.

The National Forum to Accelerate Middle-Grades Reform (1998) has articulated a vision of academic excellence, developmental responsiveness, and social equity that would lead to high-performing middle level schools' becoming the norm rather than the exception. That vision recognizes the importance of a positive, supportive climate. The Forum believes all schools are capable of achieving at high levels. Through its Schools to Watch Program now operating in 11 states, schools that are meeting the nationally recognized criteria are providing models and mentors (see www.schoolstowatch.org).

Determining the Presence of an Inviting, Supportive, and Safe Environment

A successful middle school is one that links students, staff, parents, and the community in a variety of ways. All stakeholders are involved in evaluating the environment just as they had been in determining the mission. Three key conditions that indicate a supportive and inviting environment are

- The environment promotes creativity, responsible risk-taking, cooperation, and mutual trust and respect.
- Staff and students feel safe at school and in work-related activities.
- Staff, students, and parents report that the learning environment is academically stimulating.

The foundation of Central Middle, why we are doing so well, is that the staff members bring a family environment to the school.

— James Harrison, Security Guard, Central MS, "Safe Environment"

Good communication is vital for maintaining positive interactions within a school community. An excellent way to evaluate any program is to conduct an annual survey of a random sample of school and community members to check the current perceptions of various individuals and groups. Other evidence of a positive school climate includes

- A high degree of community involvement (parents, volunteers, and community business partners)
- A higher than usual attendance rate
- Positive attitudes of teachers, students, and parents apparent in informal conversations
- Expressions indicating pride in the school
- High degree of participation in school-wide and system-wide activities.
- A positive tenor of media coverage

- Recognition of high academic expectations for every student
- Ability to handle and spring back from adversity.

The way in which a school handles an adverse situation is a particularly strong indicator of the school's supportive environment. A school with a positive climate is able to approach each day and each situation as an opportunity for growth and community building. When faced with the sudden death of a student, for instance, Mount View Middle School in Marriottsville, Maryland, was forced to come together with the community and work through this death. From the onset of the tragedy, the school became a place to gather for comfort, information, planning, discussion, and grieving. Individuals in the community dealt with all aspects of this traumatic experience. Staff members were given released time to either meet with a counselor or take time for themselves. A cadre of parents established a highly comforting presence and at the same time did not permit the media to interfere with the safe haven within. One family chartered a bus to provide transportation for any students who wanted to attend the funeral. This unfortunate incident revealed that the positive school climate had depth and was strengthened significantly by people pulling together in a time of need.

The way in which a school handles an adverse situation is a particularly strong indicator of the school's supportive environment.

Everyone in an inviting school works proactively to eliminate harassment, verbal abuse, bullying, and name calling. Students and teachers understand that they are part of a community where differences are respected and celebrated.

Strong leadership that promotes healthy, respectful relationships is the foundation on which a school creates a safe and secure environment. — DVD, Central MS, "Safe Environment"

The multiple incidents of increased terrorism worldwide and the heightened sensitivity to individual and personal security in the United States have resulted in all schools paying greater attention to safety measures. The presence of uniformed school resource officers or security guards, and even metal detectors at entrances has become reality in many places. Uniforms for students, required student and staff picture identification badges, and more sophisticated sign-in and sign-out procedures are ways many schools have responded to the need for a safe environment. Given such conditions, special efforts to maintain a warm, friendly environment became even more critical.

Maintaining an Inviting, Supportive, and Safe Environment

Like the young adolescents themselves, the climate of developmentally responsive middle level schools requires constant nurturing. A positive middle school climate encourages students' interest in learning and ultimately, becoming lifelong learners. Likewise, teachers who work in a positive environment feel good about themselves and their work, thereby creating a positive environment for their students. Improving school climate may depend more on the behavior of adults than any other single factor. Changing takes time and effort, but is possible if all adults work together toward a common goal. The law of positive reinforcement makes clear the influence of positive leaders: "In the absence of positive reinforcement from appointed leaders, negative human attitudes and behaviors are most likely to emerge from the group being led" (DeBruyn, 1996, p. 1). Maintaining a positive school climate is, therefore, an ongoing process requiring almost daily reaffirmation from all parties.

In *If You Don't Feed the Teachers, They Eat the Students*, Connors (2000) wrote, "Every day, students from all walks of life arrive at school hoping they will be safe, fed and assisted in realizing dreams. . . . To ensure that teachers are supportive of all students, we must create professional, safe, secure and encouraging environments where everyone feels appreciated, listened to, and respected" (p. 12). This is a message school leaders must not miss. The best leaders actively focus on providing a climate in which teachers are encouraged to take risks and willingly serve as coaches—guiding students through the trials and tribulations of early adolescence.

In Savannah's Mercer Middle School, a Georgia Lighthouse School to Watch, the school staff has grounded an inviting, supportive, safe environment in the basic curriculum of the school. In addition to dynamic and visionary leadership and collaborative teaching teams, an enrichment cluster program is a major factor in contributing to a positive, student-centered climate and has helped to propel this school to exemplary status. The distinctive enrichment program (see list of clusters at right) is centered on semester-long academies, outgrowths of academic programs. Students, irrespective of grade level, select their choices among several different clusters. Once placed in a cluster they remain in it for the semester and may elect to change or stay for the following semester. The options are numerous and appealing to students. At the end of the year, the

MERCER MIDDLE SCHOOL 2004-2005 ENRICHMENT CLUSTERS

Action, Lights, and Camera
- History of the motion picture

Artists' Palette
- Ceramics
- Designing edge
- Drawing and painting
- Keepsakes and gifts
- Knotting and beading
- Why knot?

Beauty Within
- Chick flicks
- Cosmetology
- Nefertiti Sisters
- Runway-Modeling

Champions of Fitness
- Introduction to golf
- Tae-Bo
- Tumbling

Math, Science, and Inventions
- Chessmasters
- Math games and puzzles
- Design

Pen and Ink
- Express yourself
- Mystery madness in the media center
- Literature circle

The Show's the Thing
- Bits and puppets: The art of puppetry
- Chorus
- Creative dance of the arts
- Jazz band
- Soul speaks
- Soul stepping
- Storytelling cluster

Young Apprentices
- Carpentry
- Logo tech
- Opening your own business
- Recipes that rock
- Web design using html

school hosts a very well-attended showcase night for parents and the community where students share the products of their long-term exploratory experiences.

A school's environment is revealed through its activities, relationships, programs, and decisions. — DVD, Scuola Vita Nuova, "Coffee House"; Warsaw MS, "Common Language"; Thurgood Marshall MS, "School Climate"

A Word of Caution

Collins (2001) has warned us: "Good is the enemy of great. And that is one of the key reasons why we have so little that becomes great. We don't have great schools principally because we have good schools" (p. 1). Taken for granted, our generally good public schools are readily criticized whenever society recognizes a failing.

Middle level reform in recent decades has helped to shift schools from being bureaucratic organizations to being communities of learners. Although many middle school classrooms still exist as independent entities operating in isolation from each other, Purkey and Strahan (2002) pointed out that everything in the school is really connected. To illustrate this, they present the Jell-O Principle:

> The school and everybody in it are like one big bowl of Jell-O: if you touch it anywhere, the thing jiggles; everything is connected to everything else. Understanding the Jell-O principle helps the teacher to remember that everything—temperature, time of day, color of walls, how the teacher dresses—adds to or subtracts from positive classroom discipline. No effort to make the school more inviting is wasted. (p. 42)

Turning Points 2000: Educating Adolescents for the 21st Century (Jackson & Davis, 2000) made a strong case for teacher collaboration, problem solving, and high-quality professional development, all operating on a foundation of communication and trust. The authors' prognosis for progress seems to be that reform is moving slowly at best. Although middle schools have continued to improve, it is clear that many thousands of young adolescents continue to attend middle schools where the programs and practices do not reflect what is known about exemplary middle level teaching and learning, nor what has been advocated by National Middle School Association for more than 30 years. Although the middle school movement has achieved remarkable success organizationally speaking, it has been less successful making changes in curriculum and instruction. For example, while the majority of middle level schools organize interdisciplinary teams, they rarely practice integrated curriculum, maintaining departmentalized instruction, while only occasionally correlating subjects. Middle grades teachers still rely heavily on direct instruction methods and coverage, less often using strategies such as investigations and cooperative learning groups. The existence of a positive school environment is a prerequisite for achieving such reforms. A personalized school environment strengthens students' commitment to school, enhances their engagement in learning, and paves the way for faculty and staff to move the middle school beyond its organizational successes and tackle the difficult but critical matter of curriculum and instruction. Without the catalyst of an inviting, supportive, and safe environment, organizational changes seldom result in positive curricular and instructional changes.

In Summary

With increased student achievement and accountability as priorities at this period of history, establishing and maintaining a positive school climate is crucial. A school's administrators have the major responsibility for seeing that the desired atmosphere exists to carry out the mission of the institution; it cannot be achieved without their active leadership. As many misguided efforts to implement easy, but unproven practices are undertaken to meet the requirements of No Child Left Behind, maintaining an emphasis on collaborative problem solving is especially important. Attempts to separate school climate issues from the academic mission are doomed to fail in the long run. Only as a school proactively provides a warm, positive environment will young adolescents succeed in all aspects of their education.

References

Collins, J. (2001). *Good to great.* New York: Harper Collins Publishers.

Connors, N. (2000). *If you don't feed the teachers, they eat the students.* Nashville, TN : Incentive Publications.

DeBruyn, R. L. (1996). Why administrative assistance and positive reinforcement are necessary on a weekly basis for teachers. Manhattan, KS: *The MASTER Teacher.*

Jackson, A. W., & Davis, G. (2000). *Turning points 2000: Educating adolescents in the 21st century.* New York: Teachers College Press and Westerville, OH: National Middle School Association.

National Middle School Association. (2003). *This we believe: Successful schools for young adolescents.* Westerville, OH: Author.

National Forum to Accelerate Middle-Grades Reform. (1998). *Vision Statement.* Retrieved April 11, 2005, from www.mgforum.org/about/vision.asp

Purkey, W., & Strahan, D. (2002). *Inviting positive classroom discipline.* Westerville, OH: National Middle School Association.

Van Hoose, J., Strahan, D., & L'Esperance, M. (2001). *Promoting harmony–Young adolescent development and school practices.* Westerville, OH: National Middle School Association.

High Expectations for Every Member of the Learning Community

Candy Beal
John Arnold

Holding high expectations for all is a phrase used so loosely in education circles that its essential meanings and implications are frequently lost. Sometimes the phrase refers to little more than abstractly "raising standards" without thought or money given to the support necessary for all students to meet those elevated standards. Too often, holding high expectations is limited to admonitions about raising students' scores on mandatory, statewide tests or improving their behavior, accompanied by strategies for teaching to these tests or firming up discipline. This one-size-fits-all approach is unrealistic and ultimately ineffective, given the fact that each child is at his or her own place on the learning continuum. Moreover, such an approach does not begin to deal with important aspects of growth and learning. Intellectual curiosity, initiative, divergent thinking, risk taking, the capacity to work with others, and a whole host of developmental factors are largely ignored.

The intentions of the section on holding high expectations in *This We Believe: Successful Schools for Young Adolescents* (NMSA, 2003) go far beyond these facile interpretations. These intentions involve seeing and appealing to the best in young adolescents in all their diversity, making sure that those expectations are achievable, realistic ones, and promoting ways to help them realize their potential in every realm of development. Further, they extend to the teachers, counselors, administrators, parents, and community members who work to support this development. This chapter will elaborate on these intentions and their implications.

It is well documented that expectations relative to students become self-fulfilling prophecies. As one student commented, "My teacher thought I was smarter than I was . . . so I was." Positive expectations promote positive attitudes and motivation to achieve; negative expectations lead to alienation, discouragement, and lack of effort. In the classic *Pygmalion in the Classroom* study (Rosenthal, 1968), teachers were assigned groups of students with similar IQs and past school performances. However, some teachers were told that their students had high IQs while other teachers were not told this. Students in the supposed high IQ groups outperformed the other students by a significant margin. In studies cited by George (1988) and Wheelock (1994), students with the same abilities tended to regard themselves and their peers as "dumb" if placed in a "low" group but "smart" if placed in a "high" group. Teachers' curriculum strategies differed markedly depending upon their perceptions of student ability. Clearly, adult expectations have a profound effect upon students' performances and attitudes. Recent studies cited by Sanders, Field, and Diego (2001) indicate that not only are teachers' and administrators' expectations highly correlative with academic achievement, but parents' academic expectations for their children significantly influence academic achievement as well.

"My teacher thought I was smarter than I was . . . so I was."

The importance of positive expectations is magnified with regard to young adolescents because of the negative stereotypes about them, which abound in our society. Popular wisdom regards them to be innately full of storm and stress, opposed to adult values, dominated by peer opinion, and disinterested in any intellectual concerns. As elaborated elsewhere (Arnold, 1993), this characterization is demonstrably untrue and highly destructive. While early adolescence is a difficult time for some, it is not unduly so for the vast majority. Studies show that young adolescents exhibit no more neurotic behavior than any other age group (Peterson, 1987), choose friends whose parents' values are consonant with those of their parents (Bandura, 1964), rely on significant adults in making important decisions (Lamb, Ketterlinus, & Fracasso, 1992), and are intellectually curious and alert (Keating, 1990). Predominant negative stereotypes are based largely on media images of "in your face" adolescent behavior and psychiatric accounts of disturbed youth. They fail to realize that while puberty is undeniably a biological phenomenon, "adolescence" as we know it today is to a great extent the result of social forces that have increasingly isolated young people from the adult world and have created a youth culture. The starting point for high expectations and developmentally responsive middle schools, then, is ridding ourselves of negative stereotypes about young adolescents and becoming proactive supporters of our youth.

Beyond ridding ourselves of negative images, we must realize that young adolescents, given the opportunity and support, are capable of far more than most of us ever imagine. Three examples, cited by Arnold (1990), powerfully illustrate that crucial fact.

Young adolescents, given opportunity and support, are capable of far more than most of us ever imagine.

Students in Alan Haskvitz's seventh grade class at Suzanne Middle School, a large Los Angeles County school that is 60% Mexican American, proposed legislation that enables California to save billions of gallons of water annually; persuaded the county sheriff of the need to fingerprint all area children so that runaways and kidnapped children could be traced more easily; and helped the county registrar rewrite voter instructions when they discovered those at the polls were written on a college level of readability.

In Sam Chattin's seventh-grade science classroom in William H. English Middle School, Scottsburg, Indiana, students ran the largest animal refuge shelter in the Midwest. While nursing animals back to health, they studied about living creatures, environmental policies, and a host of other biological issues. They have shared their work and insights through presentations in ten states and as special guests of the International Animal Rights Convention in Russia.

For more than two decades, seventh- and eighth-grade students of Erick Mortensen and Larry O'Keefe in the Paradise Project at Edmunds Middle School, Burlington, Vermont, traveled an average of 40,000 miles a year. All details of each trip were planned and carried out by students, and twice yearly they published a literary journal about their learning adventures. Further, they engaged in an "achievement program," learning practical skills and teaching them to one another. To advance to level six of this Boy Scout-type program, one student organized a weekend cleanup of the Lake Champlain waterfront that mobilized some 1,000 citizens and another student made all arrangements for a month's stay in the school by a blind artist-in-residence.

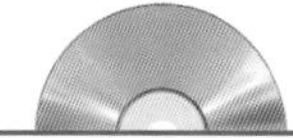

You can do and you can re-do, but you can't "not do"—and that has become a norm.
— Joyce Southern, Counselor, Chapel Hill MS, "Shared Vision"

It is noteworthy that in all three of these examples, students' test scores *skyrocketed*, though test scores had not been the focus of attention. Haskvitz's students' average scores jumped from around the 20th to higher than the 90th percentile; Chattin's students, through special testing by the National Science Foundation, achieved scores in the upper 90th percentiles in knowledge of science information and interest in science; and the Paradise students outperformed non-project students by large margins.

Two more recent examples drawn from middle schools in the Raleigh, North Carolina, area drive home the fact that middle school students, indeed, are capable of high-level accomplishment.

Recapturing the history of their school, a formerly all-black high school desegregated in the 1970s, became the mission of students at Ligon Middle School. They tracked down and interviewed graduates, published alumni memoirs, and produced a video of graduate biographies. They also used Geographic Information Systems (www.gis.com) to trace the ongoing development of the black community surrounding the school and built a community Web site to share historical information. Students were empowered by their mission as "keepers of the history" and learned firsthand about life in the Jim Crow era (Alibrandi, Beal, Wilson, & Thompson, 2000; Alibrandi, et al., 2001).

As part of North Carolina's Sixth Grade Goes to Russia (a North Carolina State curriculum integration-research project involving 5,000 students), Natalie Bates' social studies students at Dillard Drive Middle School chose their fields of inquiry and formulated "Big (research) Questions" about Russia. Merging individual findings with interview data gleaned from Russian citizens via an interactive project Web site, they formulated answers to their questions. Bates and her students also planned and hosted a statewide Global Connections Conference for North Carolina students to share their culminating projects—original dances to Russian classical music; handmade matrushka dolls, "Faberge" eggs and balalaikas; scale models of cathedrals; and newly composed folk tales. Research showed that Bates' students showed improved academic achievement, decreased absences, and an increased appreciation of social studies. Of special note were students' journal entries that stated that Bates' belief in their ability to achieve extraordinary results made the difference in students' interest and participation level (Beal, 2002; Beal, Cuper, & Dalton, 2004).

Effective schools expect and help students develop the range of capacities necessary for responsible citizenship. — DVD, Chapel Hill MS, "School-Wide Reading," "Physical Fitness"

As these examples indicate, if high expectations are to be realized, we must empower students to become intellectually engaged and to develop skills to be responsible citizens by putting forth sustained effort. Our concern must encompass their social, psychological, and moral development as well as their academic growth.

Owing to students' developmental diversity and individual differences, holding high expectations can seldom mean having the same expectations for all students. A developmentally responsive approach to teaching and learning necessarily implies one that is differentiated and personalized, taking into account individual needs, interests, and abilities. Such an approach is characterized by

- *Starting where students are, gearing instruction to their levels of development and understanding.* In virtually every middle level classroom, there will be many students who have limited capacity for complex, abstract reasoning, some who are comfortable with it, and a majority who are somewhere in transition from concrete to more abstract modes of thinking. To deal with this spectrum, teachers must be keen observers who provide a rich variety of materials, opportunities for hands-on and experiential learning, and tasks that appropriately stretch students toward the next level.
- *Varying degrees of structure.* Some students will need, at least initially, very explicit, straightforward assignments; others can handle choices from a limited menu; others will be capable of initiating projects on their own. The aim is to move students as they are able toward increasing autonomy.
- *A varied pace of learning.* A friend once commented, "In business, we expect employees to do high quality work, but vary the time needed to accomplish it. In education, you seem to vary the quality, but hold time constant." Where learning is self-paced or the amount of time students have to complete certain assignments is flexible, students are often able to improve the quality of their work considerably (see Bishop & Pflaum, 2005).
- *A variety of teaching and learning strategies.* Tomlinson (2001) noted that teaching today requires that teachers differentiate their instruction, assignments, and assessment methods. Multiple approaches that involve whole groups, small groups, and individuals are needed to meet the different learning styles and types of intelligences that exist in middle level classrooms. In general, most effective strategies are activity-oriented and inquiry-based (Bishop & Pflaum, 2005). They include integrative learning, cooperative learning, independent study, peer tutoring, service learning, apprenticeships, and a host of other approaches.
- *A curriculum that is rich in meaning, one that helps students make sense of themselves and their world.* Among other things, this implies that the content of what is studied deals with substantive issues and values, is related to students' own questions, opens doors to new learning, and is integrative in

nature (Bishop & Pflaum, 2005). Studies on alternatives to tracking (Oakes, 1985; Wheelock, 1994; Beane, 1997; Beal, 2002) indicate that curriculum rich in meaning enhances student performance at all levels.

- *Significant opportunities for students to assume initiative and responsibility with regard to curriculum and school life.* Where students are enabled to make decisions and increasingly to take control of their own learning, their motivation and achievement flourish. The common ingredient in the innovative programs described earlier is that students "own" the programs.

High Expectations for Teaching

We base our whole school on expectations—high expectations for the administration, faculty, staff, clerks, parents, students—high expectations permeate this school.
— Bill Foster, Principal, Chapel Hill MS, "High Expectations"

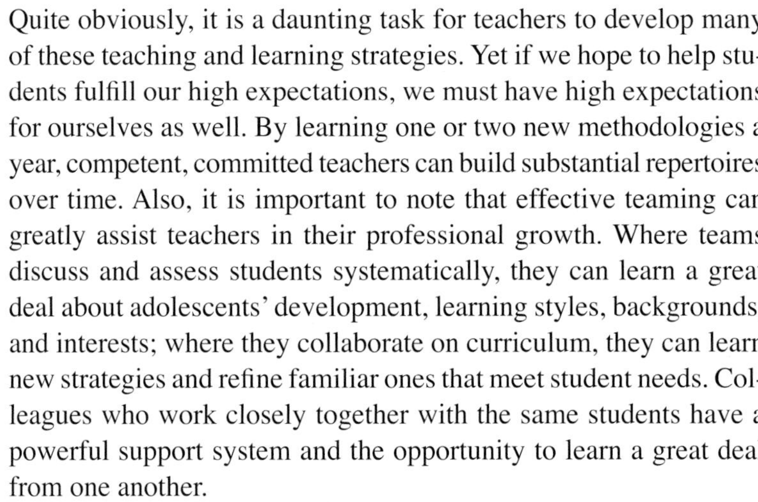

Quite obviously, it is a daunting task for teachers to develop many of these teaching and learning strategies. Yet if we hope to help students fulfill our high expectations, we must have high expectations for ourselves as well. By learning one or two new methodologies a year, competent, committed teachers can build substantial repertoires over time. Also, it is important to note that effective teaming can greatly assist teachers in their professional growth. Where teams discuss and assess students systematically, they can learn a great deal about adolescents' development, learning styles, backgrounds, and interests; where they collaborate on curriculum, they can learn new strategies and refine familiar ones that meet student needs. Colleagues who work closely together with the same students have a powerful support system and the opportunity to learn a great deal from one another.

In schools truly responsive to young adolescents, the holding of high expectations is not limited to views about students. Administrators, parents, teacher educators, and the community at large, as well as teachers hold high expectations for themselves and for one another. It is well known that effective principals are essential to successful schools, doing much to set the tone, promote positive relationships, and keep the focus on student needs, development, and learning. Where principals have high expectations of teachers and support them in their efforts, teachers are much more likely to respond to students in a similar manner. Comer (2004) states the case when he quoted a parent saying, "Teachers don't feel celebrated and rewarded enough. And in some ways, I think that is a reflection of their inability to offer praise at times [to children]" (p. 36).

Educators in developmentally responsive schools understand that virtually all parents want their children to be successful and approach them from this perspective. They are aware that parental attitudes toward learning greatly influence student progress, and that a partnership between home and school is necessary. As the work of Comer, Haynes, Joyner, and Ben-Avie (1996) has shown, this partnership is especially important relative to minority students. Impressive gains have been made where parents are incorporated into the goal-setting process for schools, faculty is helped to understand students' needs, and parents are taught to support the learning process.

In addition to teachers, administrators, and parents, it is obvious that teacher educators play a significant role in building and holding high expectations. Up-to-date knowledge about young adolescent development, pedagogy and methodology, curriculum, and school organization is surely important, but this knowledge must be modeled and applied in the educator's own teaching if it is to be effective. And it is critical to inspire aspiring teachers to care deeply about young adolescents and to be advocates for their full development.

Knowledge about young adolescent development, pedagogy, and curriculum must be modeled by the teacher educator.

Help Yourself, Yourself (HYY) (Beal, Dalton, & Ross, 2003), a study begun several years ago at North Carolina State University, takes a novel approach to teacher education. Preservice teachers study child development theories and their application to teaching and learning and are then teamed with practicing classroom teachers knowledgeable about all aspects of adolescent development. Both then work together to teach development theories to middle school students in hopes that this information will enable the students to make improved academic and social choices. After all, why keep this useful information a mystery from those who need it most, the middle school students themselves?

Through discussions, journals, and other methods, all parties discuss questions such as these: Were they more deliberate when a moral issue presented itself? Did they better understand what was going on socially in their lives? Did understanding their style of learning and types of intelligence (Gardner & Boix-Mansilla, 1994) make it easier for them to choose assignments that played to their strengths? Did they stick with difficult problems and concepts long enough to explore their complexities? Were they empowered to make changes at home and school and did that give them some measure of control in directing their own lives? Did they have the tools to take responsibility for their own learning?

Preliminary results are extremely positive. HYY found that academic work, test scores, and behavior improved for middle schoolers in all areas and among all levels of students and was extraordinarily popular with them. Teachers pushed to differentiate instruction saw the immediate benefit from motivated and focused learners. High expectations that students who were fully informed could make the right choices paid off for both the learners and teacher.

Holding high expectations for all and translating them into meaningful actions is surely not a simple task. It is an ongoing effort that changes and grows as we meet new challenges and have fresh insights. As in all aspects of middle level education, the key to success lies in keeping our eye on the prize: the growth and development of young adolescents. Stevenson (2002) has poignantly and powerfully reminded us of this potential:

> My middle school teaching experience has left me with immutable optimism about the potential of young adolescent children. Given learning opportunities that truly challenge, the responsibility to exercise meaningful choice, and respect for their ideas and dignity, youngsters are capable of tremendous commitment and dazzling originality. Underneath the confounding, frustrating, often exhausting surface, there lies an indomitable human spirit, capable of the exceptional. (pp. 331-332)

Holding high expectations is not an empty exhortation. It is the bedrock of our efforts to create schools that truly honor young adolescents, schools that help them to become all that they can be.

References

Alibrandi, M., Beal, C., Wilson, A., & Thompson, A. (2000). Reconstructing a school's history using oral histories and GIS mapping. *Social Education, 64* (3), 134-140.

Alibrandi, M., Beal, C., Wilson, A., Thompson, A., Mackie, B., Sinclair, N., et al. (2001). Students reclaim their community's history: Interdisciplinary research with technological applications. In M. Christenson, M. Johnston, & J. Norris (Eds.), *Teaching together: School/university collaboration to improve social studies education* (pp. 61-70). Washington, DC: National Council for the Social Studies.

Arnold, J. (1990). *Visions of teaching and learning: 80 exemplary middle level projects*. Columbus, OH: National Middle School Association.

Arnold, J. (1993) A curriculum to empower young adolescents. *Midpoints Occasional Paper, 4* (1). Columbus, OH: National Middle School Association.

Bandura, A. (1964). The stormy decade. Fact or fiction? *Psychology in the Schools, 1*, 224-231.

Beal, C. (2002). To Russia with technology. *Social Education, 66* (3), 166-172.

Beal, C., Dalton, P., & Ross, M. (2003, November). *Forming a help yourself, yourself (hyy) club: Teaching development theory to your students to help them better understand their own adolescence and take responsibility for their futures.* Paper presented at the annual conference of the National Middle School Association, Atlanta, GA.

Beal, C., Cuper, P., & Dalton, P., (2004). The Russia research project: building digital bridges and meeting adolescent needs. *The International Journal of Social Education, 19* (2), 1-18.

Beane, J. (1997). *Curriculum integration: Designing the core of democratic education.* New York: Teachers College Press.

Bishop, P. A., & Pflaum, S. W. (2005). Student perceptions of action, relevance, and pace. *Middle School Journal, 36* (4), 4-12.

Comer, J. (2004*). Leave no child behind. Preparing today's youth for tomorrow's world.* New Haven, CT: Yale University Press.

Comer, J., Haynes, N., Joyner, E., & Ben-Avie, M. (Eds.). (1996). *Rallying the whole village: The Comer process for reforming education.* New York: Teachers College Press.

Gardner, H., & Boix-Mansilla, V. (1994). Teaching for understanding—and beyond. *Teachers College Record, 96*, 198-218.

George, P. S. (1988). Tracking and ability grouping. *Middle School Journal, 20* (1), 21-28.

Keating, D. (1990). Adolescent thinking. In S. S. Feldman & G. I. Elliot (Eds.), *At the threshold: The developing adolescent* (pp. 54-89). Cambridge, MA: Harvard University Press.

Lamb, M., Ketterlinus, L., & Fracasso, M. (1992). Parent-child relationships. In M. Bornstein & M. Lamb (Eds.), *Developmental psychology: An advanced textbook* (pp. 465-518). Hillsdale, NH: Lawrence Erlbaum.

National Middle School Association. (2003). *This we believe: Successful schools for young adolescents.* Westerville, OH: Author.

Oakes, J. (1985). *Keeping track: How schools structure inequality.* New Haven, CT: Yale University Press.

Peterson, A. (1987, September). Those gangly years. *Psychology Today, 21*, 28-34.

Rosenthal, R. (1968). *Pygmalion in the classroom: Teacher expectations and pupils' intellectual development.* New York: Holt, Rinehart and Winston.

Sanders, C., Field, T., & Diego, M. (2001). Adolescents' academic expectations and achievement. *Adolescence, 36,* 795-802.

Stevenson, C. (2002). *Teaching ten to fourteen year olds* (3rd ed.). Boston: Pearson Allyn & Bacon.

Tomlinson, C. (2001). *How to differentiate instruction in mixed ability classrooms* (2nd ed.). Alexandria, VA: Association for Supervision and Curriculum Development.

Wheelock, A. (1994*). Alternatives to tracking and ability grouping*. Alexandria, VA: Association for Supervision and Curriculum Development.

7

Students and Teachers Engaged in Active Learning

Gert Nesin

Middle school educators regularly affirm the desirability of active learning, but many limit the definition to the physical, hands-on activity of the learners. Although physical activity certainly should be considered an important aspect of learning, active learning entails much more. According to *This We Believe: Successful Schools for Young Adolescents* (National Middle School Association, 2003), it involves teachers and students collaborating in "hands-joined" (p.16) learning. Active learning engages the intellect and social and moral sensibilities of the learners, based on the characteristics and individual needs of young adolescents. Active learning thrives in a classroom community built on trust and democratic participation. Active learning, as discussed in this chapter, not only affects students, but also the teacher's role, curriculum, and assessment.

Building a Community for Active Learning

Active learning requires participants to take risks intellectually, socially, and emotionally. Willingness to take risks depends on the safety net built in the classroom through providing a safe and supportive classroom environment (Charney, 2002; Knowles & Brown, 2000; National Research Council [NRC], 2000). This is especially critical for young adolescents who are regularly concerned about peer acceptance and belonging to a group (NMSA, 2003). A community for active learning means that students recognize, respect, and value the diversity that each participant brings to the learning. Every young person learns at different rates and in various ways. An effective classroom community values the richness of that variety, thus making each member feel safe and willing to take risks to learn.

To be engaged in the learning environment, students must, in collaboration with teachers, build the classroom environment around clear and common expectations for their learning and their interactions with others. Expectations guide learning and social behavior. Infringements of the guidelines offer opportunities for personal and community growth rather than just punishments for noncompliance. Missteps also enrich and guide academic growth. According to the NRC (2000), "Learning seems to be enhanced by social norms that . . . allow students (and teachers) the freedom to make mistakes in order to learn" (p. 145). Thoughtful consideration of the development and growth of the classroom community involves students and teachers joined in taking responsibility for growth and interactions, setting the stage for learning that is active intellectually, socially, morally, and physically.

Active Cognitive Learning

Young adolescents begin to think abstractly and see shades of gray rather than only black and white.

Young adolescents are at a unique place in their intellectual and cognitive development. With a newfound awareness of their surroundings, they show intense curiosity about the world and how it works. They begin to think abstractly and see shades of gray rather than only black and white. As they develop an awareness of their own strengths and challenges, they compare themselves to others and often lose confidence in their own abilities to learn and achieve. With active learning strategies, young people can develop self-awareness and a sense of self-efficacy as well as a deeper understanding of content and the world beyond the classroom.

Cognitive science informs active teaching and learning strategies. Although a relatively new field of study, it is based on sound research from cognitive psychology, social psychology, and neuroscience. Cognitive scientists define worthwhile education as

> Helping students develop the intellectual tools and learning strategies needed to acquire the knowledge that allows people to think productively about history, science and technology, social phenomena, mathematics, and arts. Fundamental understanding about subjects, including how to frame and ask meaningful questions . . . contributes to individuals' more basic understanding of principles of learning that can assist them in becoming self-sustaining, lifelong learners. (NRC, 2000, p. 5)

Such an active approach to learning can assist students in understanding themselves and their worlds now and throughout their lives. Essential components of active learning, according to cognitive science, are a view of intelligence, concept learning based on existing knowledge, learning transfer, and metacognition.

Beliefs About Intelligence

Beliefs about intelligence influence active learning (Deci, Vallerand, Pelletier, & Ryan, 1991; Dweck, 2000; Maehr & Anderman, 1993; NRC, 2000). On the one hand, students may believe intelligence to be a fixed entity that one possesses in a set quantity. While being adept at and willing to tackle easy tasks, this view of intelligence causes learners to balk at challenges to avoid making mistakes. They believe lack of immediate success provides proof of limited intelligence. These students shy away from active learning because it may confirm their fears of limited abilities.

In contrast, intelligence can be viewed as incremental, flexible and expanding, depending on the effort applied. Students who have this view of intelligence expect to make mistakes and approach new situations and challenges with enthusiasm and a belief that they can learn. Most learners do not believe strictly in one or the other view of intelligence, but rather fall somewhere on the continuum between them. The challenge for educators is to teach students in a way that encourages them toward the incremental view of intelligence and more active participation in their learning. Rather than having students focus on being smart or accomplishing a task quickly or correctly the first time, teachers should recognize that effort and perseverance are associated with a more incremental view of learning.

The challenge for educators is to teach students in a way that encourages them toward the incremental view of intelligence and more active participation in their learning.

Young adolescents, who are beginning to intellectually identify themselves, can benefit tremendously from an incremental view of intelligence. Instead of seeing themselves as individuals locked in a box determined by fixed intelligence, they instead recognize the expanded possibilities open to them through effort and perseverance. Students realize they can impact their learning and their futures—that through active participation and with support, they can shape who they are and who they will become.

Building Advanced Concepts

In *How People Learn: Brain, Mind, Experience, and School,* the NRC (2000) described how learners develop sophisticated understanding. Students bring existing knowledge, concepts, and misconceptions with them into a learning situation. Simple concepts are a hallmark of beginning learning, and the goal for educators is to help learners achieve expert understanding. Experts find key information and patterns based on a deep understanding of fundamental concepts, and apply the concepts to new situations.

Teachers guide students in actively building understanding rather than telling them what they should understand.

Building expert understanding requires extended time to question misconceptions, work with resources to explore meanings, and develop patterns and concepts based on this exploration. In developing concepts, teachers guide students in making observations, asking pertinent questions, identifying other resources, and using effective methods to answer the questions. In short, teachers guide students in actively building understanding rather than telling them what they should understand.

Some teachers assume that middle school students are ready for extended lectures when new material is presented. Students continually complain about lectures being overused, unengaging, and boring; and cognitive science supports that perception. A lecture or oral presentation can be an effective teaching tool in small doses, but only after students have been given time to question misconceptions, investigate patterns, and build concepts based on personal interaction with events and ideas. In this way, lecture becomes part of an active learning process rather than a passive absorption of new information.

Experts understand and can apply their content and disciplines because they have developed deep and lasting concepts rather than just possessing a collection of facts (NRC, 2000). New facts and understandings are built into the schema of the existing concepts, allowing for further understanding, retrieval, and application. Facts are like sets of earrings. If they are thrown together in a pile, they are difficult to find, not easy to examine when making a selection, and likely to get lost. Concepts are like an earring tree; the earrings (facts) can be attached to the tree in an order that is logical to the owner and easily retrieved as needed. Other earrings can be added to the tree, and the earrings may even need to be re-ordered on occasion to incorporate new types.

Incorporating previous experiences with new ones to develop increasingly sophisticated concepts requires active cognitive learning. The learner must be engaged in the process for it to happen. Facts are necessary; they are the stuff of which concepts are built. On their own, however, they do not build themselves into understanding. Young adolescents crave interaction with facts and ideas so that they can build concepts to help make order out of their expanding reality.

Learning transfer

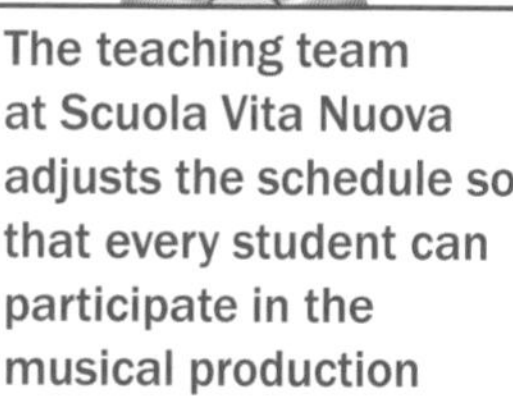

The teaching team at Scuola Vita Nuova adjusts the schedule so that every student can participate in the musical production during the school day. — "Theater Production"

Young adolescents often ask the question, "When will I ever use this?" They express frustration about the lack of transfer of learning to the real world. The ultimate goal of learning should be application in other contexts and situations, particularly beyond the classroom. According to the NRC (2000), learning transfer is a "dynamic process that requires learners to actively choose and evaluate strategies, consider resources, and receive feedback" (p. 66). This differs from the more passive view of learning in which teachers present students with some initial information and then immediately ask them to solve several problems obviously connected to the new information. Learning for transfer gives students significant responsibility in the process of collecting, evaluating, and analyzing information to build concepts and understanding. Not only do students learn the content, but they also better understand the process of learning.

Producing a musical provides students and teachers with active learning opportunities as they work together learning roles, sewing costumes, and building sets. — DVD, Scuola Vita Nuova, "Theater Production"

Motivation and multiple contexts also contribute to transfer of learning (NRC, 2000). Motivation can be increased through meaningful curriculum that is applicable to the outside world. Multiple contexts refers to using new learning to solve a variety of related but unique problems. However, what is usually requested is for students to learn an algebraic concept and apply it to similar algebra problems. Even if they do several problems in algebra class that vary slightly from the original, students will likely not be able to transfer that concept to anything else in algebra and almost surely not outside of the class. If, on the other hand, the same concept is used to solve very different algebra problems, problems related to other subjects, and especially problems existing in the real world, the students practice transfer and will be able to use the concept in the future.

Metacognition

Throughout the process of learning, metacognition defines the last fundamental cognitive aspect of active learning. According to the NRC (2000), metacognition includes

> Knowledge about learning, knowledge of their own learning strengths and weaknesses, and the demands of the learning task at hand. Metacognition also includes self-regulation—the ability to orchestrate one's learning: to plan, monitor success, and correct errors when appropriate. (p. 97)

Young adolescents become increasingly capable of self-regulation and reflection, making them active participants in their learning.

Young adolescents become increasingly capable of self-regulation and reflection, making them active participants in their learning. These skills, however, do not happen automatically. As with any other new skills, metacognition must be taught, practiced, and developed. To be learned well, metacognition should be repeatedly incorporated into learning activities. Students should regularly think and talk about group and individual learning goals, progress toward goals, and further their plans to reach the goals. In this way, they actively orchestrate their own learning.

Active learning calls for cognitive engagement, which requires teaching students to take responsibility for planning and assessing their learning. Students must also adopt an incremental view of intelligence, realizing that effort coupled with support increases learning. Thoughtful participation leads to learning transfer, which is a major goal and one especially important to young adolescents.

Active Social, Moral, and Physical Learning

Collaborating with peers in learning also engages young adolescents socially.

In addition to cognitive activity, young adolescents crave social, moral, and physical involvement. Socially and morally, they begin to be concerned about others, often the downtrodden. They want to make a difference in the world. They are concerned about inconsistencies they notice in others and in society, and they need peer interactions (NMSA, 2003). Active learning in this context means being involved in the world outside of the classroom, in a way that improves society and addresses injustices.

Service learning offers one way to engage young adolescents in their communities and beyond (Fertman, White, & White, 1996; Jackson & Davis, 2000; Schine, 1997). In this model, service in the community becomes embedded in the curriculum. Through their classroom learning, students discover and investigate a problem in their community, state, country, or even the world. Students, in collaboration with teachers and community representatives, then devise and carry out a plan to address that problem. Not only does this kind of learning actively engage young adolescents' social and moral sensibilities, it also increases motivation for learning because it is connected to something that matters.

Collaborating with peers in learning also engages young adolescents socially. Throughout the strategies previously described, interaction with peers must be a prime consideration. In many learning situations these interactions offer an opportunity to further develop learning, to foster respect for each other, and to provide a chance to socialize around some common purpose. Students may not necessarily conduct interactions in an appropriate or productive way—especially with peers not considered friends—but with explicit teaching, needed skills, too, can be learned.

Although active learning encompasses much more, physical activity remains an important consideration. Young people need to move (NMSA, 2003)—to release energy, engage all of their senses, and give their growing bodies an opportunity to stretch. Hands-on learning continues to be as important for middle school students as it was for them in elementary school. Experiments, manipulatives, and group challenges are examples of some of the ways to engage young adolescents physically.

French teacher Ty Bryant leads students in a game of academic "Simon Says" to engage them and sharpen their command of the language. — Chapel Hill MS

Implications for Curriculum, Assessment, and the Teacher's Role

Active learning is inseparable from curriculum and assessment. To create a learning environment where students want to become engaged requires a meaningful curriculum. For young adolescents, meaningful curriculum directly relates to their interests and concerns in the context of the world in and out of school. Curriculum must be important to them now, not just for some vague future use in academics or even in life. Curriculum that young people perceive as important and relevant will likely engage them in meaningful learning.

Curriculum must be important to students now, not just for some vague future use in academics or even in life.

Assessment plays a key role in active learning as well. However, common grading practices often disengage learners from active participation. If based on an average or percentage of correct answers, it reinforces the fixed view of intelligence. Averaging also punishes students for making mistakes, even if those mistakes are later understood and corrected. Further, traditional grades discourage students from taking intellectual risks and challenges because anything other than immediate success negatively affects the final grade. The more difficulty students face in learning quickly, the more likely these practices will disengage them from learning.

Assessment, if focused on learning concepts and goals, can encourage active learning and offer feedback. If students clearly understand the goals, they can make individual and group plans to meet those goals. Teachers and peers provide frequent and specific feedback on progress toward the goals, which in turn leads to further development and adjustment to the plans for meeting goals. Mistakes become part of the feedback, and plans for further learning become not only essential, but also valued. Metacognition, an incremental view of intelligence and concepts—all components of active learning—are embedded in this view of assessment.

The teacher's role becomes primarily collaborative rather than predominantly directive.

To create the active learning described in this chapter, the teacher's role becomes primarily collaborative rather than predominantly directive. Instead of telling students what and how to learn, providing resources, and assessing student learning, the teacher facilitates students in making those decisions. The teacher remains the educational expert and assures that student decisions move them toward stated ends, but the teacher's goal becomes teaching students how to monitor and control their own learning. For students to become active in their learning, teachers have to surrender some control.

Contrasting Passive and Active Learning: An Example

In this chapter, active learning is described in the context of cognitive, social, moral, and physical development of young adolescents and the implications it carries for curriculum, assessment, and teachers. Two examples of classroom learning follow; one illustrates predominantly passive learning and the other active learning. The example of predominantly passive learning does not represent the extreme of passive learning, but one that might typically occur in any middle school. The second represents how a similar situation, with moderate changes, becomes active learning.

Example #1: Predominantly passive learning

A team of middle school teachers looks at the curriculum and determines that a unit on drug abuse and addiction will meet standards and likely appeal to their group of students. They plan lectures and activities to teach students about addiction, environments, and choices around substance use. The teachers review resources in and out of school and select what they believe are the best and most interesting. During the next few weeks, students move through the activities that teachers planned and construct posters on some facet of the unit.

Example #2: Active learning

A group of young adolescents and their teacher collaboratively pose the questions "Why do only certain people become addicted to drugs and alcohol?" and "What are the chances that I will become addicted to some substance?" The students, with the teacher as facilitator, discuss possible ways to answer the questions and develop a list that includes researching the genetics of addiction, investigating family histories, reading about environmental factors that increase addictive behaviors, conducting a confidential survey among their peers, and interviewing addicts, counselors, and doctors.

They search for resources that best answer their questions and find that some Internet resources are reliable and valid while others are biased, incomplete, or just plain incorrect. They find that some primary sources interview well, but others cannot seem to help them understand. They discover that lecture from the teacher or a guest speaker at just the right time can be informative and interesting. As they progress through their list of activities, they collaborate with their teacher to determine what they have learned about their questions and what they still have to learn. They develop a few additional activities to address weaknesses in their understanding. When they finally develop some possible answers to the original question, they go back to their human sources for feedback on their answers. Finally, they develop a plan to present to the school board about how to effectively teach their peers about substance abuse.

Buy-in to learning increases significantly when students such as Maggie are partners with their teachers in designing curriculum.
— DVD, Maranacook Community MS, "Curriculum Development"

In the first example, students may well have been engaged in learning about substance abuse because it is a topic of high interest. They may gather similar information as the second group of students and may even build similar concepts. They have not, however, actively participated in their own learning to any significant degree.

The second group consciously became motivated because the questions belonged to the students. They found and evaluated their own resources and sought feedback to assess their progress toward their goal of answering the questions. They collaborated with each other and engaged with their communities to develop a solution for substance abuse among their peers. In short, they became active participants, taking increasing responsibility for every aspect of their learning. The teachers in the second example allowed the learning to be more active for students by collaborating with the students rather than controlling and directing the learning themselves.

Young adolescents are not only capable of active learning, but they learn best when they are allowed to take responsibility for significant decisions in their educational lives. They have important questions and concerns; they are ready to engage. Educators have only to share the reins.

References

Charney, R. (2002). *Teaching children to care: Classroom management for ethical and academic growth, K-8* (Rev. ed.). Greenfield, MA: National Foundation for Children.

Deci, E., Vallerand, R., Pelletier, L., & Ryan, R. (1991). Motivation and education: The self-determination perspective. *Educational Psychologist, 26*(3 & 4), 325-346.

Dweck, C. (2000). *Self-theories: Their role in motivation, personality, and development*. Florence, KY: Psychology Press.

Fertman, C., White, G., & White, L. (1996). *Service learning in the middle school: Building a culture of service*. Columbus, OH: National Middle School Association.

Jackson, A. W., & Davis, G. (2000). *Turning points 2000: Educating adolescents in the 21st century.* New York: Teachers College Press and Westerville, OH: National Middle School Association.

Knowles, T., & Brown, D. (2000). *What every middle school teacher should know.* Portsmouth, NH: Heinemann.

Maehr, M., & Anderman, E . (1993). Reinventing schools for early adolescents: Emphasizing task goals. *The Elementary School Journal, 93,* 593-620.

National Middle School Association. (2003). *This we believe: Successful schools for young adolescents.* Westerville, OH: Author.

National Research Council. (2000). *How people learn: Brain, mind, experience, and school.* Washington, DC: National Academy Press.

Schine, J. (1997). Service learning and young adolescents: A good fit. In J. L. Irvin (Ed.), *What current research says to the middle level practitioner* (pp. 257-263). Columbus, OH: National Middle School Association.

An Adult Advocate for Every Student

Ross M. Burkhardt
J. Thomas Kane

A wink from a teacher during a presentation indicating a good job, a hug in the hall on a bad hair day, a stern lecture on accountability, or even a call to parents to alert them of a situation are the kinds of support that keep middle schoolers on track. How and what allows these gestures to be accepted by a young adolescent? Advocacy!

Advisory to Advocacy: Meeting Every Student's Needs
James & Spradling, 2002, p. 5

Advocacy: *The particular role that middle level educators play as active supporters of and intercessors for young adolescents. While each student should have an adult who is primarily responsible for the academic and personal growth of that individual, advocacy should be inherent in the school's culture and in shared responsibility.*

Understanding and Implementing This We Believe: First Steps
Lounsbury & Brazee, 2004, p. 11

The heart of a successful advisory program is the development of a trustful, caring community in which students perceive their advisor as demonstrating unconditional support for their growth.

What Every Middle School Teacher Should Know
Knowles & Brown, 2000, p. 154

"Mr. B., I got a 93 on my test!" Marisa rushed into my classroom between second and third period to tell me the good news. For several weeks we had been discussing her lack of success in math. An honor student in seventh grade, Marisa was unexpectedly receiving Cs and Ds on her eighth-grade algebra tests. She had considered a tutor or possibly dropping to a lower ability level; recently she had begun attending math extra-help sessions. In my dual role as Marisa's advisor and teacher, I saw her four times daily—morning advisory, English, advisory lunch, and social studies. Once a month I had a 40-minute advisory conference with Marisa to discuss school issues and life in general. An accomplished actress who was learning to play Lacrosse, Marisa regularly shared with me the joys and the woes of being 13. And math was one of her burdens. I listened sympathetically as she voiced her frustrations; she knew that I believed in her eventual success. After hearing her plight, I suggested the math extra-help sessions. That is about all I did, besides listening to her. Marisa did the rest.

Advocacy lies at the heart of middle level education, and every middle level educator needs to be an advocate for young adolescents. National Middle School Association (2003) in its position paper *This We Believe: Successful Schools for Young Adolescents* asserts that successful schools for young adolescents are characterized by, among other things, "an adult advocate for every student" (p. 7), one "who is knowledgeable about young adolescent development in general, who self-evidently enjoys working with young adolescents, and who comes to know students well as individuals" (p. 16).

As young adolescents navigate the transition from elementary school to middle school, as their bodies grow and change, as they develop new interests and expand peer relationships, as they probe boundaries and test limits both at home and in school, as they explore a rapidly changing world through the Internet, as they are subjected to daily bombardments of enticing advertisements on television and in magazines, as they consider alluring messages embedded in the lyrics of current popular songs, as they confront sensational headlines, and as they edge tentatively yet inexorably towards maturity, advocating for young adolescents is necessarily problematic. Some of these youngsters weather the turbulence with few upsets; others inhabit self-centered lives redolent with roller-coaster drama; still others experience pain and suffering resulting from abusive settings or unhealthy choices, or both. All experience momentous changes when growing from ages 10 to 15.

Clearly, educating today's youth is as great a challenge as it ever was, and middle level teachers "are engaged in the most important work on the planet" (NMSA, 1996, p. 3). J. H. Lounsbury (personal communication, December 30, 2004) put it this way:

> As young adolescents undergo the many changes that occur in this transition stage of life, they need the support and guidance of adults who understand them and can put into perspective their occasionally belligerent ways, their often silly manner, their sometimes hurtful nature, and their incessant questioning. Young adolescents want desperately to talk to adults, to engage in informal conversations about things that interest them, and to hear the opinions of adults they like. Middle school teachers are in a unique position to be the advocates these vulnerable youth need; for, as professional educators, they understand human growth and development, have an established relationship with them, and are present among them and their peers in the ongoing life of school. Middle school teachers cannot and should not try to escape the critical responsibility they inevitably carry as significant others in the lives of these young people who quite literally are making up their minds about the values, attitudes, and dispositions that will direct their behavior in the years to come. It is an awesome responsibility and an opportunity to influence lives that must be taken willingly and seriously. I firmly believe that fulfilling this role well will lead to increased academic achievement.

Many middle level schools respond to this "awesome responsibility" by instituting advisory programs designed to address the affective needs of young adolescents while supporting their academic development. Most advisory programs share several common attributes: (a) a designated staff member responsible for a small group of students; (b) regularly scheduled meetings of the advisory group; (c) ongoing individual conferences between advisor and advisees during the school year; (d) administrative support for advisory activities; (e) parent contact with the school through the child's advisor; and, most importantly, (f) an adult advocate for every young adolescent.

Advocacy and advisory are closely related. If advocacy is an operational mindset, an attitude about how to engage with and support young adolescents during these important years of growth, then advisory refers to specific programs designed by middle level educators to address the needs and interests of kids. In *From Advisory to Advocacy*, James and Spradling (2002) offered this distinction:

> An advocacy program is not a curriculum printed in a manual. It is a process developed through a set of experiences that establishes rapport between adults to students as well as students to adults and students to students, practices those students can internalize and use with others over a lifetime. (pp. 5-6)

According to *This We Believe* (NMSA, 2003), one obligation of a successful middle level school is to provide "an attitude of caring that translates into action when adults are responsive to the needs of each and every young adolescent in their charge" (p. 16). Successful schools demonstrate "a continuity of caring and support that extends throughout a student's middle level experience" (p. 17). An advisory program enables such a "continuity of caring" to take root. Schools that have instituted and maintained successful advisory programs note greater academic achievement, fewer alienated students, increased attendance, less vandalism, more student-centered learning activities, and a better educational climate permeating the building. As Galassi, Gulledge, and Cox (1998) pointed out:

At Warsaw Middle School, every student is a part of a focus group, three from each grade 5-8, that stays together over their middle school years.
— "Focus Group"

> Research indicates that students who receive adequate support become better adjusted to middle school and have a more positive self-concept, lower feelings of depression, and greater liking of middle school (e.g., Dubois, Felner, Meares, & Krier, 1994; Dubois & Hirsch, 1990). (pp. 58-59)

In a watershed research report on the impact of the 1989 *Turning Points* recommendations, Felner and associates (1997) reported that

> Small teams and teacher-based advisory programming in particular . . . appear to enable students to make the transition into middle-grades schools without the pronounced declines in socio/emotional well-being and academic achievement that have been reported in some studies of students moving into middle-grades schools and junior high schools. (p. 549)

Doda (2003) spoke to the importance of middle level educators creating caring schools for young adolescents:

> Advisory, or whatever we choose to call it (i.e., Home Base, Prime Time, Morning Meeting, etc.) is our commitment to creating caring schools—schools dedicated to building community where our children are actively

> respected, valued, taken seriously, understood; where they can learn to care about each other, develop compassion, participate in a model democratic, humane community; where they can be encouraged, coached, supported; and where student voice can be at the forefront of curriculum. . . . If we embrace advisory . . . as a powerful opportunity to enhance our efforts to reach and teach our young people, then affect and achievement become codependent and no middle school should be without it. (p. 21)

In its 1989 landmark publication *Turning Points: Preparing American Youth for the 21st Century*, the Carnegie Council on Adolescent Development advanced eight recommendations for transforming the education of young adolescents and middle grades schools. The first recommendation endorsed the creation of smaller communities of learning and called for an adult advisor for each student. "The effect of the advisory system," noted the report, "appears to be to reduce alienation of students and to provide each young adolescent with the support of a caring adult who knows that student well. That bond can make the student's engagement and interest in learning a reality" (p. 41). This recommendation—"smaller learning communities"—was reaffirmed in *Turning Points 2000: Educating Adolescents in the 21st Century* (Jackson & Davis, 2000, p. 24).

At Thurgood Marshall Middle School all students and teachers are looped and spend two years together. "They know me, I know them. I know their stories. I know what to expect of them, and they know what to expect of me."
— Renee Robinson, Teacher, "Introduction"

In 1981 when Joan Lipsitz visited Shoreham-Wading River (SWR) Middle School to conduct research for her acclaimed book *Successful Schools for Young Adolescents*, she encountered a phenomenon, the absence of alienation, when she was told by a seventh grade girl, "They absolutely know me here" (Lipsitz, 1984, p. 129). Would that every middle school student in every middle level school could make the same declaration!

That notion—students being known and knowing that they are known by the adults in the building—is at the heart of advocacy. The two most important jobs middle level educators have are to know the students they teach and to address their learning needs. The National Board for Professional Teaching Standards is unambiguous on this point: "Accomplished [middle level] generalists draw on their knowledge of early adolescent development and their relationships with students to understand and foster their students' knowledge, skills, interests, aspirations, and values" (National Board for Professional Teaching Standards [NBPTS], 1994, p. 9). If teachers expect students to become engaged learners, they must communicate to those students that they are welcomed, respected, and appreciated. Young adolescents need affirmation and support. They need to know that those who are charged with educating them are also concerned about them. Advisory programs help to make this concern an everyday reality for students.

And yet, some schools that initiated advisory programs during the past three decades lost sight of this concern. Too many programs floundered because advisory was seen as a curriculum to be covered rather than a relationship to be nurtured. And while it is more difficult to develop positive relationships than it is to conduct scripted activities, one goal of every middle level educator ought to be the creation of a more intimate school setting for students. J. Burns (personal communication, January 11, 2005) recently remarked

> Advisory means attentive relationship-building work with kids. We have recently coined the term "relational work" between teachers and students. Advocacy means knowing who young adolescents are and speaking out for them and their interests. However, this does not mean defending the student right or wrong. It is not about that. I am seeing advocacy more as what we do with kids across the day. Teachers also bring parents into it, bring the community into it. In my conversations with students, I have been told the things they really like in advisory are food and time to socialize. What they really dislike in advisory are pencil and paper activities, because they get so much of that elsewhere during the day. Both advisory and advocacy are about relationships that grow as people figure out what really matters in school achievement.

Advocacy speaks to a dynamic relationship between middle level educators and those they serve—the emerging adolescents in our schools. Knowles and Brown (2000) asserted that "advisors must be willing to develop a relationship with students different from the one they experience as a regular classroom teacher—one characterized by caring, not authoritarianism" (p. 153).

When students make a lasting connection with at least one caring adult, academic and personal outcomes improve.

The Carnegie Corporation of New York underscored the direct connection between advocacy and academic achievement, stating, "When students make a lasting connection with at least one caring adult, academic and personal outcomes improve. . . .When it is well implemented, our sense is that the advisory can be effective in developing relationships that support learning" (Jackson & Davis, 2000, p. 143).

In his seminal work, *A Middle School Curriculum: From Rhetoric to Reality*, Beane (1993) argued "the central purpose of the middle school curriculum should be helping early adolescents explore self and social meanings at this time in their lives" (p. 18).

Teachers who serve as advisors to sixth, seventh, and eighth graders receive daily, if not hourly, reminders of what it is like to be a young adolescent in today's fast-paced world. Through conversation and contact with their charges, teachers gain useful insights into early adolescence that they can then weave into the ongoing classroom experience over the course of the school year.

Teachers and staff make a point of talking with students outside of class, attending performances and sporting events, and generally being available. — DVD, Warsaw MS, "Focus Group"; Scuola Vita Nuova, "Community Liaison"; Maranacook Community MS, "Ice Fishing"

Young adolescents *are* concerned about issues other than school, and they need assistance in facing the future. Rubinstein (1994) observed

> Often, the predominant question teens have while trying to exist in the larger, more anonymous middle schools is whether life is really worth living. If we want them to answer this question with "Yes, life is worth living," then we must find the ways and time to give them the personal attention and support they need to grow up as healthy people in both body and mind. Support must come before challenge to help young people grow. (p. 26)

Advisory programs that focus on the needs of young adolescents provide such attention and support. As the adage goes, "Kids don't care how much you know until they know how much you care."

Initiating Advocacy

How to begin? One useful approach is to have a faculty committee frame a mission statement that describes the nature and purpose of advocacy. In 1973 a group of advisors at SWR Middle School drafted the following passage, which continues to be used more than three decades later as the basic definition of its nationally recognized program:

> Advisory is essentially a comprehensive, school-oriented, one-to-one relationship between the advisor and

> the advisee for the purposes of communication and direction. . . . Advisory enables each student to have an adult advocate in the school; the advisor is a person who can champion the advisee's cause in student-teacher, student-administrator, and student-student interactions.
> (SWR Middle School, 2004)

Advisors need to know what is expected of them as they advocate for young adolescents. A staff committee can compile a list of responsibilities—a job description—that may include taking attendance, disseminating school announcements, collecting lunch money, handling minor discipline issues, and communicating with the families of advisees. *This We Believe* describes the advisor as "the primary liaison between the school and family [who] often initiates contact with parents, providing pertinent information about the student's program and progress, as well as being ready to receive calls from any parent with a concern" (NMSA, 2003, p. 17). When teachers "make themselves available to counsel and advise students on a wide range of issues from academic progress to peer relationships to extra-curricular opportunities," they form "constructive relationships" which support students in becoming better learners and more responsible citizens. Such relationships provide teachers with "a window to see more sharply aspects of their students' character, values, interests, and talents that might otherwise be overlooked" (NBPTS, 1994, pp. 9-10).

Constructive relationships provide teachers with a window to see more sharply aspects of students' character, values, interests, and talents.

How does a teacher learn to be an effective advisor? Staff development sessions are helpful, especially when veterans share their experiences with beginning advisors. Also, a positive attitude can lead to expertise over time. Jane Wittlock, a former teacher and administrator at SWR Middle School responded to the question, "What kind of training should an advisor have?" in the following manner: "I don't think training could really help. If you don't love 10- to 14-year-olds initially, *nothing* could help you become an advisor. If you think this age group is *truly special*, then you'll be a good advisor" (SWR Middle School, 1989). This response emphasizes the attitudinal nature of advocacy—a positive relationship between the advisor and the advisee.

Chris Stevenson described the Alpha Program in Shelburne, Vermont, which has educated young adolescents for more than a third of a century, as "a community of adults and young adolescents who willingly learn, work, and live together in a harmonious climate driven by high expectations, initiative, individual choices, and remarkable degrees of responsibility and accountability well beyond what is even expected, much less accomplished through conventional school practices" (Kuntz, 2005, p. vi). Advocacy thrives at Alpha largely because of

> Teachers who believed that teaching involved making connections with each student on many levels, intellectual, personal, social. They defined successful teaching as "getting to know the hopes, fears, and potential of each student." They did not follow a standard approach to learning or teaching; they individualized expectations and activities for students. They were as concerned about student identity and self-understanding as they were about the content presented and activities planned. (p. 39).

Administrative support is one key to a vibrant advocacy program in middle school. The school principal must engage in three activities that support advisory activities: mentoring, monitoring, and maintenance. The principal as mentor ensures that new staff members understand the school's philosophy and mission statement on advisory. Initially, new teachers can be paired with successful veteran advisors. To enhance their in-depth understanding of the role that advocacy plays in a caring school community, the principal can supply novice advisors with pertinent reading materials.

Administrative support is one key to a vibrant advocacy program in middle school.

The principal should monitor advisory experiences that take place in the school through dialogue with staff members and students by witnessing, from a distance, the interactions that occur between advisors and advisees, and by orchestrating sharing sessions for teachers at faculty meetings. Such occasions provide a venue for exchanging tales of success and failure that can inform future advocacy activities.

Maintenance of a middle school's program begins with the principal's keeping current his or her own expertise regarding early adolescence and advocacy by reading timely journal articles and new publications focused on advocacy. The principal can propose advisory program enhancement opportunities as teachers design their yearly personal professional development plans.

Through mentoring, monitoring, and maintaining a school's relational work with young adolescents, principals become visible witnesses for advocacy and promoters of the advisory program. They understand the long-term gains that an advisory program can provide. MacLaury (2002) reported:

> Many principals perceive supportive advisory programs to also have a long-term, positive effect by helping to prevent students from dropping out of school. George and Oldaker (1985) determined that 93% of such exemplary schools had advisory programs for all their students and

that 62% of these children enjoyed "consistent academic improvement," while schools reported an 80% reduction in referrals for behavioral problems. (p. 17)

A school's priorities show up in the master schedule. In order for effective advisor-advisee relationships to blossom, the schedule must allow time for advisory activities to occur. Group meetings, individual conferences, parent conferences, program evaluation—all of these will appear in the school calendar where and when there is genuine commitment to making advisory work.

When creating advisory groups, small works best. If every educator in the building serves as an advisor, the load is shared evenly, and more students are better served. An ideal advisory group contains 10 to 12 students. Advocacy takes time; the smaller the group size, the more effective the advisor can be.

For many parents of middle school children, early adolescence is a developmental labyrinth. Confused about what makes their youngster tick, parents do not always fully grasp the format, design, and intent of a developmentally responsive middle level school. This is especially true when parents are themselves products of a traditional junior high school experience.

If parents are to become genuine partners with and supporters of their child's middle school, every effort should be made to educate them regarding the format and functioning of an effective middle school. Parents should have a clear picture of how a middle school operates and, as part of their orientation to the early teen years, understand the importance of advisory and advocacy. Back to School Night provides an annual opportunity to inform parents. The *first* stop on such an evening should be a meeting with their youngster's advisor. After explaining the program to parents, advisors can engage them in an advocacy exercise that will help them appreciate how advisory can serve their child.

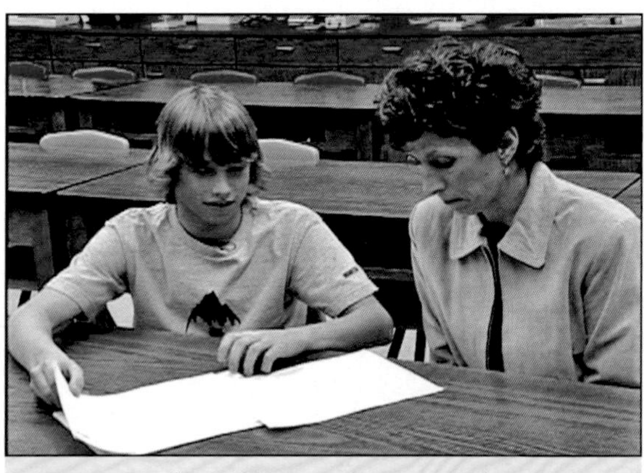

Advocating for students includes collaboration between home and school.
— DVD, Warsaw MS, "Focus Group"

Whether beginning an advisory program from scratch or evaluating one that has been in place for many years, staff members need occasions to discuss and modify the operational aspects of the program. Faculty meetings can be used for this purpose. The following set of questions may prove helpful:

1. What does the school's mission statement say regarding advisory?
2. What does "advocacy" mean? What are its parameters?
3. What does the advisory program mission statement say?
4. What are the basic responsibilities of an advisor?
5. Who in the school will manage and maintain the advisory program?
6. How will advisory groups be formed?
7. When do advisors meet with advisees in groups? When do advisors meet individually with advisees?
8. How will issues of confidentially be handled?
9. Who will mediate differences of opinion among advisors regarding the resolution of problems with students?
10. What happens when a student wants to switch from one advisory group to another?
11. Should advisory groups contain students all at the same grade level, or should more than one grade level be represented?
12. Should the advisor continue with his or her advisees all through middle school, or should students have new advisors each year?
13. Should an advisee participate in an advisor-parent conference?
14. What happens when parents want to meet with a teacher other than the child's advisor?
15. How, when, and by whom will the advisory program be evaluated?

J. Silverstein, an English and social studies teacher who also served as an advisor for 30 years, understands how advisory made his teaching tasks easier (personal communication, January 19, 2005):

> When visitors came to Shoreham-Wading River, they often said that they could not imagine adding the workload of being an advisor to their already overbooked schedules. What they did not realize was that the advisory system made so many aspects of their job easier, and that the dividends were well worth the effort. The advisory system, for example, cut down on discipline problems and gave me a natural support system when dealing with students who had poor work habits, troubled home situations, or even those who had behavioral or learning disabilities. Whenever I, as a teacher, had difficulties with a student, an advisor was there to help me find a solution, and often the knowledge that they brought provided the perspective needed to solve any problem.

Ultimately, "an advisory system is a simple method that ensures that no secondary school (middle school, junior high school, or high school) student becomes anonymous" (Goldberg, 1998, p. 1). Anonymity leads to alienation, and, unfortunately in the minds of some young people, feelings of alienation sanction antisocial behavior. Advocacy for all minimizes the number of students who fall through the cracks. Education has always been a human business, and an advisory program "will appeal to any middle, junior high, or high school that wishes to emphasize personalization" (Goldberg, 1998, p. ix). The more humane and caring the school, the more readily a sense of community will take root and flourish.

Why, then, an adult advocate for every student? Because the roles and responsibilities of today's middle level teachers call for it and because Marisa and all other middle level students deserve it. As Rubinstein (1994) so eloquently maintained in *Hints for Teaching Success in Middle School*, "The most critical need for any person is to find meaning, purpose, and significance. In order to do this, that person must feel understood, accepted, and affirmed" (p. 26).

Advocacy provides young adolescents with affirmation and acceptance at a critical time in their lives; it is an essential element of the successful middle level school. After all, "middle level schools are in a particularly critical position because of the opportunity they have to influence, for better or worse, not only the students themselves but society at large. The future for our society hangs in the balance" (NMSA, 2003, p. 36).

References

Beane, J. A. 1993. *A middle school curriculum: From rhetoric to reality* (2nd ed.). Columbus, OH: National Middle School Association.

Carnegie Council on Adolescent Development. (1989). *Turning points: Preparing American youth for the 21st century.* New York: Carnegie Corporation.

Doda, N. (2003). Relationships in the middle school: Rethinking advisory. *In Transition, 31* (1), 20-24.

DuBois, D.L., Felner, R.D., Meares, H., & Krier, M. (1994). Prospective investigation of the effects of socioeconomic disadvantage, life stress, and social support on early adolescent adjustment. *Journal of Abnormal Psychology, 103,* 511-522.

DuBois, D. L., & Hirsch, B. J. (1990). School and neighborhood friendships of Blacks and Whites in early adolescence. *Child Development, 62,* 524-536.

Felner, R. D., Jackson, A. W., Kasak, D., Mulhall, P., Brand, S., & Flowers, N. (1997). The impact of school reform for the middle years: A longitudinal study of a network engaged in Turning Points-based comprehensive school transformation. *Phi Delta Kappan, 78,* 528-532, 541-550.

Galassi, J. P., Gulledge, S. A., & Cox, N. D. (1998). *Advisory: Definitions, descriptions, decisions, directions.* Columbus, OH: National Middle School Association.

Goldberg, M. F. (1998). *How to design an advisory system for a secondary school.* Alexandria, VA: Association for Supervision and Curriculum Development.

Jackson, A. W., & Davis, G. A. (2000). *Turning points 2000: Educating adolescents in the 21st century.* New York: Teachers College Press and Westerville, OH: National Middle School Association.

James, M., & Spradling, N. (2002). *From advisory to advocacy: Meeting every student's needs.* Westerville, OH: National Middle School Association.

Knowles, T., & Brown, D. F. (2000). *What every middle school teacher should know.* Portsmouth, NH: Heinemann.

Kuntz, S. (2005). *The story of Alpha: A multiage, student-centered team —33 years and counting.* Westerville, OH: National Middle School Association.

Lipsitz, J. (1984). *Successful schools for young adolescents.* East Brunswick, NY: Transaction.

Lounsbury, J. H., & Brazee, E. N. (2004). *Understanding and implementing This We Believe—First steps.* Westerville, OH: National Middle School Association.

MacLaury, S. (2002). *Student advisories in grades 5-12: A facilitator's guide.* Norwood, MA: Christopher-Gordon.

National Board for Professional Teaching Standards. (1994). *Early adolescence/generalist standards for National Board certification.* Washington, DC: Author.

National Middle School Association. (1996). *National Middle School Association 1996 Annual Report.* Columbus, OH: Author.

National Middle School Association. (2003). *This we believe: Successful schools for young adolescents.* Westerville, OH: Author.

Rubinstein, R. E. (1994). *Hints for teaching success in middle school.* Englewood, CO: Teachers Ideas Press.

Shoreham-Wading River Middle School. (1989). *Advisory activities at Shoreham-Wading River Middle School.* Shoreham, NY: Author.

Shoreham-Wading River Middle School. (2004). *Advisory handbook.* Shoreham, NY: Author. Retrieved January 22, 2005, from *http://www.swrcsd.com/schools/pms.asp*

School-Initiated Family and Community Partnerships

Joyce L. Epstein

This We Believe, the position paper of National Middle School Association (2003), discusses 14 characteristics of responsive middle level schools. The beliefs set high expectations for good people, good places, and good programs in the middle grades. They are presented as important goals to improve the quality of life in schools and the quality of education for all young adolescents.

One characteristic of a responsive middle level school is "family and community partnerships." A goal of good partnerships is on every list for school improvement, but few schools have implemented comprehensive partnership programs. This chapter addresses three questions to help middle level educators move from beliefs about the importance of family and community involvement to action:

1. What is a comprehensive, goal-oriented program of school, family, and community partnerships in the middle grades?
2. How does family and community involvement link with the other elements of an effective middle level school?
3. How can schools answer the call for action to develop and sustain productive partnership programs?

A Framework for a Comprehensive Program of Partnerships: Six Types of Involvement

For decades studies have shown that families are important for children's learning, development, and school success across the grades. Research is accumulating that extends that social fact by showing that school programs of partnership are needed to help all families support their children's education from preschool through high school (Epstein, 2001; Henderson & Mapp, 2002; Sanders & Epstein, 2000; Sanders & Simon, 2002; Sheldon & Epstein, 2005; Sheldon & Van Voorhis, 2004).

Studies show that if middle level schools implement comprehensive and inclusive programs of partnership, then many more families respond, including those who would not become involved on their own.

Left on their own, few families continue as active partners in the middle grades. Still, most families want and need more information about early adolescence, middle level education, the school system, special programs that are available to their children, and other issues and options that affect students in the middle grades. Studies show that if middle level schools implement comprehensive and inclusive programs of partnership, then many more families respond, including those who would not become involved on their own.

What is a comprehensive program of partnerships? From many studies and activities with educators and families, I developed a framework of six types of involvement that helps schools establish full and productive programs of school-family-community partnerships (Epstein et al., 2002). This section summarizes the six major types of involvement with a few sample practices that are important in the middle grades. Also noted are some of the challenges that must be met in order to involve all families, and examples of the results that can be expected in the middle grades from each type of involvement if activities are well implemented.

Type 1 – Parenting

Type 1 activities help families understand young adolescent development, acquire parenting skills for the age group, and set home conditions to support learning at each grade level. Other Type 1 activities help schools obtain information from families so that educators understand families' backgrounds, cultures, and goals for their children. Type 1 activities reinforce the fact that educators and parents share responsibility for students' learning and development through the middle grades, and help develop trust and mutual respect for each other's efforts in guiding student development.

Sample practices. Among Type 1 activities, middle level schools may conduct workshops for parents; provide short, clear summaries of important information on parenting; and organize opportunities for parents to exchange ideas on topics of young adolescent development including health, nutrition, discipline, guidance, peer pressure, preventing drug abuse, and planning for the future. Type 1 activities also provide parents with useful information on children's transitions to the middle grades and to high school, attendance policies, and other topics that are important for young adolescents' success in school. Middle schools may offer parent education classes, family support programs, family computer classes, family literacy programs, parent-to-parent panels, and other services for parents. To ensure family input, at the start of each school year or periodically, teachers and counselors may ask parents to share insights about their children's strengths, talents, interests, needs, and goals. See in Salinas and Jansorn (2004), for example, how Sunset, Utah, Junior High School organized parenting classes (p. 84) and how Lowndes County, Georgia, schools organized workshops at a "parent university" (p. 108).

Challenges. One challenge for successful Type 1 activities is to get information to parents who cannot come to meetings and workshops at the school building. This may be done with videos, tape recordings, newsletters, cable broadcasts, phone calls, computerized messages, school Web sites, and other print and non-print communications. Another Type 1 challenge is to design procedures and opportunities that enable all families to share information about their children with teachers, counselors, and others.

If families are part of their children's transitions—elementary to middle and middle to high school—more students adjust well to their new schools, and more parents remain involved.

Expected results. If information flows to and from families about young adolescent development, parents should increase their confidence about parenting through the middle grades, students should be more aware of parents' continuing guidance, and teachers should better understand their students' families. For example, studies show that if practices are targeted to help families send their children to school on time, then student attendance should improve (Epstein & Sheldon, 2002; Sheldon & Epstein, 2004). If families are part of their children's transitions from elementary to middle school and from middle to high school, more students should adjust well to their new schools, and more parents should remain involved across the grades (Seidman, Lambert, Allen, & Aber, 2003).

Type 2 – Communicating

Type 2 activities keep families informed about school programs and student progress with school-to-home and home-to-school communications such as notices, memos, conferences, report cards, newsletters, phone and computerized messages, the Internet, open houses, and other innovative communications. Schools tend to send a lot of information home, but two-way channels of communication are needed in successful partnership programs.

Sample practices. Among many Type 2 activities, middle level schools may provide parents with clear information on each teacher's criteria for report card grades, how to interpret interim reports, and, as necessary, how to work with students to help them improve their grades. Type 2 activities include conferences for parents with teams of teachers, or parent-student-teacher conferences (Tuinsta & Hiatt-Michael, 2004) to ensure that students take personal responsibility for learning. Schools may organize class parents, block parents, or telephone trees for more effective communications and set up the equivalent of an educational welcome wagon for families who transfer to the school during the school year. Activities may be designed to improve school newsletters to include student work and recognitions, parent columns, important calendars, and parent response forms. See, for example, how an e-mail system was organized by Madison Junior High School in Naperville, Illinois, (Salinas & Jansorn, 2004, p. 79).

Schools bear responsibility for providing consistent and varied means to maintain communication and build supportive relationships with students' families. — DVD, William Thomas MS, "Student-Led Conferences"; Chapel Hill MS, "Student Agenda Books"; Scuola Vita Nuova, "Community Liaison"

Challenges. One challenge for successful Type 2 activities is to make communications clear and understandable for all families, including parents who have less formal education, speak languages other than English at home, or do not read English well. All families must be able to process and respond to the information they receive. Another key Type 2 challenge is to develop effective two-way channels of communication so that families can easily contact teachers or counselors, offer ideas and suggestions, request conferences and information. Middle level schools also must make sure that students understand their roles in facilitating and participating in all school-family-community partnerships, including delivering home-to-school and school-to-home communications.

Expected results. If information is clear and two-way channels of communication are established, home-school interactions should increase. More families should understand the school's programs and teachers' expectations, follow their children's progress, and attend parent-teacher conferences. Specifically, if e-mail, voice mail systems, and Web sites are used to communicate information about homework, more families should know more about their children's daily assignments. If newsletters include respond-and-reply forms, more families should offer ideas, questions, and comments about school programs and activities. Studies indicated that good communications with families were consistently important for helping schools improve student behavior (Sheldon & Epstein, 2002) and math achievement (Sheldon & Epstein, 2005).

Type 3 – Volunteering

Type 3 activities improve recruitment, training, and schedules to involve parents and others as volunteers and as audiences at the school or in other locations to support students and school programs. Type 3 activities improve the adult-student ratio in a school and make it possible to offer more varied learning opportunities, and for teachers to provide students with more individualized attention.

A school-community liaison with social work background serves a vital role for teachers, students, and their families.
— Scuola Vita Nuova, "Community Liaison"

Sample practices. Among many Type 3 activities, middle level schools may collect information on family members' talents, occupations, interests, and availability to serve as volunteers to enrich students' academic classes; improve career explorations; serve as foreign language translators; conduct attendance monitoring and phone calls; work on "parent patrols" for safety; organize and improve activities such as clothing and uniform exchanges, school stores, fairs, and many other activities. Schools may also create opportunities for mentors, coaches, tutors, and leaders of after-school programs to ensure that middle grades students have engrossing and safe activities that expand their skills and talents. For example, middle level schools may establish a Family Center where parents can obtain information, conduct volunteer work for the school, and meet with other parents (Johnson, 1996).

Challenges. Challenges for successful Type 3 activities are to recruit widely so that many parents feel welcome as volunteers; make hours flexible for parents and other volunteers who work during the school day; provide training; and enable volunteers to contribute productively to the school, classroom curricula, and after-school programs. It helps if one or two volunteers serve as coordinators to match all volunteers' times and skills with the needs of teachers, administrators, and students. Another Type 3 challenge is to change the definition of "volunteer" to mean any one who supports the school and students' activities at any time and in any place. This opens options for parents and others who serve as audiences at school concerts, assemblies, sports activities, and other events to be recognized for volunteering their time. A related challenge is to help students in the middle grades understand how volunteers help their school, and to encourage students to volunteer, themselves, to help their school, family, and community.

If tasks, schedules, locations, and training for volunteers are varied, more parents, family members, and others in the community will support the school and students' activities.

Expected results. If tasks, schedules, locations, and training for volunteers are varied, more parents, family members, and others in the community will support the school and students' activities. If a useful directory is available of parents' time, talents, and resources, more teachers will call upon volunteers to improve school programs and activities. More parents should attend student performances and other events as members of the audience, if they know that their support is viewed as "volunteering." Specifically, if volunteers serve as attendance monitors, more families will be alerted and able to help students improve attendance (Sanders, 1999). If volunteers conduct a "hall patrol" or are active in other locations, school safety should increase and student behavior problems should decrease due to a better student-adult ratio and more supervision. If volunteers serve as tutors for particular subjects, student tutees should improve their skills in that subject. If volunteers discuss careers, students should be more aware of their options for the future. One study found that when parent volunteers shared art work linked to social studies units, students in the middle grades gained art appreciation experiences and knowledge about art and artists that they did not have before (Epstein & Dauber, 1995). Thus, if the volunteers have appropriate training for working with middle school students, they can assist teachers in improving student learning in particular subjects.

Type 4 – Learning at home

Type 4 activities involve families with their children in academic learning activities at home that are coordinated with classwork and contribute to success in school. This includes interactive homework, goal setting, and other curriculum-linked activities and decisions about academic courses and school programs. Type 4 activities link every teacher with every student and parent on curricular issues.

Sample practices. Among many Type 4 activities, middle level schools may provide information to students and to parents about the skills needed to pass each course and about each teacher's homework policies. Schools also may implement activities that help families encourage, praise, guide, and monitor their children's work using interactive homework, student-teacher-family contracts, long-term projects, summer home-learning packets, student-led conferences with parents at home, goal-setting activities, homework hotlines of daily assignments, or other interactive strategies that keep students and families talking about schoolwork at home. For example, the Teachers Involve Parents in Schoolwork (TIPS) process guides students to share and discuss their work and ideas with a family partner so that parents can see how and what students are learning in math, science, and language arts in the middle grades (Epstein, Salinas, & Van Voorhis, 2001; Epstein & Van Voorhis, 2001; Van Voorhis & Epstein, 2002).

Challenges. One challenge for successful Type 4 activities is to implement a regular schedule of interactive homework that requires students to take responsibility for discussing with family members important things they are learning, interviewing family members, recording reactions, and sharing their work and ideas at home. Another Type 4 challenge is to create procedures and activities that involve families regularly and systematically with students on short-term and long-term goal setting for achievement, behavior, attendance, development of personal talents, and plans for high school and post-secondary education.

Expected results. If Type 4 activities are well designed and well implemented, students should improve their homework completion, report card grades, and test scores in specific subjects. More families should know what their children are learning in class and how to monitor, support, and discuss homework. There should be more positive conversations between students and family members about their school work and academic ideas. Students and teachers should be more aware of family interest in students' work. Several studies show that interactive homework in the middle grades increases parental involvement with students about their schoolwork in math (Balli, Demo, & Wedman, 1998) and improves homework completion and report card grades in language arts (Epstein, Simon, & Salinas, 1997) and in science (Van Voorhis, 2003).

A partnership with a local music store enables students to take piano lessons at school at no charge to the family.
— DVD, William Thomas MS, "Piano Lab"

Type 5—Decision making

Type 5 activities include families' voices in developing a school's vision and mission statements, and in designing, reviewing, and improving school policies and other school decisions. Family members are participants on school improvement teams, committees, PTA/PTO or other parent organizations, and district councils. Parents also may be part of independent advocacy groups and task forces for school improvement.

Sample practices. Among Type 5 activities, middle level schools may organize and maintain an active parent association and include family representatives on all committees for school improvement, including curriculum, safety, supplies and equipment, partnerships, and career development committees. Schools may offer parents and teachers special training in leadership, decision making, and collaboration. Type 5 activities may be designed to distribute information for families about school policies, course offerings, special services, and tests and assessments. Middle level schools may use a variety of technologies including low-tech summaries and high-tech e-mail lists to share information and gather parents' ideas and reactions to policy questions. In particular, parents, other family members, teachers, administrators, students, and community partners are members of the Action Team for Partnerships, which plans and monitors the development of the school's program of family and community involvement.

One challenge is to ensure that there are parent representatives on school committees from all of the racial and ethnic groups, socioeconomic groups, and geographic communities present in the school.

Challenges. One challenge for successful Type 5 activities is to ensure that there are parent representatives on school committees from all of the racial and ethnic groups, socioeconomic groups, and geographic communities present in the middle level school. A related challenge is to help parent leaders serve as true representatives to obtain information from and provide information to other parents about decisions. An ongoing challenge is to help parent and teacher members of committees trust, respect, and listen to each other as they work toward common goals for school improvement.

Expected results. If Type 5 activities are well implemented, more families will have input into decisions that affect the quality of their children's education; students should increase their awareness that families have a say in school policies; and teachers should increase their understanding of family perspectives on policies and programs for improving the school.

Type 6—Collaborating with the community

Type 6 activities coordinate the work and resources of community businesses; agencies; cultural, civic, and religious organizations; colleges and universities; and other groups to strengthen school programs, family practices, and student learning and development.

Other activities enable students, staff, and families to contribute their services to the community.

Sample practices. Among many Type 6 activities, middle level schools may inform students and families about programs and resources in their community, such as after-school recreation, tutorial programs, health services, cultural events, service opportunities, and summer programs. Schools may arrange "gold card" discount programs with local merchants to recognize students who improve attendance and report card grades, or who demonstrate other accomplishments. Collaborations with community businesses, groups, and agencies also may strengthen the other types of involvement. For example, parent education workshops or meetings for families may be conducted at community or business locations (Type 1); local radio and TV (including foreign language stations), churches, clinics, supermarkets, and laundromats may help schools communicate about school events (Type 2); people from businesses and the community may serve as school volunteers (Type 3); artists, scientists, writers, mathematicians, and others in the community may enrich student learning in specific subjects (Type 4); and community members may serve on school and district decision-making councils and committees (Type 5).

A partnership with Youth Guidance, a community group that provides arts activities for special education students, has had a positive impact on students' academics and self-confidence.
— DVD, Thurgood Marshall MS, "Art-Based Partnerships"

Challenges. One challenge for successful Type 6 activities is to increase the equity of access for diverse students and families to community resources and programs. Another challenge is to solve "turf" problems such as who will fund and who will lead school-community collaborations. Still another Type 6 challenge is to link students' valuable learning experiences in the community to the school curriculum, including lessons that build on non-school skills and talents, such as students' work as volunteers and as members of student clubs and groups. A major challenge is to inform and involve the family in community-related activities that affect their children, so that families are aware of how others are assisting their children.

Expected results. Well-implemented Type 6 activities should help families, students, and educators know about the resources and programs in their community that can help students attain important school goals. By increasing equal access to community programs, more and different students and families should participate and benefit from various programs. Coordinated community services could help more students and their families solve problems that arise in early adolescence before they become too serious. Type 6 activities also should support and measurably enrich school curricula and extracurricular programs (Sanders, 2001; in press).

Not every practice to involve families will result in higher student test scores. Rather, practices for each type of involvement can be selected to help students, families, and teachers reach specific school improvement goals and results.

Summary. The six types of involvement create a comprehensive program of partnerships, but the implementation challenges for each type must be met in order for school programs to effectively inform and involve all families. The expected results are directly linked to the quality of the design and goal-oriented content of the activities. Not every practice to involve families will result in higher student test scores. Rather, practices for each type of involvement can be selected to help students, families, and teachers reach specific school improvement goals and results. The summary above includes a few examples from hundreds of possible activities that may help middle level schools improve their partnership programs.

Linking Partnerships to Other Recommended Middle Level Characteristics

The 14 characteristics of responsive middle levels schools in *This We Believe* are important. In excellent schools, educators who work with young adolescents share a vision of high expectations for all students. The school provides strong support, through an adult advocate, for every student and its partnerships with all students' families and communities. Academically, each subject's curriculum is relevant, challenging, integrative, and exploratory. Teachers are flexible in their uses of varied instructional approaches, assessments, and evaluations. Students are offered good guidance and programs that promote their health and safety. Instruction emphasizes students' active learning and inspired teaching, which motivates students to set high goals and take responsibility for progress in learning. These elements combine to promote all students' learning in a climate that is inviting, challenging, and joyful. With courageous and collaborative leadership, district leaders, principals, teachers, parents, students, and community partners work together to develop programs and practices that ensure successful middle level schools and successful students.

All of the characteristics of a good middle level school are interrelated (Epstein & Connors, 1995). It is particularly important for middle level educators to understand how a strong program of *School-initiated family and community partnerships* (described above) is linked to the other recommended elements so that family and community involvement is not something extra, separate, or different from the "real work" of the school. There are several ways that family and community involvement enhance the other recommendations in *This We Believe*.

Educators who value working with this age group and are prepared to do so

To understand young adolescents, educators need to know their students' family backgrounds, cultures, hopes, and dreams. If a school has a strong partnership program, with activities for the six types of involvement, more families will understand young adolescents, middle level schools, peer pressure, and other topics of importance. And, educators will better understand students' families. Indeed, middle level educators serve as role models for students by the ways they talk about and work with students' families. Many young adolescents are trying to balance their love for their family, need for guidance, and need for greater independence. Middle level educators who understand students' families can help students see that these seemingly contradictory pressures can coexist. See, for example, how Westminster Community School #68 in Buffalo, NY, conducted a *Legacy Quilt* project to help students talk with parents about their heritage (Salinas & Jansorn, 2003, p. 72).

Courageous, collaborative leadership

It takes courage and collaborative leadership, along with thoughtful and persistent action, to implement all 14 characteristics of an excellent middle level school. This kind of management and mettle requires effective teamwork, not only among administrators and teachers, but also parents, community partners, and students. Working together, all partners in education form the school's *learning community* (Epstein & Salinas, 2004) and may develop a goal-oriented program of school, family, and community partnerships.

A comprehensive program of family and community involvement takes more than organizing a discussion group or implementing incidental projects. Rather, each school must have an Action Team for Partnerships consisting of teachers, administrators, parents, and

Each school must have an Action Team for Partnerships of teachers, administrators, parents, and community partners, which serves as a permanent committee of the School Improvement Team or Council.

community partners, which serves as a permanent committee of the School Improvement Team or Council. The Action Team writes an annual Action Plan for Partnerships, including a detailed schedule of family and community involvement activities linked to school improvement goals for a welcoming school climate and for student achievement, attitudes, behavior, health, and other indicators of success. The plans and activities must be evaluated and continually improved from year to year. Research and field work show that comprehensive partnership programs help improve school climate and courses, strengthen families, invigorate community support, and increase student achievement and success in school (Epstein, 2001; Henderson & Mapp, 2002; Sheldon, 2003).

There is a growing consensus that educators must be competent in working on teams, sharing leadership, and conducting partnership activities with families in diverse communities (Fullan, 2001; Murphy, 2002). Of course, principals play key roles as school leaders and as members of the Action Team for Partnerships, even as teachers, parents, and others take leadership for planning and implementing family and community involvement activities to increase student learning and success (Epstein et al., 2002; Epstein & Jansorn, 2004).

A shared vision that guides decisions

Along with educators and students, families and community members must contribute to the shared vision of a responsive middle level school. Schools need to have well-designed practices as part of their partnership program that enable parents and community members to give input to a new vision or mission statement for a school or school district, and to periodic revisions of those documents. School vision and mission statements should be presented and discussed each year as new families and students enter the middle level school.

An inviting, supportive, and safe environment

A safe, welcoming, stimulating, and caring environment describes a good school for students, educators, families, and the community. In a school with strong partnerships, family and community members are more likely to volunteer to help ensure the safety of the playground, hallways, and lunchroom; to share their talents in classroom discussions; and lead or coach programs after school to create a true school community. Some schools discuss school climate only in terms of student attitudes and behavior. However, other aspects of school life, including teachers' professional relationships and school, family, and community partnerships are aspects of a positive school climate. See in Salinas and Jansorn (2004), for example, many different ways to develop a welcoming climate, such as Thompson Middle School's Family Fun Fair in Newport, Rhode Island (p. 71), Meany Middle School's Family Enrichment Center in Seattle, Washington (p. 81), and Franklin D. Roosevelt Middle School's Spring Family Affair, in Cleveland, Ohio (p. 80).

High expectations for every member of the learning community

National and local surveys of middle grades students and their families indicate that they have very high expectations of success in school and in life. Fully 98% of a national sample of eighth grade students plan to graduate from high school; and 82% plan at least some post-secondary schooling, with 70% aiming to complete college (Epstein & Lee, 1995). Responsive middle level schools must incorporate students' and families' high aspirations with educators' high expectations for all students. Teachers and parents must work together to guide students in taking the courses they need to meet their goals, in selecting electives, in choosing summer programs, and in taking advantage of extra time and extra help, as needed, in coaching classes before and after school and on Saturdays.

Students and teachers engaged in active learning

Excellent middle level schools emphasize active learning as an important instructional approach to make school subjects real and relevant to students. Families need information and guidelines on how to support young adolescents as active learners who can set learning goals, take responsibility for short-term and long-term projects, and monitor their own progress. See in Salinas and Jansorn (2003), for example, the Book Buddies program in Thurmont Middle School in Thurmont, Maryland, which helped parents learn about and celebrate the growth of their middle school students' skills and confidence as they read aloud with preschool and elementary children (p. 14). And in Salinas and Jansorn (2004) see another example of how a K-8 school, Southside Elementary in Buffalo, New York, conducted Science Mystery Nights to help parents understand inquiry-based instruction to increase students' critical thinking, lab skills, and science knowledge (p. 37).

Families need information and guidelines on how to support young adolescents as active learners who can set learning goals, take responsibility for short- and long-term projects, and monitor their own progress.

An adult advocate for every student

School-based advocates and teacher advisors need to know each student's family. In some schools, students have the same advisor or advocate every year. This makes it possible for the advisor and students' families to get to know each other well. The advocate may serve as a key contact for the family should questions or concerns arise, facilitating two-way channels of communication before problems become too serious to solve.

Curriculum that is relevant, challenging, integrative, and exploratory

Teachers work together to improve their course content to challenge and motivate student learning. Families and communities need to know about the courses, special programs, and services that are offered to increase student learning in the middle grades. Good information about the curriculum helps families discuss important academic topics with their young adolescents (Epstein & Salinas, 2004). Families also need good information about how their students are progressing in each subject, how to help students set and meet learning goals, how to monitor and discuss homework, and how to work with students to solve major problems that threaten course or grade level failure. Some middle level schools create student educational and occupational plans based on conferences with students and parents (Lloyd, 1996). If schools are serious about student learning, school-family-community partnerships must include information on and involvement with the curriculum.

Multiple teaching and learning approaches that respond to their diversity

Families benefit from knowing about the varied instructional approaches that middle grades teachers use in all subjects, including group activities, problem-solving strategies, writing prompts and prewriting strategies, students as historians, hands-on science, and other challenging innovations that promote learning. Many new instructional approaches are unfamiliar to families. They need information on the varied ways that students learn different subjects. Workshops for parents and "family nights" are common activities that may be organized in many different ways to help parents understand state and local standards in specific subjects; units of work covered in various courses; teaching methods; state tests and sample items; how to help their children at home; and other subject-specific information.

Families benefit from knowing about varied instructional approaches—group activities, problem-solving strategies, prewriting strategies, hands-on science, and other challenging innovations.

Some instructional approaches can be designed to involve parents in appropriate ways. For example, students are guided to demonstrate skills, share ideas, and conduct conversations with parents about real-world applications of school subjects in the Teachers Involve Parents in Schoolwork (TIPS) interactive homework process, noted above as a Type 4 activity. Also see how families may be helped to understand instructional approaches in teaching science methods with the thoughtful organization of a Science Fair, conducted by Murray Junior High School in Saint Paul, Minnesota (Salinas & Jansorn, 2004, p. 35).

Assessments and evaluation programs that promote quality learning

Families and community members need to know about the major tests, new or traditional assessments, report card criteria, and other state and local standards that schools use to determine children's progress on their learning paths. For example, many schools conduct evening meetings for parents to learn about and try items on the state tests that are administered for the No Child Left Behind Act (Epstein, 2004). Families also can help students set learning goals and strategies for reaching goals. Families, teachers, and students may discuss progress in parent-teacher-student conferences, through student self-report cards, and family-report cards. Programs such as Project Write in Massachusetts required students to share their writing portfolios with a parent and obtain reactions and suggestions. Students may conduct "home conferences" to share writing and other work with a parent, and to develop plans for how to improve their skills over the next marking period. Students and families also should have opportunities to rate the quality of school programs each year. There are many ways to include students and families in important assessments and evaluations in order to make those measures more meaningful.

Flexible organizational structures that support meaningful relationships and learning

Families need to understand interdisciplinary teams, middle level "houses," schedules, electives and exploratories, and other arrangements that define middle level school organizations. Every middle level school should have annual group and individual meetings of parents, teachers, and advisors to ensure that families understand how classes are organized and to gather family input for the decisions that affect their children's experiences and education.

See in Salinas and Jansorn (2003), for example, how Washington Junior High's Sixth Grade Family Picnic in Naperville, Illinois, introduced parents to the organization of the middle level school that their children were entering (p. 55).

Every middle level school should have annual group and individual meetings of parents, teachers, and advisors to ensure that families understand how classes are organized and to gather family input.

School-wide efforts and policies that foster health, wellness, and safety

Families have major responsibility for students' growth and development and health related outcomes concerning nutrition; weight management; physical strength; exercise; sex education; prevention of the use of drugs, alcohol, and tobacco; and other health topics that are important in the middle grades. Programs of family and community involvement may include activities to improve the health and safety standards for the school as a whole (Gerne & Epstein, 2004). Students' health and safety out of school are directly linked to their work and achievements in school. Students, families, and community members may work in partnership with educators to develop and review safety policies, health policies, dress codes, lunch menus, facilities and equipment, and other policies and conditions that affect children's health and safety. If educators identify students' health problems, parents must be partners in decisions about health services. See in Salinas and Jansorn (2003), for example, Visiting Nurses, an immunization project for students and families at the Byrd Middle School in Sun Valley, California (p. 44), varied health activities such as Lowndes Middle School's Fitness Fair in Valdosta, Georgia (p.45), the Alberta, Canada, Good Shepherd School's Try it at Lunch (p. 47), and Rosary School's, You Go, Girl (p. 48).

Multifaceted guidance and support services

Families need to know about the formal and informal guidance programs at the school. This includes knowing the names, phone numbers, e-mail addresses, or voice-mail boxes of their children's teachers, counselors, advocates, or administrators in order to reach them with questions about their children's lives and work at school. In some middle level schools, guidance counselors are members of interdisciplinary teams and meet with teachers, parents, and students on a regular schedule and in other meetings as needed. If students need counseling services, families also must be part of those decisions. See, for example, how Lowndes Middle School in Valdosta, Georgia, involved parents in increasing understanding among racial groups at the school with Family Night Teaches Tolerance (Salinas & Jansorn, 2004, p. 60).

The examples discussed above show clearly that school, family, and community partnerships have important connections with all of the elements of effective middle level schools. A comprehensive program of family and community involvement will include activities that ensure that families remain important, positive influences in their young adolescents' education.

Call to Action: National Network of Partnership Schools

Most middle level educators want to build strong school-family-community partnerships, but most have not reached this goal. Indeed, developing good connections of home, school, and community is an ongoing process that takes a bit of courage to change old ways, a lot of teamwork, and a reasonable investment of time and effort. Based on research and the work of many educators, parents, and students, a program has been developed to help all elementary, middle, and high schools develop strong and sustainable goal-oriented programs of partnerships with families and communities (Epstein et al., 2002).

Schools, districts, and state departments of education are invited to join the National Network of Partnership Schools (NNPS) at Johns Hopkins University to obtain assistance in improving their plans and activities for productive family and community involvement. District and state leaders are helped to organize leadership activities to assist increasing numbers of schools to conduct successful partnership activities. Schools are assisted to organize an Action Team for Partnerships, write an annual One-Year Action Plan for partnerships, implement and coordinate activities, evaluate results, monitor progress, publicize activities, and report regularly on the school's partnership program. Each ATP tailors its plans with activities for the six types of involvement to meet specific school improvement goals, including goals for improving student achievement, attitudes, behaviors, and the climate of partnerships. The One-Year Action Plan for partnerships is appended to the School Improvement Plan so that educators, parents, and community partners can see that everyone has a role to play in helping students achieve success in school. In this way, a program of school, family, and community partnerships is not an "extra" program, but is part of every school improvement plan and an integral part of an excellent school.

To obtain an invitation and membership forms for schools, districts, states, and organizations write to: Dr. Joyce L. Epstein, Director, National Network of Partnership Schools, Center on School, Family, and Community Partnerships, 3003 North Charles Street,

Suite 200, Baltimore, MD 21218, or contact Mr. Kenyatta Williams, tel: 410-516-2318, fax: 410-516-8890, nnps@csos.jhu.edu.

References

Balli, S. J., Demo, D. H., & Wedman, J. F. (1998). Family involvement with children's homework: An intervention in the middle grades. *Family Relations, 47*, 149-157.

Epstein, J. L. (2001). *School, family, and community partnerships: Preparing educators and improving schools*. Boulder, CO: Westview Press.

Epstein, J. L. (2004). How middle schools can meet NCLB requirements for family involvement. *Middle Ground, 8*(1), 14-17.

Epstein, J. L., & Connors, L. J. (1995). School and family partnerships in the middle grades. In B. Rutherford (Ed.), *Creating family/school partnerships* (pp. 137-166). Columbus, OH: National Middle School Association.

Epstein, J. L., & Dauber, S. L. (1995). Effects on students of an interdisciplinary program linking social studies, art, and family volunteers in the middle grades. *Journal of Early Adolescence, 15*,114-144.

Epstein, J. L., & Jansorn, N. R. (2004). Developing successful partnership programs: Principal leadership makes a difference. *Principal, 83*(3): 10-15.

Epstein, J. L, & Lee, S. (1995). National patterns of school and family connections in the middle grades. In B. Ryan, G. Adams, T. Gullotta, R. Weissberg, & R. Hampton (Eds.), *The family-school connection. Theory, research and practice* (pp. 108-154). Thousand Oaks, CA: Sage.

Epstein, J. L., & Salinas, K. C. (2004). Partnering with families and communities. *Educational Leadership, 61*(8), 12-18.

Epstein, J. L., Salinas, K. C., & Van Voorhis, F. L. (2001). *Teachers Involve Parents in Schoolwork (TIPS) manuals and prototype activities for the elementary and middle grades*. Baltimore, MD: Center on School, Family, and Community Partnerships, Johns Hopkins University.

Epstein, J. L., Sanders, M. G., Simon, B. S., Salinas, K. C., Jansorn, N. R., & Van Voorhis, F. L. (2002). *School, family, and community partnerships: Your handbook for action* (2nd ed.). Thousand Oaks, CA: Corwin Press.

Epstein, J. L., & Sheldon, S. B. (2002). Present and accounted for: Improving student attendance through family and community involvement. *Journal of Educational Research, 95*, 308-318.

Epstein, J. L., Simon, B. S., & Salinas, K. C. (1997, September). Involving parents in homework in the middle grades. *Research Bulletin 18*. Bloomington, IN: Phi Delta Kappa, CEDR.

Epstein, J. L., & Van Voorhis, F. L. (2001). More than minutes: Teachers' roles in designing homework. *Educational Psychologist, 36,* 181-194.

Fullan, M. (2001). *Leading in a culture of change*. San Francisco: Jossey Bass.

Gerne, K. M., & Epstein, J. L. (2004). The power of partnerships: School, family, and community collaboration to improve children's health. *RMC Health Educator, 4*(2), 1-2, 4-6.

Henderson, A. T., & Mapp, K. L. (2002). *A new wave of evidence: The impact of school, family, and community connections on student achievement.* Austin, TX: Southwest Educational Development Laboratory.

Johnson, V. R. (1996). *Family center guidebook.* Baltimore: Johns Hopkins University Center on Families, Communities, Schools and Children's Learning.

Lloyd, G. M. (1996). Research and practical applications for school, family, and community partnerships. In A. Booth & J. F. Dunn (Eds.), *Family-school links: How do they affect educational outcomes?* (pp. 255-264). Mahwah, NJ: Lawrence Erlbaum Associates.

Murphy, J. (Ed.). (2002). *The educational leadership challenge: Redefining leadership for the 21st century (*101st Yearbook of the National Society of the Study of Education, Part 1). Chicago: University of Chicago Press.

National Middle School Association. (2003). *This we believe: Successful schools for young adolescents.* Westerville, OH: Author.

Salinas, K. C. & Jansorn, N. R. (2003). *Promising partnership practices 2003.* Baltimore: Johns Hopkins University Center on School, Family, and Community Partnerships.

Salinas, K. C., & Jansorn, N. R. (2004). *Promising partnership practices 2004.* Baltimore: Johns Hopkins University Center on School, Family, and Community Partnerships. (Note: Annual collections from 1999 are available on the Web site of the National Network of Partnership Schools at www.partnershipschools.org in the section In the Spotlight.)

Sanders, M. G. (1999). Improving school, family, and community partnerships in urban schools. *Middle School Journal, 31* (2), 35-41.

Sanders, M. G. (2001). Schools, families, and communities partnering for middle level students' success. *Bulletin of the National Association of Secondary School Principals, 85* (627), 53–61.

Sanders, M. G. (in press). *Building school-community partnerships: Collaboration for student success.* Thousand Oaks, CA: Corwin Press.

Sanders M. G., & Epstein J. L. (2000). Building school, family and community partnerships in secondary schools. In Mavis G. Sanders, (Ed.), *Schooling students placed at risk: Research, policy and practice in the education of poor and minority adolescents.* Mahwah NJ: Lawrence Erlbaum Associates.

Sanders, M. G., & Simon, B.S. (2002). A comparison of program development at elementary, middle, and high schools in the National Network of Partnership Schools. *The School Community Journal, 12*(1), 7-27.

Seidman, E., Lambert, L. E., Allen, L., & Aber, J. L. (2003). Urban adolescents' transition to junior high school and protective family transactions. *Journal of Early Adolescence, 23*, 166–193.

Sheldon, S. B. (2003). Linking school-family-community partnerships in urban elementary schools to student achievement on state tests. *Urban Review, 35*(2), 149-165.

Sheldon, S. B., & Epstein, J. L. (2002). Improving student behavior and discipline with family and community involvement. *Education in Urban Society, 35*, 4-26.

Sheldon, S. B., & Epstein, J. L. (2004). Getting students to school: Using family and community involvement to reduce chronic absenteeism. *School Community Journal, 4*(2), 39-56.

Sheldon, S. B., & Epstein, J. L. (2004). School programs of family and community involvement to support children's reading and literacy development across the grades. In J. Flood & P. Anders (Eds.), *Literacy development of students in urban schools: Research and policy* (pp. 107-138). Newark, DE: International Reading Association (IRA).

Sheldon, S. B., & Epstein, J. L. (2005). Involvement counts: Family and community partnerships and math achievement. *Journal of Educational Research, 98, 196-206.*

Sheldon, S. B., & Van Voorhis, F. L. (2004). Partnership programs in U.S. schools: Their development and relationship to family involvement outcomes. *School Effectiveness and School Improvement, 15*, 125-148.

Tuinsta, C., & Hiatt-Michael, D. (2004). Student-led parent conferences in middle schools. *The School Community Journal, 14*(1), 59–80.

Van Voorhis, F. L. (2003). Interactive homework in middle school: Effects on family involvement and students' science achievement. *Journal of Educational Research, 96*, 323-339.

Van Voorhis, F. L. & Epstein, J. L. (2002). *Teachers Involve Parents in Schoolwork (TIPS): Interactive homework CD for the elementary and middle grades*. Baltimore: Center on School, Family, and Community Partnerships at Johns Hopkins University.

Curriculum that Is Relevant, Challenging, Integrative, and Exploratory

Chris Stevenson
Penny A. Bishop

One sunny, early fall afternoon, Chris left his office a bit early to catch the second half of a soccer game on campus. As he climbed into the sparsely filled grandstand, he noticed a row of seven or eight young adolescent girls and boys chattering among themselves while watching the game together. Not one to pass up such a good opportunity for a "double feature," he took a seat behind the middle of their row. This was an irresistible opportunity to unobtrusively check out a sample of adolescent culture while at the same time, watch some soccer.

The kids' talk was wide ranging, jumping quickly from topic to topic. Sometimes they seemed to agree, but more often it was as if the conversation was a competition for the most profound statements of fact and opinion. Unable to detect any coherent theme from the center of the row, Chris eased his way to one end where Joe was attempting to explain soccer rules to Amy, who was earnestly attentive. An apparent novice to the sport, she struggled to understand and to reassure him that his tutorial made sense to her. Try as he might, however, Joe's explanations of the offside rule in particular did not quite clear up Amy's confusion. Although she tried mightily, it was clear that she was just not getting it. Joe finally concluded his lesson with the reassurance that, "it makes a lot more sense when you're doing it."

When one is 11, 12, or 13 years old, enduring, useful knowledge is associated with firsthand engagement of the subject matter.

We think Joe is onto something fundamentally important to our quest for middle level curriculum and pedagogy. Especially among young adolescents, "it makes a lot more sense when you're doing it." Joe understands that when one is 11, 12, or 13 years old, enduring, useful knowledge is associated with firsthand engagement of the subject matter. While this truth is widely espoused among middle level educators, it is all too infrequently a primary focus affecting adults' curricular decisions.

From the earliest beginnings of the middle school concept the most steadfast rationale in approaching curriculum decisions has been a dogged emphasis on educational methods that complement the "unique characteristics and needs of young adolescents" (NMSA, 2003, p. 3). Somehow, however, our search for the composition of that curriculum has seemed inevitably reduced to discussions and proposals within "disciplines vs. interdisciplinary" or "subject specific vs. integrated" dualities. Interesting and often entertaining but irresolvable debates have too easily diverted us from our espoused goal of creating successful matches between our kids and their studies. The issue is not whether life is inherently discipline-based or interdisciplinary. We submit that Joe would have us seek and find our direction by examining more closely the interactions between the subject matter (e.g., soccer rules) and the learner's derivation of meaning (e.g., his and Amy's separate understandings). Authentic learning leaves unmistakable tracks in learners' talk with each other and adults. Consider some examples of students whose engagement in learning at the middle level is self-evident. Who could dispute these examples as *relevant* to them, *challenging*, *integrative,* and *exploratory*?

Kids Genuinely Engaged in Curriculum

Snapshot I

Authentic learning leaves unmistakable tracks in learners' talk with each other and adults.

Brian and Amelia, eighth graders at a charter middle school in the Pacific Northwest, returned from their winter break filled with questions about the recent and devastating tsunami in Asia. Questions and commentary about the tragedy rang through the halls as students jostled one another, trying to fit bulky backpacks into their lockers. Students informally debated these recent events on their way to class, with Amelia arguing, "I think it was an earthquake," while Brian asserted, "No, I heard it was a tidal wave." Their friend Etienne overheard them as he scooted through the doorway at the last minute and interjected, "I heard more than 100,000 people died. My mom said that's bigger than our city."

Although their first-year science teacher, Ms. Joyner, had spent most of her break carefully planning their next unit on forensic science, she recognized the teachable moment inherent in her students' discussion. She decided that morning, therefore, to postpone the forensic science unit and turn to the study of tsunamis, capitalizing on her students' obvious and intense interest. She began class by inviting students to share what they already knew about tsunamis and this recent event. As they spoke, she listed their thoughts on the white board at the front of the room. Their prior knowledge was based primarily on images from network news coverage and fell into three broad categories: scientific perspectives on how tsunamis are formed; a geographical knowledge of the region in Asia where the tsunami occurred; and widely ranging thoughts on the degree of the devastation, including the number of deaths and damaged or destroyed villages.

Next Ms. Joyner encouraged students to pose questions in pairs about the natural disaster. Students turned to their neighbors and began to list on notepaper the questions that had emerged for them as well as ones provoked by their class discussion. She then asked them to share their questions aloud while she again made notes on the white board for all to see. The questions included, What is the difference between a tidal wave and a tsunami? How does a tsunami begin? Can anything stop it? Has it ever happened before? How many cities and villages were hit? How many people died? Could the same thing happen here? What will happen to the children who have no parents? What can I do to help?

With assistance from their teachers, students develop curriculum which helps them answer questions about their world and themselves. — DVD, Maranacook Community MS, "Sled Project," "Curriculum Development," "Ice Fishing"

The students' questions formed the foundation for a three-week unit on tsunamis, the force and physics of water, soil salinity, and geography. Students helped construct a wave pool with materials donated from a local plastics plant, and then they used the apparatus to reconstruct and analyze the force of water. As is often characteristic of young adolescents, they felt a call to action. Brian and Amelia decided to host a community-wide pancake breakfast to raise money to donate to tsunami relief, and they quickly earned the support of their peers. Ms. Joyner helped the class to brainstorm various jobs that are necessary to sponsor such an event. They formed committees to handle the project: Public Awareness, Donations, Food Prep, Serving, and Clean-up. The team's teachers devoted their usual 40-minute advisory time each day to planning the event. The Donations Committee solicited donations of ingredients from local grocery stores while students on the Public Awareness Committee busily prepared posters, advertising copy, and letters to the editors of surrounding newspapers urging citizens to donate generously.

> In integrated curriculum, we each come up with ideas we want to learn about. We put them all on a poster and narrow it down to the top 10 ideas and vote. It is much more fun to learn about stuff you want to learn about rather than what you are given.
> — Maggie, Maranacook Community MS, "Curriculum Development"

When the designated Saturday morning arrived, the school's cafeteria was taken over by the Food Prep, Serving, and Clean-up teams, who enthusiastically rolled up their sleeves as they greeted and served their neighbors. The fundraiser was very successful, and they donated their proceeds to a relief organization aimed at helping surviving children of the tsunami. Ms. Joyner felt a lot of satisfaction in such successful curriculum that grew out of her students' concerns and questions. In observing their deep engagement in the subject matter, she knew with no doubt that the project was a great educational success. Students gained a new sense of personal efficacy as they learned about what was timely and relevant, and they gave to their global community from their local community in the purest spirit of "think globally, act locally."

Snapshot II

Meg and Sara, seventh graders on the Harmony Team, attend an urban middle school. They have also recently become best friends, prompted in part by a shared traumatic experience: legal separations and impending divorce by both sets of parents. One part of the curriculum provided by Harmony is comprised of independent studies called "Orbital Studies" that can be carried out by individuals or combinations of students who have a shared interest (Stevenson, 2002, pp. 162, 202). Meg openly wanted to know more about what divorce meant for her and her family, and although Sara tends to keep her feelings more private, she agreed with Meg that exploring divorce and its effects on everyone in their two families was highly relevant and worthy as a focus for an orbital study. One of their teachers, Mrs. Redmond, was eager to support them, in part because she has been divorced for three years and is the custodial parent for her two children in elementary school.

Mrs. Redmond helped them get started by inviting them to compile three lists: things they already know about separation and divorce; questions they want to answer; and issues and questions they want to discuss with their parents. She also helped them identify possible resources for their investigations: court-related children's service providers, attorneys who specialize in family matters, judges, and published materials about divorce for children their age, of which they found very few. The girls were especially interested in learning about the experiences and opinions of other students whose families had split. Even before they finished creating a web of resources and expanding their lists of questions and issues—harmony requirements for orbital studies—their investigation was well under way. Every couple of days they met with Mrs. Redmond to show her their progress, ask questions, and get her advice.

After less than two weeks they decided on a culminating product: they decided to write a book for kids their ages about separation and divorce. Since they had found almost nothing written by kids for kids, Mrs. Redmond helped them see that they could address a literary niche. The material for the book would come from print and human resources readily available in their school and community, but the approach and voice would be uniquely theirs.

The volume they eventually produced, *Kids Helping Kids with Divorce,* evolved as a blend of personal stories, mostly from other adolescents, with information learned from people and community agencies dealing with divorce. For Meg and Sara it was a giant stride in conceptualizing and producing a volume of such magnitude, but it also showed them a constructive way to deal with painful personal issues. Even during a time of their own intense personal struggle, the girls' parents trusted Mrs. Redmond and the other Harmony teachers to help the girls with both their scholarly and personal needs over the several weeks of their investigation. Interest in their study by other adolescents and parents triggered the formation of a "Divorce Group" taught by the school's counselors and made up of students across the school who share personal experience with separation and divorce. Meg and Sara's book became required reading. Everyone benefited from this experience of creating an authentic opportunity for firsthand inquiry and learning about an issue that matters to growing numbers of young adolescents. Meg and Sara learned about a difficult issue in their lives, and their study helped other kids going through the same difficult time. Mrs. Redmond and her colleagues also gained both personally and as teachers from the girls' work.

The volume students eventually produced evolved as a blend of personal stories, mostly from other adolescents, with information learned from people and community agencies dealing with divorce.

Snapshot III

Casey is a sixth grader on an interdisciplinary team in a New England middle school. Afternoons on his team are dedicated to the integrated study of science and social studies called Life Studies.

Students sign up for Life Studies groups based on their interests and the state's approved standards that link to their personal and academic goals for the month. One month Casey's Life Studies group focused on inventing new technology. The students were to select technology that is commonly used today, research the historical evolution of that technology, and speculate about how it might evolve 20 years from now.

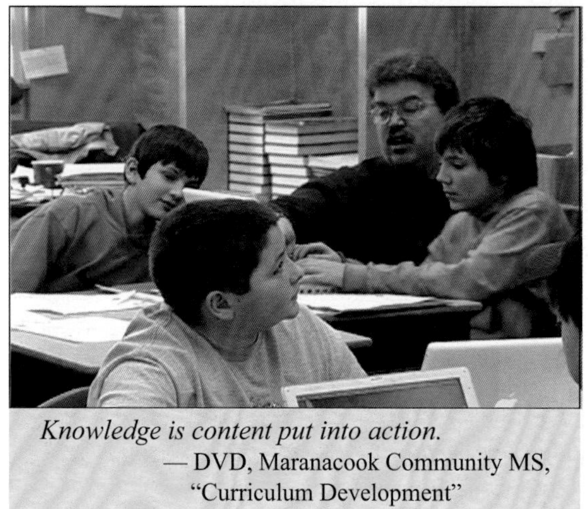

Knowledge is content put into action.
— DVD, Maranacook Community MS, "Curriculum Development"

Casey loves working with computers and so became quite excited about this task. He contributed eagerly to the class, brainstorming various technologies on which they might focus. He is, by self-admission, stubborn at times and as a result often finds collaboration on projects a challenge. He was greatly relieved when his teacher, Mr. Edwards, told students they could choose their own partners. Casey teamed up with his good friend, Jared, and they excitedly moved to a computer to begin to capture their ideas.

Casey and Jared began talking about a friend who suffers from diabetes. They were interested in the fact that her "state of the art" insulin pump had already broken five times. They did not understand why it should break with so many filters on it to ensure that it is reliable. Mr. Edwards circulated around the room, and crouched by the computer to listen to the boys' conversation. He encouraged them to pursue this important question and guided them to several diabetes Web sites to learn more about the disease and various insulin pumps on the market

The two boys spent three weeks learning about diabetes, the role of insulin in the body, and current biomedical technology. Their work culminated in the design of an implanted insulin pump that would be inserted into the body with multiple filters to automatically monitor a person's insulin levels. Mr. Edwards introduced them to new software that assisted them with multidimensional graphics and with which they were able to construct their new technology on the computer, finally uploading it to their Web page. Casey and Jared felt a sense of competence and accomplishment in designing a tool that could respond to real needs in the world, as well as to the needs of someone they know and care about. Mr. Edwards especially enjoyed his role as a facilitator in the boys' work, watching two capable and motivated students find real-world relevance in their learning.

Attributes of Effective Curriculum

What do the students in the middle schools framed by these snapshots have in common? Certainly they exhibit a deep engagement with curriculum that is relevant, challenging, integrative, and exploratory. None of these studies would have taken place without the support, encouragement, and guidance of savvy, student-oriented teachers. In each case, students enjoyed rich and substantive learning experiences because they first felt confident enough in relationships with their teachers to be able to express their ideas, interests, and questions. When students find teachers indifferent to their ideas, then such ideas do not get expressed. These youngsters were also blessed with teachers who not only were open to the possibility of authentic student choice but who understood and valued the power of learning driven by strong personal motivation. Showing eager learners how to plan and proceed, staying in touch with them as they progress, and helping them wrap up their study is the proverbial "piece of cake." It gives meaning to teaching in ways that transcend the usual.

Showing eager learners options about how to plan and proceed, staying in touch with them as they progress, and helping them wrap up their study gives meaning to teaching in ways that transcend the usual.

Relevant

"Curriculum is relevant when it allows students to pursue answers to questions they have about themselves, content, and the world" (NMSA, 2003, p. 20). Unquestionably, the Asian tsunami, divorce, and diabetes are content of momentous personal relevance to these students. Based on their own questions, excellent curriculum emerged from their earnest desire to understand new concepts and world events. Helping others is a common thread running through each of the snapshots: designing an implanted insulin pump to help a friend, composing a book to help kids get through divorce, raising money to help victims of a natural disaster thousands of miles away. In each case, students found personal relevance in following their own lines of inquiry to understand the world around them. Their needs for relevance are increasingly addressed by service learning initiatives, heightening their personal involvement in academic and civic life (Allen, 2003). It is encouraging to see more and more service learning opportunities in middle schools. These snapshots meld service with academic learning, drawing together the best of both worlds. Young adolescents long to make a real and felt difference, and they love to be recognized for their intelligence and expertise.

Challenging

The teacher's role in moving beyond mere coverage of content to curriculum that "addresses substantive issues and skills, is geared

Young adolescents long to make a real and felt difference in the world, and they love to be recognized for their intelligence and expertise.

to (students') levels of understanding, and increasingly enables them to assume control of their own learning" (NMSA, 2003, p. 21) is critical. The snapshots above illustrate learning that is grounded in substantive and rigorous concepts and skills and that also teach students how to develop personal responsibility for their own learning. Mrs. Redmond, for example, began by working closely with Meg and Sara to help them identify questions and locate resources. She gradually moved into more of an advisory role, interjecting advice or questions when needed, but allowing Meg and Sara to direct their work and learning in accord with their own inclinations. Similarly, Mr. Edwards skillfully guided Casey and Jared in finding resources for their study and taught them to use new software. At the same time, he ensured that they addressed their substantive questions and controlled their project. In all cases, the concepts under study were challenging for young adolescents and the tasks were achievable.

Integrative

In addition to helping youngsters make sense of the world around them, curriculum is integrative when students explore their own agendas and make meaningful decisions about their learning, often defying "arbitrary subject boundaries" (NMSA 2003, p. 22). In each of the three snapshots, students were deeply immersed in acquiring concepts that by nature crossed the lines of subject-specific disciplines. In the study of a tsunami tragedy, for example, Brian, Amelia, and their peers acquired and applied map reading and other geography skills to contrast world regions affected by the natural disaster. They used scientific methods to design and conduct their own investigation of the connections between the earth's crustal plates and the force of water. And they honed persuasive writing skills as they carefully composed and revised their letters to the community, ever aware of the authentic audience. In each case, students made ongoing and meaningful decisions about their learning, critiquing, and modifying their approaches along the way. Without Ms. Joyner's willingness to ground curriculum in students' questions, or her ability to see the possibilities beyond her personal academic discipline, the students' investigation would have been limited to a relatively conventional science class. Instead, their eyes were opened to the rich and inherently interdisciplinary world in which they live.

Curriculum is integrative when students explore their own agendas and make meaningful decisions about their learning, often defying "arbitrary subject boundaries."

Exploratory

National Middle School Association (2003) urges middle level educators to consider exploration as "an attitude and approach, not a classification of content" (p. 23). For too long the term "exploratory" has referred to unified arts or other classes thought to be outside the realm of the "core" academic areas such as technology education or family and consumer science. We argue that all curricula for middle grades students must involve exploration. Young adolescents are by nature intensely inquisitive. A rich middle level program capitalizes on that intellectual curiosity by opening up young people's potential for future career interests and recreational pursuits. It enables students to investigate beyond their immediate realm, regardless of gender, social class, ethnicity, or life circumstances, and to consider limitless possibilities. As they empowered their students to become authors, scientists, human service advocates, and inventors, Mrs. Redmond, Ms. Joyner, and Mr. Edwards created activities that broadened students' views of the world, themselves, and their futures. These teachers embody exploration as an attitude and approach, regardless of their specific subject matter specializations.

For too long the term "exploratory" has referred to classes thought to be outside the realm of the "core" academic areas such as technology education or family and consumer science.

Gathering plant and animal specimens from the school pond and studying the ground water system are two ways that the region's ecology provides context for learning science.
— DVD, Jefferson MS, "Prairie Curriculum"

Student Engagement

Savvy middle level teachers know from experience that if you want to understand how learning happens for young adolescents, the quickest way to find out is to simply ask them. We do not refer here to occasional conversational inquiries, although such occasions may produce valuable insights. What we are recommending is a foundational assessment that invites students on a regular schedule to reflect on current and recent experiences and identify factors that have been effective in helping them learn. Such inquiries require young people to become reflective and analytical about their progress as learners. Students learn about their strengths and their continuing learning needs, and this data informs their planning of subsequent studies.

Similarly, teachers improve their own practice by creating a formal time to listen to students reflect on what works, and what does not. For too long educators have underestimated or neglected entirely the knowledge to be gained from engaging students in self-assessment and formal documentation of their strengths and needs as learners. As Cook-Sather (2002) asserted, "We as educators . . . must seriously question the assumption that we know more than the young people of today about how they learn or what they need to learn in preparation for the decades ahead" (p. 3).

In order to understand how middle school students learn, and to help them come to know themselves well as learners, we have found the concept of *engagement* to be a helpful one. Since we know that engaged students learn more (Finn, Pannozzo, & Achilles, 2003), inviting students to consider times of engagement and times of disengagement in learning can reveal powerful insights for learners and teachers alike. For example, recent interviews with middle schoolers from six schools (Bishop & Pflaum, 2005a, 2005b) revealed the critical role of relevance in curriculum just mentioned. When asked to describe any time in her schooling when she felt deeply engaged in her learning, eighth grader Amelia was eager to talk about her literature group's recent discussion of Kafka's *Metamorphosis*. She explained that this was the first time she had learned about the concept of alienation. Amelia explained, "I didn't know it was such a big issue and then I came into the course and then I realized that it was like pretty important. . . . Most everybody is alienated, so just, like, think how *you're* alienated" (2005a, p. 36). For Amelia, finding relevance in a topic such as alienation engaged her deeply. Knowing that relevance can help engage her, therefore, increases her learning, Amelia can consider how to find relevance when designing her own learning. Her teacher can build on this knowledge to ensure Amelia makes connections between her studies and her life.

Other students found they were most successful when working at their own individual pace. Again asked to describe a time of engagement, one fifth grader, Nad, explained that he loved sustained silent reading because, "I like going at my own pace. . . . Some kids in my group, they don't read with any expression. And they read really slowly, even though I understand that they can't read as well but . . . I really, I like to just, I really like to read alone" (p. 9). He contrasted that with a math class in which he was unsuccessful and disengaged, confiding that, "I don't usually get it in my head the first time he explains it" (p. 10). With these insights, Nad discovered the importance an individualized pace plays in his learning, and he can consider that when planning future work. His teacher gains important information that Nad might otherwise not offer, given the class-wide novels and whole group math instruction that are the norm in his class.

Our point is not that there is a recipe for engaging middle school students in relevant, challenging, integrative, and exploratory curriculum. On the contrary, young adolescents are constantly changing and are by nature a developmentally diverse group. Rather, we believe that students who are invited into a reflective dialogue about learning enhance their ability to set demanding yet achievable personal and academic goals for themselves. They are equipped with growing self-knowledge. Amelia and Nad are two of many examples of youngsters involved in reflecting on their learning needs and on the curriculum in relation to these needs. Such opportunities enhance students' sense of personal efficacy; they enable teachers to reflect on their teaching and the inherent match or mismatch between their approaches and the youngsters in their classrooms.

Students who are invited into a reflective dialogue about learning enhance their ability to set demanding yet achievable personal and academic goals for themselves.

Curriculum and Adolescent Development

Looking comprehensively at young adolescents' healthy and enthusiastic learning would cause one to consider the curriculum in relation to the learner himself or herself. What should be the primary purpose of curriculum at the middle level? *This We Believe* posits that middle level curriculum must be "relevant, challenging, integrative, and exploratory" (2003, p. 7). It is fair to rejoin, "To whom?" Might sincere adults use such descriptors to justify any curriculum content or program or guide for any age students? If our focus is truly on young adolescent learners, then we will emphasize ***their*** challenging and being challenged by their schoolwork, ***their*** successfully integrating new learning into their continuously modified existing knowledge, and ***their*** exploring the ideas and questions that interest them.

Hamburg (1993) has stated well the primary purpose and nature of middle level curriculum:

> What are the requirements for healthy adolescent development? In my view, it is essential that we help young adolescents to acquire constructive knowledge and skills, inquiring habits of mind, dependable human relationships, reliable basis for learning respect, a sense of belonging in a valued group, and a way of being useful to their communities. (p. 467)

Given the range of developmental diversity among children during these years, it does not seem feasible for any single curriculum plan conceived by adults in isolation from a particular group of students and administered to all students at the same time to possibly accommodate everyone. Fortunately, such a single plan is not our only option. One of the great benefits of working with these students is their readiness to make responsible choices as to what they will study and learn. The more choices they are able to make, the more seriously they are inclined to trust the choices adults are also making

What should be the primary purpose of curriculum at the middle level?

Perhaps the greatest challenge to educators is to summon the courage to form partnerships with students by which they share curriculum planning.

for them. Perhaps the greatest challenge to educators is to summon the courage to form partnerships with students by which they share curriculum planning. Beane's (1993) work compels teachers to enter into just such coalitions, and student-maintained records of their work in portfolios enables teachers to more fully understand the extent to which curriculum is actually cultivating competence and responsibility as well as testimonials of affiliation, awareness, and ethical perceptions of themselves.

Middle level educators should focus on the ways students are growing and changing during these transition years between childhood and late adolescence. We know with certainty that they undergo distinctive changes from the ways of their earlier childhood. We also know that there is a great deal of variability among them; differentness is the norm in early adolescence. Individuals change according to idiosyncratic schedules, and they also develop uniquely in terms of intelligence, disposition, attitudes and tastes, interests, work habits, and aspirations. It seems to us that the abundance of possibilities for children during this brief period of human life invites curriculum initiatives that complement individual differences and transcend established curriculum paradigms. This perspective does not demean those curricula; rather, it ensures that our focus on the growth and development of individual children is preserved. For this brief period of schooling, our abiding concern should be the effectiveness with which our children learn both how to learn and the disposition that they can learn successfully.

What if our primary purpose in planning curriculum is to ensure the healthy development of young adolescent learners? What are their predominant needs as learners and citizens? Three decades of interviews with young adolescent students and countless collaborations with middle level teachers point to some developmental needs that can be satisfied through curriculum designs that preserve learner efficacy as the focal point. Students who demonstrate personal efficacy in school and in their relationships with peers and adults exhibit some essential traits: competency, responsibility, affiliation, awareness, and ethical perception of self.

Competence

Young adolescents care a great deal about being competent. Successful students identify themselves by the things they do well, and they relish opportunities to do those things. Whether it is running, or spelling, or shooting baskets, or solving equations, a powerful need for personal expertise perseveres. It does not follow that individuals have to be the very best at their particular competency, that no one else is equally as good as they are. But it does seem to matter that one be somewhat set apart from others by this expertise. The very best of circumstances is when classmates and significant others, especially older adolescents and adults, also acknowledge one's competence. Good curriculum from students' perspectives assures that they grow steadily in competencies that they acknowledge as useful and worthwhile. When youngsters are failing to grow in competence in their own eyes and in the perceptions of others, a fundamental developmental need is being denied.

Responsibility

A second attribute of young adolescent learners who seem to be thriving is their perception of themselves as accountable and responsible in ways that approximate adulthood. They know they are not yet ready for a more fully independent adult role, but they value being able to take greater responsibility for themselves as well as being recognized for evidence of greater maturity. Initiative, dependability, and resourcefulness are qualities they value in themselves and each other. They care about being at ease with planning and organizing learning, working either alone or with selected peers. They prefer to think of themselves as good choosers and fair judges, and their personally constructed academic portfolios exude personal accountability and self-awareness. Curriculum that matches well with these qualities cultivates the very self-reliance we know to be essential to successful learners and strong individuals.

Affiliation

As longtime teachers of young adolescents and as observers of others who teach them well, we have noted that when curriculum is at its best it takes on something of a life of its own. There is a palpable "curriculum transcendence" through which students derive remarkable degrees of engagement and energy. Observe students preparing a drama production or doing a project together: they give lots of energy to such work, and in turn they are energized. Such experiences become benchmarks of future learning, and students articulate intense feelings of affiliation with those learning events. Sometimes the significance of the experience comes from the value of the compelling working relationships with peers or with teachers in the school; oftentimes significant relationships are created while working with other adults in the community. At its very best, after all, learning is an energy loop: one invests energy in a process that in

> When curriculum is at its best it takes on something of a life of its own.

turn energizes that same individual. Whatever curriculum unit middle level teachers may choose to teach, if there is no evidence of passion and ownership, enduring learning is not likely to occur.

Awareness

No one likes to be taken for a fool, especially young adolescents. Perhaps because of the intensity of the identity formation process, these youngsters are especially sensitive about how they are perceived and treated. Note their language, humor, dress, and interactions with peer groups as evidence of their need to be regarded by others as "with it." Being involved, savvy, and "tuned in" are paramount. Believing that "I know what's going on," affirms a sense of worth. Insights about one's abilities and strengths give rise to reflections and theories about how things are and how things should be done. We have found young adolescents to be especially responsive to inquiries designed to explain their perceptions about the dynamics of peer relationships, their school, and the community (Stevenson, 2002). Curriculum that serves these students well provides a climate and context in which they recognize the relevance of their studies and have ample opportunities to demonstrate their knowledge to others, especially parents, older adolescents, and community people.

Young adolescents are especially responsive to inquiries designed to explain their perceptions about the dynamics of peer relationships, their school, and the community.

Ethical perception of self

Perhaps the most reassuring indicator of sound education and human development is evidence of our children's natural inclination toward moral ideals. It is crucial for them to regard themselves as good people of high moral standing. Their growing interest in existential questions, concern about injustices, and readiness for activism in worthy causes signals the youngster's need to believe in himself or herself as a good person, an individual of worth who is making a difference in the world. Advocacy for animals, stewardship of the environment, and compassion for the needy and disadvantaged are natural causes they are eager to support as a matter of principle. As they grow in knowledge of the exigencies of political and economic systems, they come to recognize both the promise and vulnerabilities of democracy. A growing sophistication about how things work in a morally conscious and responsible community portends active citizenship that brings vitality to the school today and the larger community tomorrow. Any curriculum design that does not provide opportunities and support for students to do "right things" alongside the significant adults in their lives is sadly incomplete. Kids understand the value of being good through doing good.

Perhaps the most reassuring indicator of sound education and human development is evidence of our children's natural inclination toward moral ideals.

A Caveat for the Bold

Pressures on all teachers to stick to prescribed curriculum are greater today than they have ever been. Under the illusion of "accountability," school system policies emphasize regular paper and pencil testing covering specific prescribed content, and the media extends this illusion of "quality" by reporting test scores and comparing schools' performance as an indication of "excellence." Further, most middle level teachers are licensed to teach only one or two subject matter areas, and this very designation can discourage them from teaching beyond their subject areas. Federal injunctions contained in the No Child Left Behind Act easily intimidate many administrators, if not most teachers, from deviating from assumed deductive, prescriptive teaching, and textbook-centered modes of instruction that have long proved inadequate and inappropriate to the experienced observer of young adolescents' learning and healthy development.

We should not be surprised at these developments, given the extent to which politicians who have no experience with the actualities of children's learning and development are issuing mandates about the content of curriculum and methods of evaluation. The public appears to be amazingly gullible in accepting this falsification of education. Even more disappointing, it does not appear likely that in the near future we can expect a national or even local political initiative to restore the kind of curriculum and pedagogy that successful middle level teachers know to be best suited for their particular students.

The good news is that there remain numbers of middle level teachers like Ms. Joyner, Mrs. Redmond, and Mr. Edwards who grasp early adolescence and who also have a strength of professional conviction to trust both their understanding and their students to pursue curriculum that is relevant, challenging, integrative, and exploratory. We know there are numerous other committed middle level teachers who are following suit, nurturing and building on their students' interests, ideas, and questions to pursue learning opportunities that effectively change kids' lives and advance far more valid definitions of "accountability" and "excellence." It is not too extreme to also point out that these are the teachers who are achieving immortality with their students by their readiness to teach beyond the externally mandated box of what is politically correct today. These are also the teachers we must seek out, learn from, and encourage; they are the ones who will preserve the wisdom of the middle level concept that provoked the reform movement in the first place.

Back in the earliest days of middle level reform a now long-forgotten source caught our attention with a persuasive argument that middle level curriculum was urgently in need of major overhaul. The writer cautioned, however, that to throw out existing programs in favor of all new designs would bring about certain catastrophe. The essay went on to encourage that educators resolve to build 15% of their curriculum around the expressed needs and interests of their students. We were advised to treat that modest 15% as professional inquiry conceived to better understand the studies and pedagogy that best served our students. The remaining 85% of our curriculum could remain unchanged for the moment. The crucial advice was that we incorporate insights drawn from the 15% into the remaining 85%, and thereby remake subsequent curriculum in ways that will be more closely aligned with the particular characteristics and needs of our students. In so doing, we affirm ourselves as professionals who adapt practices according to insights resulting from our inquiries. Young people like those reported in this chapter will thank us for our wisdom, actions, and courage.

References

Allen, R. (2003). The democratic aims of service learning. *Educational Leadership 60*(6), 51-54.

Beane, J. A. (1993). *A middle school curriculum: From rhetoric to reality* (2nd ed.). Columbus, OH: National Middle School Association.

Bishop, P., & Pflaum, S. (2005a). *Reaching and teaching middle school learners: Asking students to show us what works.* Thousand Oaks, CA: Corwin Press.

Bishop, P., & Pflaum, S. (2005b). Student perceptions of action, relevance, and pace. *Middle School Journal, 36*(4), 4-12.

Cook-Sather, A. (2002). Authorizing students' perspectives: Toward trust, dialogue and change in education. *Educational Researcher, 31*(4), 3-14.

Finn, J.D., Pannozzo, G.M., & Achilles, C.M. (2003). The why's of class size: Student behavior in small classes. *Review of Educational Research, 73*, 321-368.

Hamburg, D. A. (1993). The opportunities of early adolescence. *Teachers College Record, 94*, 466-471

National Middle School Association. (2003) *This we believe: Successful schools for young adolescents.* Westerville, OH: Author.

Stevenson, C. (2002). *Teaching ten to fourteen year olds* (3rd ed.). Boston: Pearson Allyn & Bacon.

Multiple Learning and Teaching Approaches that Respond to Their Diversity

Barbara Brodhagen
Susan Gorud

Schools can be thought of as collections of opportunities to learn (Hammond, 1997). Student achievement is affected positively when those learning opportunities capitalize on students' cultural, experiential, and personal backgrounds. Teachers who recognize and honor the wide diversity among young adolescents are able to maximize student learning within the curriculum. Diversity has many facets that influence young adolescents and their learning environment: gender, socio-economic class, intellectual capacity, and linguistic and ethnic backgrounds among them. This diversity among young adolescents provides opportunities for sharing personal and cultural experiences to enrich relationships within the classroom community. Evidence suggests that students who have positive affiliations with their teachers are more likely to achieve academically than those who do not (Anfara et al., 2003; Dilg, 2003; Wehlage, Rutter, Smith, Lesko, & Fernandez, 1989).

This chapter describes developmentally responsive approaches to teaching and learning that respond to the diversity among today's young adolescents. Strategies will include use of learning inventories, a variety of teaching approaches, question posing by young adolescents, projects, knowledge performance, and student reflection. Within each description, examples will show how these strategies can celebrate and address student diversity within a heterogeneous classroom. Finally some attention will be given to professional development for teachers who want to create a classroom environment that welcomes students' diversity and offers open access to academic and social success.

Inventories: Learning and Cultural

Teachers serious about responding to the diverse skills, abilities, and prior knowledge of young adolescents take time to learn about the range of students' multiple intelligences, learning styles, and individual experiences. Some teachers use formal inventories or assessments to help discover students' strengths, talents, learning preferences, and areas to improve upon. Other teachers have students complete a questionnaire that might include open-ended statements such as the following:

- I learn best when I . . .
- In my spare time I really like to . . .
- I know when I really want to concentrate I have to . . .
- The best time for me to read is . . .
- When I think about making something with my hands I . . .

Still other teachers recognize that young adolescents have had many learning experiences in school and simply ask their students to describe how they believe they learn best. By posting a list of these strategies and activities teachers are reminded to include them throughout the year. Through a good understanding of students' learning strengths and weaknesses, the teacher can effectively plan formative and summative assessments that allow students' fair treatment when asked to demonstrate learning.

An aspect of curriculum planning that is often neglected or overlooked is learning about and gaining understanding of how students' cultures influence classroom relationships. A cultural inventory provides the teacher with information that can be used to help select curriculum content and to choose particular teaching strategies that are responsive to student make up. The information gained can "ensure learning approaches and options that span the full range of culture-influenced possibilities" (Tomlinson & Eidson, 2003, p. 234). Information can be shared by conducting beginning of the year activities that ask students to share multiple aspects of their lives. Students could bring in photographs that provide a visual sampling of who they are as people. An assignment that asks students to list their ethnic backgrounds, then display the information in the form of a graph that shows the entire class profile, and lets everyone see the class diversity in a visual way.

A cultural inventory can be used to determine the social skills that may be needed by students to forge relationships and effectively work together, with some of these behaviors needing to be directly taught and modeled (Banks et al., 2005). Cultural understanding is sometimes attained after a conflict arises in the classroom. By administering a cultural inventory students can achieve a better understanding of their peers' cultural needs to avoid conflict. It might ask students to describe how close a person should stand near them without violating their personal space or what would be a comfortable voice volume to use in class. Other inventory questions could address eye contact, appropriate physical contact, and sensitivity around personal property. Teachers or students could read "Ann Landers"-type letters that can focus discussions that address these social and relational situations. A classroom that responds to diversity must include explicit instruction that places intercultural relations in the forefront of classroom dialogue.

A cultural inventory helps teachers and students build on the strengths each brings to the classroom. — DVD, Scuola Vita Nuova, "First Graders"; Thurgood Marshall MS, "Art-Based Partnership"

In addition to these strategies for gathering information about students' learning styles and cultural traits and preferences, it is a good idea to explain to students the reason for these inventories. By explaining the idea of multiple learning styles, students might be able to understand times when they have been unsuccessful in their learning or peer relationships and begin to articulate how other strategies might help them learn (Feinberg, 2004). A simple statement as, "Say it another way," cues the teacher into rephrasing or using visuals to give the direction. Some students might not want the entire class to become aware of language challenges or processing difficulties. By asking students to write their learning requests in a classroom journal that will be read by the teacher allows this to happen in a safe and non-intrusive manner.

Teaching Approaches

This We Believe states that successful schools for young adolescents provide a curriculum that is relevant, challenging, integrative, and exploratory. That section goes on to describe the kind of curriculum needed and deserved by young adolescents, including using teaching approaches that respond to student diversity (see Chapter 10). Teachers have always used a variety of teaching approaches—direct or whole group instruction, flexible grouping, and cooperative learning to name a few. Each of these approaches can have strengths and weaknesses, depending on the composition of the classroom learning community. A teaching approach or approaches should be selected by first determining the diverse learning needs present in the classroom and which approach will have more likelihood of increasing students' acquisition of skills and knowledge.

Connecting learning to real-life situations within multiple contexts makes learning more meaningful and accessible.

Presenting information through both visual and auditory means increases retention of material. The use of advanced organizers, anticipatory sets, or scaffolding (see Combs, 2004) helps students understand and remember more when new ideas or information are connected to prior learning. Connecting learning to real-life situations within multiple contexts makes learning more meaningful and accessible.

Some less obvious teaching approaches offer possibilities that can tap into individual student learning strengths while responding to classroom diversity and learning challenges. Parallel teaching, station teaching, collaborative teacher-student planning, and the use of balanced literacy are teaching and learning approaches that can help address classroom diversity. These teaching approaches should be targeted to individual or small group needs and used sparingly, but not on a regular basis.

Parallel teaching, where two teachers are teaching essentially the same content at the same time to two different groups, allows teachers to tailor the instruction to a specific group of students. Both groups of students would interact with essential and enduring concepts that are integral to the unit of study. For example, in a lesson on using metaphors and similes, one group of students could be introduced to advanced examples from a variety of texts, with students explaining and recording where the author used them and why. In the other group, visuals along with concrete examples are used with students who are linguistically challenged so these students could come to understand these literary structures without pressure of a text. Both groups could learn about metaphors and similes at their appropriate level of developmental readiness (Tomlinson & Eidson, 2003).

Station teaching allows students to encounter the essential and enduring concepts in a variety of ways. Within a unit about money and economics, "All About Franklin," small groups of students move between various stations where information about the four great ancient river civilizations and their contributions to economic development and the history of money are presented. The students would view videos, see pictures of artifacts, timelines, and read selections with students helping each other at each station. Station teaching allows opportunities for peer interactions and gaining knowledge through a variety of modalities. By learning at stations, students can see their own cultures' contributions. This practice allows the teacher to join groups of students who may need targeted teacher assistance.

Collaborative teacher-student planning creates many opportunities to address diversity in the classroom. Students can first write questions, ideas, issues, or suggestions for resources in classroom journals that are also read by teachers, and then contribute their ideas in classroom sharing discussions. If some students are not comfortable making their ideas public, teachers can bring their suggestions to the group for them. Teachers can bring the unit idea to the students and then have students generate questions, activities, and even assessment strategies. There are numerous collaborative approaches that ensure that all students have opportunities to offer input into the curriculum (Brodhagen, 1995). Diversity in the classroom is addressed when students' questions and ideas are included.

Efforts to improve and promote literacy should be present throughout the curriculum. A balanced literacy program gives students choice in readings within any important knowledge or skill being taught, teaches explicit reading strategies, and offers choice in trade books, especially when these books are intended to teach aspects of the larger curriculum. If students need to have instruction about certain reading or writing skills, it is provided. Reading logs or journals should be used so students can answer comprehension questions, make connections to their lives, or to other things they have read. Student groupings for reading or book groups would change frequently, depending on the purpose for the groups. Occasionally, students who have similar skills might be in the same group, or there might be a need for gender-based groups, or

Reading fluency and instruction are integrated throughout the curriculum. — DVD, William Thomas MS, "Reading for Fluency"

there might even be a group who wants to read a particular author. Decisions like these are made to address the diversity of the classroom and to promote interaction and reflection among students. [Note: See themed issues of *Middle School Journal*: January 2004 "Teachers Speak Out on Creating Literate Young Adolescents" and November 2004 "Reading, Writing, and Poetry Too."]

Question Posing

"Multiple learning and teaching approaches that respond to their diversity" challenge educators to have students "acquire various ways of posing and answering questions . . . participate in decisions about what to study and how best to study the topics selected" (NMSA, 2003, p. 25). In order to do this, students need to have an opportunity to ask their own questions. Young adolescents might be asked to raise questions for a teacher-selected theme, or they might be given the opportunity to generate questions for a chapter's focus, or the students' questions might become the focus for the curriculum (Brodhagen, 1995; Beane, 1993). In each of these approaches students would be asked to think about what they already know and help determine what else needs to be learned.

To help teachers begin asking students to pose questions, we might look to our Australian colleagues and their expertise at "negotiating the curriculum" (Boomer, Lester, Onore, & Cook, 1994). They call for learner engagement, as seen when students become curious or puzzled about their learning; exploration as students take risks in their learning as they are challenged, yet supported; and reflection as students talk about what it is they have learned and experienced. These teachers help students identify and use the knowledge and skills they already possess. Four questions are presented to help learners focus on the problem, question, or issue of their intended study. Teachers in the United States use a variation of this commonly referred to as "K-W-L" (Ogle, 1986):

1. What do we know already? (Or where are we now, and what don't we need to learn or be taught about?)
2. What do we want, and need, to find out? (Or what are our questions, what don't we know, and what are our problems, curiosities, and challenges?)
3. How will we find out? (Where will we look, what experiments and inquiries will we make, what will we need, what information and resources are available, who will do what, and what should be the order of things?)
4. How will we know, and show, that we've found out when we've finished? (What are our findings? What have we

learned? Whom will we show? For whom are we doing the work? Where to next?)

Asking students to list or tell what it is they already know reinforces their view about self as a successful learner, builds upon prior learning, and begins to provide the linkage to new learning that will be integrated into existing personal knowledge and understandings. This is supported by past and emerging research in which positive effects have been reported in the areas of mathematics, science, the arts, language arts, and social studies (Cawelti, 1995).

Question posing need not be limited to core content areas. This strategy can be successfully employed in exploratory or encore classes as well. For example, in a French class studying the city of Paris, students collectively listed what they knew about the city along with what they wanted to know. Students then determined the research methods they needed to find the answers to their questions. Students divided up their questions and worked in pairs to research the answers that were used later in an all-class trivia game.

When young adolescents are invited to participate in the planning of their own learning they do suggest varied learning activities. They name activities they like and those in which they do well. This includes activities that are visual, auditory, kinesthetic, interpersonal, mathematical, artistic, and so on. Young adolescents are quite skilled at naming a wide variety of activities that can be used to construct learning situations that build upon their learning strengths (Brodhagen, 1995; Storz & Nestor, 2003).

Young adolescents are quite skilled at naming a wide variety of activities that can be used to construct learning situations that build upon their learning strengths.

For example, a question raised in one of our student-planned themes was, "Who Am I?" Students' suggestions for activities that might be used to answer that question included (a) creating a life map that highlights events in their lives by either drawing pictures or using photos with captions explaining the event, (b) interviewing a couple of their relatives to recall what the student was like earlier in her or his life, and (c) constructing a "trading card" highlighting important life statistics, and (d) completing a family tree including ancestral background. In a different theme, "Outer Space: The Mysteries Above and Beyond," the question, "What is our solar system?" generated these suggestions: (a) make a model of our solar system in the classroom, (b) do a research project on all the parts of the solar system, (c) have a guest speaker, (d) visit the university Space Place, and (e) go to Kennedy Space Center. Students were unable to do the last of these, but the point is that the students themselves were able to generate many ideas for varied learning activities.

Projects

When students participate in naming or suggesting activities they always suggest doing "projects." Project-based learning has been a part of the educational scene for nearly a century (Kilpatrick, 1918). Projects are standard in many classrooms but frequently used in classrooms where curriculum integration or multidisciplinary curriculum approaches are used. Projects are authentically integrative as they use knowledge and skills from several disciplines. Projects can provide an enriched learning experience that responds to the needs of a diverse group of learners.

Projects are authentically integrative as they use knowledge and skills from several disciplines.

According to Blumenfeld, Soloway, Marx, Krajcik, Guzdial, and Palincsar (1991), there are two essential components of projects: "they require a question or problem that serves to organize and drive activities" and "these activities [must] result in a series of artifacts, or products, that culminate in a final product that addresses the driving question" (p. 370). The question itself can be determined by either the teacher or student, however, the students' freedom to generate artifacts is critical, because it is through this process of generation that students construct their knowledge; the doing and learning are inextricable. Artifacts are representations of the students' problem solutions that reflect emergent states of knowledge.

Once again we can see how students' learning styles and strengths and cultural backgrounds would be accommodated by their involvement in creating an artifact. A project plan implicitly or explicitly requires students to state or reflect upon what it is they already know about the question or problem that is the focus of their project. The new information learned builds or is constructed upon students' existing knowledge. Projects create numerous opportunities for differentiation to occur.

The detail and depth of information that a project requires can take several weeks of class time. During this time the young adolescent can sometimes lose focus or become frustrated. Project "pauses" can be planned where students take a pause in their work to demonstrate the interim knowledge that has been acquired. For example, students can create an artifact or do a brief presentation of their work such as a trivia or board game, a written "recipe" for researching their topic, or by acting as teacher, presenting facts with visual support that they have acquired. Project pauses allow students to reflect, they support student motivation to see the project through to completion, and they allow the teacher to take an interim pulse of the students' understanding of the project. The students can record these project reflections in process logs (Tomlinson & Eidson, 2003).

By using project pauses, the teacher can address diverse learning needs more effectively throughout the project.

Projects should provide students opportunities to use multiple, multicultural resources. When students use diverse resources such as these, it is more likely they will be motivated to complete a project. Common "experts," people in their personal community who know much about a topic, and school exploratory staff can also serve as resources for specialized knowledge. Other resources can include technology and popular culture.

Technology can be a useful tool in many student- or teacher-designed projects and appeals to today's young adolescents' learning preferences. Most students are able to access more information when using technology. It allows them to get more up-to-date facts, for example weather and economic status reports; to correspond more quickly with other adolescents both at home and abroad; and to access a wider range of databases. And of course, using a word processor allows for corrections and revisions in a less labor-intensive manner, making it especially appealing to students for whom writing does not come easily.

Technology is an increasingly useful tool for both students and teachers. — DVD, Warsaw MS, "Differentiated Instruction"; Maranacook Community MS, "Curriculum Development"

Projects also provide opportunities for interaction among students as well as between students and teachers. This interaction can be instructional and evaluative, and it can even be considered social. Beane and Lipka (1984) reported three features of schooling in which students said they "felt good about themselves at school." They are "I get to work with my friends," "we have fun," and "the teacher is nice." What young adolescents were talking about is a teacher who lets kids work in pairs, cooperative groups, or as peer tutors; a teacher who has them "do" things, like projects, plays, media productions, and so on; and a teacher who treats them with respect, which includes giving them challenging work (see Bishop & Pflaum, 2005).

Fortunately, we now have many teacher accounts that include numerous examples of projects that we can refer to for ideas and guidance. Some of these are *Integrated Studies in the Middle*

Grades: Dancing Through Walls (Stevenson & Carr, 1993), *Dissolving Boundaries* (Brazee & Capelluti, 1995), *Beyond Separate Subjects: Integrative Learning at the Middle-Level* (Siu-Runyan & Faircloth, 1995), *Whole Learning in the Middle School: Evolution and Transition* (Pace, 1995), *Learning Through Real-World Problem Solving* (Nagel, 1996), *Watershed: A Successful Voyage Into Integrative Learning* (Springer, 1994), and *Democratic Schools* (Apple & Beane, 1995).

Knowledge Performance and Student Reflection

Major learning activities or units should culminate in some kind of knowledge performance and student reflection.

Major learning activities or units should culminate in some kind of knowledge performance and student reflection (Anfara et al., 2003). Knowledge performance should be demonstrated through student-centered action and activity, such as projects, presentations, debate, drama, simulations, creative writing, art work, or use of technology (Beane, 1997). The essential and enduring knowledge or "big ideas" and skills must be apparent within each knowledge performance. When students create wind-up or summary projects, which are meaningful and personal, knowledge endures.

To fairly and accurately assess students' learning within knowledge performance, teachers must consider students' learning strengths, cultural nuances, and other student learning characteristics when constructing and then completing evaluations. In the evaluation process, different looking projects could receive similar ratings, and since there was not one way to complete a project, each one can and probably will look different. As a result, students with "special needs" have opportunities to demonstrate their knowledge using the skills they do have, rather than simply failing because of those they do not have.

To facilitate student reflection a growing number of teachers have found that learning is enhanced when students participate in interaction and reflection about what is being learned. In other words, having students talk about their learning can increase their understanding and mastery of new ideas. Whole class discussions serve as a forum for students to explain learning processes and to hear strategies used by others. Partners or triad groups can be used the same way. Journal writing and end-of-week "processing" sessions offer time for reflection about personal and whole-group learning experiences. When individual students are able to express their unique learning in multiple ways, diversity of learning is addressed.

When young adolescents are asked to explain what they have read in literature, to talk through how they have solved a math problem, to draw a web, to explain their position on a social studies issue, or to discuss a final integrating project about an issue or problem, we see them use critical thinking and processing skills, synthesize content, and make evident their own meanings. This kind of interaction benefits both the speaker and the listener (Cawelti, 1995). Culminating learning experiences that require knowledge performance and student reflection, lend themselves well to standards-based assessments and student portfolios, and in turn become authentic demonstrations of knowledge.

Culminating learning experiences that require knowledge performance and student reflection, lend themselves well to standards-based assessments and student portfolios.

Parents can benefit from students having opportunities to reflect on learning too. Reflection by students can improve at-home conversations when young adolescents actually have an answer to the question, "what are you doing in school?" Parents would also observe student learning when invited to end-of-unit presentations, project fairs, and other culminating activities. Like other teachers, we have also found that student-led parent conferences are a powerful way of having students interact about and reflect on their learning. On these occasions, students explain to parents, guardians, or other significant adults what and how they have learned; how they have dealt with problems; how they have demonstrated their learning; and what goals they have set for further learning. These conferences are especially meaningful when they are a part of a comprehensive plan for students to assess their own work.

Professional Development

Student diversity within our schools continues to increase, while the cultural makeup of those who teach remains constant (Banks et al., 2005). Teachers want to do their very best. Teachers want all children to learn, but desire alone is not sufficient. Effective professional development can serve to close the cultural gap between teacher and student. There are many resources available to help educators to develop and implement equity pedagogy (Banks et al., 2005), which in turn increases the likelihood of success for young adolescents. There is an extensive research base from which to draw; and although each school context is different and individual study results might vary, enough work has been done to say that some teaching and learning strategies are better than others. Sometimes the task ahead seems overwhelming, however by systematically learning new teaching strategies and systematically implementing them in the classroom, educators will be better able to respond to the increasing diversity in middle school classrooms.

School administrators, school boards, teachers' unions, and the wider community must realize, as was reported by the National Commission on Teaching and America's Future (1996), that good teachers are the most important element of successful learning. One of the best ways to improve student achievement is to continually improve the quality of the teaching staff. This means that teachers need adequate time to master new teaching and learning strategies. A one-hour inservice presentation is not enough for teachers to implement a new teaching practice. Teachers need to read research and determine whether a strategy can serve the needs of their students.

> When teachers study their own practice and its effects on students in their classrooms, real change in teaching and learning strategies can occur.

Teachers need to come together to discuss what results or effects are seen as changes are implemented in the classroom (Burnaford, Beane, & Brodhagen, 1994). In some districts, groups of teachers are able to meet throughout the year to study their own practice. Teachers might study teaching and learning strategies that respond to a diverse group of learners, curriculum integration, or numerous other topics related to their practice. When teachers study their own practice and its effects on students in their classrooms, real change in teaching and learning strategies can occur.

Multiple and diverse opportunities for collaboration, regular workshops, visitation days, adequate planning time, access to technology, and diversity training would begin to provide the support needed to effectively teach a diverse student population. We believe that all students can learn when their individual learning strengths and challenges are honored and recognized.

Conclusion

Five days a week millions of diverse, rapidly changing young adolescents show up at schools all across the country—and no two of them are alike. This growing diversity places increased demands on all middle level educators. To meet these challenges we must recognize the need to continually learn about and implement multiple learning and teaching approaches that will best serve our diverse student population. By placing diversity in the forefront of our curriculum planning, we will afford all students the quality education they deserve. Our schools mirror our society. By honoring and celebrating the diversity in our classrooms, we are offering our nation's young people the best opportunity to become contributing members of their communities, the nation, and the world.

References

Anfara, V. A., Jr., Andrews, P. G., Hough, D. L., Mertens, S. B., Mizelle, N. B., White, G. P. (2003) *Research and resources in support of* This We Believe. Westerville, OH: National Middle School Association.

Apple, M. W., & Beane, J. A. (1995). *Democratic schools.* Alexandria, VA: Association for Supervision and Curriculum Development.

Banks, J. A., Cookson, P., Gay, G., Hawley, W., Irvine, J., Nieto, S., et al. (2005). Education and Diversity. *Social Education 69*(1). pp. 36-40.

Beane, J. A. (1993). *A middle school curriculum: From rhetoric to reality* (2nd ed.). Columbus, OH: National Middle School Association.

Beane, J. A. (1997). *Curriculum Integration: Designing the core of democratic education.* New York: Teachers College Press.

Beane, J. A., & Lipka, R. P. (1984). *Self-concept, self-esteem, and the curriculum.* Boston: Allyn and Bacon.

Bishop, P. A., & Pflaum, S. W. (2005). Student perceptions of action, relevance, and pace. *Middle School Journal, 36*(4), 4-12.

Blumenfeld, P., Soloway, E., Marx, R. W., Krajcik, J. S., Guzdial, M., & Palincsar, A. (1991). Motivating project based learning: Sustaining the doing, supporting the learning. *Educational Psychologist, 26*(3&4), 369-398.

Boomer, G., Lester, N., Onore, C., & Cook, J. (1994). *Negotiating the curriculum: Educating for the 21st century.* London: Falmer.

Brazee, E. N., & Capelluti, J. (1995). *Dissolving boundaries: Toward an integrative curriculum.* Columbus, OH: National Middle School Association.

Brodhagen, B. L. (1995). The situation made us special. In M. W. Apple & J. A. Beane (Eds.), *Democratic Schools* (pp. 83-100). Alexandria, VA: Association for Supervision and Curriculum Development.

Burnaford, G., Beane, J., & Brodhagen, B. (1994). Teacher action research: Inside an integrative curriculum. *Middle School Journal, 26* (2), 5-13.

Cawelti, G. (Ed.). (1995). *Handbook of research on improving student achievement.* Arlington, VA: Educational Research Service.

Combs, D. (2004). A framework for scaffolding content area reading strategies. *Middle School Journal, 36*(2), 13-20.

Dilg, M. (2003). *Thriving in the multicultural classroom: Principles and practices for effective teaching.* New York: Teachers College Press.

Feinberg, C. (2004, July 1). The possible dream: A nation of proficient schoolchildren. *HGSE News: The News Source of the Harvard Graduate School of Education.* Retrieved May 6, 2005, from www.gsc.harvard.edu/news/features/howard07012004.html

Hammond, L. (1997). The Right to Learn. *Social Education, 69*(1), 36-40.

Kilpatrick, W. H. (1918). The project method. *Teachers College Record, 19*, 319-335.

Nagel, N. G. (1996). *Learning through real-world problem solving.* Thousand Oaks, CA: Corwin.

National Commission on Teaching and America's Future. (1996). *What matters most: Teaching for America's future.* New York: Carnegie Corporation.

National Middle School Association. (2003). *This we believe: Successful schools for young adolescents*. Westerville, OH: Author.

Ogle, D. (1986). K-W-L: A teaching model that develops active reading of expository text. *Reading Teacher, 39,* 564-570.

Pace, G. (Ed.). (1995). *Whole learning in the middle school: Evolution and transition*. Norwood, MA: Christopher-Gordon.

Siu-Runyan, Y., & Faircloth, C. V. (Eds.). (1995). *Beyond separate subjects: Integrative learning at the middle level*. Norwood, MA: Christopher-Gordon.

Stevenson, C., & Carr, J. E. (Eds.). (1993). *Integrated studies in the middle grades: Dancing through walls*. New York: Teachers College Press.

Storz, M. G., Nestor, K. R. (2003). Insights into meeting standards from listening to the voices of urban students. *Middle School Journal, 36*(4), 4-12.

Tomlinson, C., & Eidson, C. (2003). *Differentiation in practice*. Alexandria, VA: Association for Supervision and Curriculum Development.

Wehlage, G., Rutter, R., Smith, G., Lesko, N., & Fernandez, R. (1989). *Reducing the risk: Schools as communities of support*. London: The Falmer Press.

Assessment and Evaluation that Promote Quality Learning

Sue C. Thompson
Dan French

In *This We Believe: Successful Schools for Young Adolescents* National Middle School Association (2003) urges educators to conduct continuous, authentic, and appropriate assessment and evaluation measures in order to provide evidence about every student's learning progress. The position paper goes on to state: "Such information helps students, teachers, and family members select immediate learning goals and plan further education. Grades alone are inadequate expressions for assessing and reporting student progress on the many goals of middle level education" (p. 27).

It is important to understand the difference between *assessment* and *evaluation* because the two are distinctly different functions. *This We Believe* (NMSA, 2003) emphasizes that assessment is the process of estimating a student's progress toward an objective and using that information to help students continue their learning. On the other hand, evaluation is the process of using data and standards to judge the quality of progress or level of achievement. Both assessment and evaluation have a role to play in determining the academic growth of a student.

The Impact of No Child Left Behind

The advent of No Child Left Behind (NCLB) has brought a dimension to assessment and evaluation not present when *This We Believe: Developmentally Responsive Middle Level Schools* (NMSA, 1995) was written. The federal mandate has unleashed a flood of testing as the prime means of demonstrating educational accountability. Comprehensive definitions of accountability have been replaced in some states by one single, paper and pencil, on-demand high-stakes test. As educators know, it is impossible to truly understand what a student knows and can do based on information from one single test that inevitably focuses on a very narrow range of student output.

> The advent of the *No Child Left Behind Act of 2001* has plunged us into an unprecedented era of high stakes testing, coupled with the threat of not being promoted from grade to grade and of not graduating from high school and will be the engine that drives improvement in instruction and student achievement. Yet there are many inherent flaws to this approach, an approach that, under the mantle of equity and excellence, threatens to undermine the tenets of exemplary middle grades practice, and leave behind the very students that the legislation and testing movement purport to be helping. (French, 2003, pp. 14-15)

High-stakes testing programs have moved middle schools away from the active, engaged learning experiences that truly prepare students for the world of today—and tomorrow.

George (2002) stated, "Goals and results in NCLB, it should be noted, are limited to cognitive achievement as measured by standardized tests. Middle level leaders will need to supplement test data with other evidence of student achievement and growth that matches the full range of goals and expectations for young adolescents" (pp. 7-8). High-stakes testing programs in many districts and states have resulted in a movement away from the active, engaged learning experiences that truly prepare students for the world in which they live today and the world they will occupy as adults.

> In a concerted effort to prepare students for standardized tests, in state after state the curriculum to be covered is being prescribed. These prescriptions, while seemingly sensible as a way to ensure accountability actually hinder middle level teachers in meeting the *intellectual* needs of their pupils. Courses of study with aligned and mandated curriculum are most likely to be counterproductive when presented to young adolescents. Teachers who know their students as individuals ought not be hampered unduly in exercising their professional judgment about what, when, and how to teach. In the current climate they are relinquishing much of their judgment and creativity and knuckling under [to] narrowly conceived and highly specific objectives that are purported to yield improved test scores. The best middle school teachers, however, are more nearly artists than technicians. (Lounsbury, 2004, p. xiv-xv)

According to Darling-Hammond (2004),

> NCLB's regulations have caused a number of schools to abandon their thoughtful diagnostic assessment and accountability systems—replacing instructionally rich, improvement-oriented systems with more rote-oriented punishment-driven approaches—and it has thrown many high-performing and steadily improving schools into chaos rather than helping them remain focused and deliberate in their ongoing efforts to serve students well. (pp. 4-5)

Kohn (2004), an outspoken critic of standardized testing, points out that our students are being tested to an extent that is unprecedented in our history and unparallel anywhere else in the world. Norm-referenced tests are not intended to measure the quality of learning or teaching. For educators who have a strong sense of social justice, one of the biggest concerns about standardized tests is that they are biased. "For decades, critics have complained that many standardized tests are unfair because the questions require a set of knowledge and skills more likely to be possessed by children from a privileged background" (p. 57).

Alarmingly, one district, that was committed to the middle school concept until two years ago, has returned to a departmentalized organizational structure against all evidence that this organizational structure would not support the needs of the young adolescents in their seventh and eighth grade middle schools. More alarmingly, the district has decided to move their growing population of English as a second language (ESL) learners from one middle school to another middle school every year to avoid having any one middle school fail to meet adequately yearly progress (AYP) on standardized tests. Instead of these students and their families coming over time to feel a part of a school community, they will not only have to adjust to language challenges, but also to new school environments. These are some of the very students that advocates for No Child Left Behind profess to want to help in order to close the achievement gap.

The social equity agenda has become a part of the language of middle schools, in part because the National Forum to Accelerate Middle-Grades Reform (1999) determined criteria for socially equitable schools. Two of the criteria specifically address assessment. One criterion states that students may use many and varied approaches to achieve and demonstrate competence and mastery of standards while the other states that the school continually adapt curriculum, instruction, assessment, and scheduling to meet its students' diverse and changing needs. There are two faces of standards in addressing educational equity.

> In a society like ours that is stratified by race and income, we must have standards of what all students should know and be able to do upon moving from middle to high school and graduating from high school. The absence of standards virtually guarantees stratified resources and access to knowledge, based upon income, color of skin, and the community or neighborhood in which one lives. (French, 2003, p. 15)

Arhar (2003) took a critical look at the vision of education that is advocated through the *No Child Left Behind Act* (2001) and the vision of middle level education advocated by NMSA's *This We Believe* (1995, 2003), the National Forum to Accelerate Middle-Grades Reform (1994-2003a, 1994-2003b) and *Turning Points 2000* (Jackson & Davis, 2000). "One vision (NCLB) emphasizes accountability through standardized testing and parental choice and the other (National Forum to Accelerate Middle-Grades Reform) emphasizes becoming actively involved in helping children learn" (p. 47). This belief is supported by Pate (2004) who pointed out that appropriate and developmentally responsive assessment is an integral part of middle level education and stated, "Employing a variety of assessment practices will help ensure that teachers capture student learning, for no single method can possibly encapsulate all that students have learned. Assessment in middle schools should be ongoing and include both formative and summative measures" (p. 73).

Assessment in middle schools should be ongoing and include both formative and summative measures.

Even middle school educators who are sensitive to working with young adolescents and their developmental needs and understand the value of varied assessments are in a state of confusion as a result of the emphasis on standardized test results and the sanctions being imposed on them based on these results. For example, one middle school states that it strives to incorporate the components reported as essential by the National Middle School Association for its organizational structure. The population is divided into small learning communities through the use of interdisciplinary teams. On the other hand, each content area's standards and essential questions are examined and outlined within a curriculum map that is provided to each staff member. This map indicates month by month where teachers should be in their content areas. Teachers conduct common assessments in each content area to ensure that all students are learning the same information. There is no flexibility to deviate from the curriculum maps or the common assessments.

Equally troublesome, there is no representation of other content area teachers on these content-specific committees that develop the curriculum maps or the common assessment instruments. The way team time is used has been determined by the administration, and there is little opportunity or encouragement for members of the team to work collaboratively on interdisciplinary or integrated units. On the one hand, there stands what the school's vision statement says about instructional practice and assessment that will accommodate individual differences, interests, and abilities and staff members' being committed to understanding the uniqueness of each student. In tention with these is the district's expectation for a standardized curriculum and assessment plan. As Beane (2004) reminded us, "If the separate subject curriculum and lecture-worksheet regimen worked, middle level schools would have a very different history" (p. 57).

Meaningful learning experiences occur through the complexity of integrated thematic instruction that focuses on the questions, issues, and concerns of young adolescents in relation to their world. Consequently, assessing these kinds of learning experiences should entail a wide range of authentic assessments, including projects where students are actually demonstrating what they know and can do through collaborating, exploring, making, investigating, acting, and being fully engaged in the learning experience. Such projects need not be subject specific but may use skills and knowledge from several content areas.

Meaningful learning experiences occur through integrated thematic instruction that focuses on the questions, issues, and concerns of young adolescents in relation to their world.

Mark Springer, a strong proponent of integrative curriculum who designed a broad, successful integrative program at Radnor Middle School in Wayne, Pennsylvania, says he does not believe testing generally improves education. However, even Springer sees potential for teachers' using it in a positive way. In Paterson (2004), Springer says, "Confident, well-educated, experienced teachers will simply use the tests as yet another measure of performance. These teachers will continue to individualize instruction for their students and will continue to be creative and energetic and captivating. By doing so, they will continue to educate young thinkers who, by extension, will do well on tests" (p. 12).

Chirichello, Eckel, and Pagliaro (2005) wrote about an engaging, relevant, challenging, and thought-provoking unit on African cultures that is built around concepts. Concepts are big ideas that can be taught in a variety of ways to students who come to us with varied interests and ways of learning (also see Tomlinson, 1998). The authors explain, "Concepts connect topics, and essential questions can move the level of understanding to analysis, synthesis, application, and evaluation" (p. 39). Using concepts to organize the curriculum and standards, students can "demonstrate their strengths in a variety of ways so that assessment becomes integral to learning and not merely a post-instruction accountability tool" (p. 39).

Using concepts to organize the curriculum, students can "demonstrate their strengths in a variety of ways so that assessment becomes integral to learning and not merely a post-instruction accountability tool.

Assessment and evaluation should reflect a curricular delivery model that is, like the curriculum itself, integrative, challenging, exploratory, and promotes learning through providing relevant and meaningful learning experiences for young adolescents.

Staying on the Right Track

While standardized, often high-stakes tests are a part of the landscape of American education, middle school educators who are concerned with meeting the needs of young adolescents must filter the assessment and evaluation processes and products of learning through varied and multiple procedures of assessment. There needs to be a clear distinction between standards and standardization. Standards should not lead to standardization of instruction or assessment. The tension created by high-stakes testing and other facets of standards-based reform should not impede teachers' efforts to create relevant, integrated curriculum for young adolescents. This tension can be somewhat resolved when "the standards, concepts, and essential questions within the curriculum are the first sources for ideas about authentic assessment. Teachers and students can brainstorm together, then refine and adapt their ideas to fit the standards" (Jackson & Davis, 2000, p. 59).

National Middle School Association (2003) and the National Forum to Accelerate Middle-Grades Reform (2002) both call for multiple measures to assess students' progress. Authentic assessment practices such as portfolios, exhibitions, performances, and demonstrations provide a complete picture of student learning compared to that allowed by the exclusive use of standardized tests. Both learners and learning are complex. "The work of creating academically challenging, developmentally responsive, and socially equitable middle schools that serve a diverse range of students is much more complex and messy than merely measuring students using a high stakes standardized test" (French, 2003, p. 22).

National Middle School Association published a companion book for *This We Believe,* which provides practitioners with the research and resources that support its recommendations. *Research and Resources in Support of This We Believe* (Anfara et al., 2003) provides specific citations to back up the association's advocacy of assessment and evaluation that will promote student learning. The authors emphasize that the book's goal is not to avoid accountability efforts, but to use assessment measures as tools for raising the achievement of students.

Goal Setting and the Empowerment of Young Adolescents

This We Believe . . . And Now We Must Act (Erb, 2001) emphasized the importance of using assessment to actively promote learning and encouraged student participation in all phases of assessment. In that volume, Vars (2001) stated, "Hence it is important to invite students to work with their teachers to make critical decisions at all stages of the learning enterprise, especially goal setting, establishing evaluation criteria, demonstrating learning, self-evaluation, peer evaluation, and reporting" (p. 79).

Students should be invited to make critical decisions at all stages of the learning enterprise.

Williams (2002) shared the story of how she and her students changed their classroom environment from one that was teacher-directed to one that was a collaborative, educational team of learners where all voices were valued. She stated, "By providing different forms of assessment I learned to listen to all of my students more effectively. From reading their journal responses I realized the need to include the students more fully in their education" (p. 59). Through the self-assessments, a dialogue was started in class about learning and how to improve as learners.

Young adolescents need opportunities to reflect upon the work they are producing in order to develop the ability to do so. In the area of cognitive-intellectual development, young adolescents not only display a wide range of individual intellectual development, but they are increasingly able to think abstractly, not just concretely. Scales (2003) reported, "Middle level educators are in a unique position to help build many developmental assets such as feeling empowered and playing useful roles, building social competence, and developing a commitment to learning" (p. 51).

One way that young adolescents can be empowered is to provide opportunities for them to engage in self-reflection and grow in their ability to self-evaluate and value themselves as learners. As stated by Smith and Myers (2001), "Students need time to reflect on their work, to make connections between and among tasks, and to note improvements along the way. Such personal integration of knowledge is the key to good assessment" (p. 11). Students are able to not just study science or some subject but reflect on their work as scientists, or mathematicians, or historians.

Students may also consider their feelings about the learning tasks with which they are engaged. Good middle school teachers ask students to answer questions that give them opportunities to share work they are proud of, identify what they want to improve on, and evaluate what they gained from the learning activity. Students are learning to become critical consumers of their educational experiences and realize the impact these experiences have on their lives.

Student-Led Conferences Meet Multiple Goals

We get the kids very involved in owning responsibility for their test scores. We are very honest with them about what these tests mean.
— Brenda Tolbert, Language Arts Teacher, Chapel Hill MS, "School-Wide Reading"

Turning Points (Carnegie Council on Adolescent Development, 1989) recommended that middle grades schools "*reengage families in the education of young adolescents* by giving families meaningful roles in school governance, communicating with families about the school program and student's progress, and offering families opportunities to support the learning process at home and at the school" (emphasis in original) (p. 9). *Turning Points 2000* further advanced this idea and called for middle grades schools that involve parents and communities in supporting student learning and healthy development (Jackson & Davis, 2000, p. 24).

One challenge that middle level educators face is the commonly found declining degree of parent involvement as children progress from elementary to middle school. Student-led conferences are one of the ways to keep parents actively involved as students share important information about their learning. Students take ownership in the process as they select the work to share with the parent or conference attendee. Students come prepared to explain selected papers and may even determine questions they would like the attendee to ask them about their work.

According to Farber (1999), when the students on her middle school team switched from traditional parent-teacher conferences to student-led conferences, "The long-lasting improvement in students' intellectual focus was one of the main benefits of student-led conferences. But teachers point to many other advantages, including less stress, fewer complaints, and better parent attendance on conference day" (p. 21). Dyck (2002) identified these benefits of student-led conferences:

- Encourage students to accept personal responsibility for their academic performance
- Help students recognize and take ownership for the things that interfered with their learning success
- Teach students the process of self-evaluation
- Develop students' oral communication skills and organizational skills
- Increase students' self-confidence
- Enhance communication between student and parents.

(p. 38)

The benefits of student-led conferences are manifold and certain. — DVD, William Thomas MS, "Student-Led Conferences"

Enhancing communication between student and parents can be one of the most valuable benefits of student-led conferences. Increased conversations at home between children and their parents about schoolwork inevitably follow conferences. Parents and students are living in a fast-paced world, and conversations between them are all too often limited and fleeting and not typically about school. One student on the Alpha Team at Shelburne Community School in Vermont, a multiage group of sixth, seventh, and eighth graders stated, "You know, it's a ton of work and scary at first, but now I think it's kind of fun. You get to talk with your parents for as long as you want and no one interrupts you. We bring snacks because we talk about my work for so long" (Smith & Myers, 2001, p. 14).

Technology has come into play with ways to keep home and school working together: Web sites and e-mail provide opportunities for parents, teachers, and students to connect electronically. For the foreseeable future, written reports will continue to be a tool used in communicating with the home and school, but other means are now available and are increasingly being used.

Establishing Evaluation Criteria to Demonstrate Learning

"Teachers should specify the criteria for evaluation in advance in the form of a rubric that defines levels of quality" (NMSA, 2003, p. 27). Students should be involved in developing rubrics and should have examples of quality work available. Rubrics provide directions for how to recognize whether the student has reached a certain level of mastery related to skills, knowledge, and dispositions. By making teacher expectations clear, rubrics result in a higher quality of work and enhance student learning. Students are empowered when they can use rubrics to evaluate their own work. Rubrics take the guesswork out of grades. If students have a clear target to aim for, they are more likely to hit it.

Students should be involved in developing rubrics and should have examples of quality work available.

There are many ways that students can demonstrate their learning including journals, demonstrations, peer feedback, teacher-designed tests, and audio or video evidence of learning. Portfolios are selections of student work that can be used to monitor students' efforts, their progress, and their achievements. Not only should portfolios include selections of work by the student to show evidence of growth, portfolios should also stimulate a meaningful dialogue between a student and teacher as well as with parents.

There are many ways students can demonstrate their learning.
— DVD, Chapel Hill MS, "Hot Air Balloons," "School-Wide Reading"

One district uses cross-curricular portfolios to support integrated learning. All of the middle school teachers in this district determined the essential skills, knowledge, and dispositions they wanted their students to have acquired by the end of each of the three years in middle school. The work reflected, collectively, the beliefs and mental models the middle school teachers had about curriculum and assessment in the district's middle schools. Four common strands and definitions were identified:

> *Communication:* A piece of student work that demonstrates effective written and oral student expression.
>
> *Problem Solving—Critical Thinking:* A piece of student work that demonstrates problem solving and critical thinking skills that could originate in any discipline. The skills might include identifying and solving problems, applying perspective, using manipulatives, making connections to real life, understanding one's own learning style, or gathering, processing, and producing data.
>
> *Academic Development—Integrated Studies:* A piece of student work that reflects the standards for the disciplines represented in middle school and shows the connection between the disciplines. Students demonstrate their ability to use skills and knowledge across disciplines to complete projects, exhibitions, and other assignments.
>
> *Personal and Social Awareness:* A piece of student work that demonstrates evidence of application to the life skills of appreciation of others, common sense, cooperation, effort, flexibility, goal setting, integrity, patience, respect, sense of humor, leadership experiences, caring, community

> service, curiosity, empathy, friendship, initiative, moral courage, perseverance, responsibility, and organization and time management.
>
> The standards reflected the teachers' knowledge and understanding of current cognitive research and the needs and characteristics of the young adolescent learner. The strands also indicated that the teachers valued the integrated curriculum delivery model. (Thompson, 2002, pp. 169-170)

The teachers also recognized the difficulties in trying to assess the life skills of the students under the Personal and Social Awareness strand and developed a self-assessment checklist so students could rate themselves and their growth in this area—another example of student empowerment and valuing student voice.

Conclusion

Middle schools today face tremendous pressures related to assessment and evaluation. These tensions can either be used to create meaningful dialogue about the role and nature of assessment and evaluation in middle schools or can result in schools' simply giving in to pressures. Educators and parents should have opportunities to view students' progress through multiple lens, ones that reflect their growth and development in several dimensions.

> In developmentally responsive middle level schools, assessment and evaluation procedures also reflect the characteristics and uniqueness of young adolescents. Since early adolescence is a critical period of building a clear self-concept and positive self-regard, assessment and evaluation should emphasize individual progress rather than comparison with other students and should not rely on extrinsic motivation. (NMSA, 2003, p. 28)

Schools, however, in expedient attempts to raise test scores, are promoting all kinds of incentive programs, from special treats for those students who do well on tests, to certificates indicating the achievement of certain students to the exclusion of others. Valuable time away from learning is being used for All-School Assemblies to "pump" students up for testing days. But as Kohn (1993) points out, "Punishment and rewards are not opposite at all; they are two sides of the same coin. And it is a coin that does not buy very much" (p. 50).

National Middle School Association understands that successful schools for young adolescents are undergirded by an interdependent web of beliefs and characteristics that do not operate independently. When all of the characteristics of *This We Believe* (2003) are in place and working in concert, the sum is greater than the parts. Every decision made in a successful middle school should support what is in the best interests of students. A broad program of assessment and evaluation, therefore, is a necessary component of a successful middle level school.

Sue Swaim (2005), executive director of National Middle School Association, has stated well the need to avoid evaluating schools and students on the basis of a test:

> No one argues the importance of accountability in our schools and classrooms, nor does anyone dispute the fact that, when appropriately developed and implemented, tests are important tools for evaluating schools' progress in achieving academic excellence. Today, however, school success is too often defined solely by the results of high-stakes tests. This is a mistake. When considered by themselves, test scores are an inadequate yardstick by which to measure a person's education or a school's success. We must acknowledge the serious limitations of standardized tests in evaluating the adequacy of an individual's education and the competency of a faculty. Middle school accountability must be based on a broader database. (p. 5)

References

Anfara, V. A., Jr., (Ed.), Andrews, P.G., Hough, D., Mertens, S., Mizelle, N., & White, G. (2003) *Research and resources in support of* This We Believe. Westerville, OH: National Middle School Association.

Arhar, J. (2003). No Child Left Behind and middle level education: A look at research, policy, and practice. *Middle School Journal, 34*(5), 46-51.

Beane, J. (2004). Creating quality in the middle school curriculum. In S. Thompson (Ed.), *Reforming middle level education: Considerations for policymakers* (pp. 49-63). Greenwich, CT: Information Age Publishing.

Carnegie Council on Adolescent Development. (1989). *Turning points: Preparing American youth for the 21st century.* New York: Carnegie Corporation.

Chirichello, M., Eckel, J., & Pagliaro, G. (2005). Using concepts and connections to reach students with integrated curriculum. *Middle School Journal, 36*(5), 37-43.

Darling-Hammond, L. (2004). From "separate but equal" to "No Child Left Behind": The collision of new standards and old inequalities. In D. Meier & G. Woods (Eds.), *Many children left behind* (pp. 4-5). Boston: Beacon Press.

Dyck, B. (2002). Student-led conferences up close & personal. *Middle Ground, 6*(2), 39-41.

Doda, N. (2004). Creating socially equitable middle grades schools. In N. Doda & S. Thompson (Eds.), *Reforming middle level education: Considerations for policymakers* (pp. 65-84). Greenwich, CT: Information Age Publishing.

Erb, T. O. (Ed.). (2001). *This we believe . . . And now we must act.* Westerville, OH: National Middle School Association.

Farber, P. (1999). Speak up: Student-led conference is a real conversation piece. *Middle Ground, 2*(4), 21-24.

French, D. (2003). The new vision of authentic assessment to overcome the flaws of high stakes testing. *Middle School Journal, 35*(1), 14-23.

French, D. (2004). The role of accountability in middle level schools. In S. Thompson (Ed.), *Reforming middle level education: Considerations for policymakers* (pp. 85-107). Greenwich, CT: Information Age Publishing.

George, P. (2002). *No child left behind: Implications for middle level leaders.* Westerville, OH: National Middle School Association.

Jackson, A. W., & Davis, G. A. (2000). *Turning points 2000: Educating adolescents in the 21st century.* New York: Teachers College Press and Westerville, OH: National Middle School Association.

Kohn, A. (1993). *Punished by rewards: The trouble with gold stars, incentive plans, A's, praise, and other bribes.* Boston: Houghton Mifflin.

Kohn, A. (2004). *What does it mean to be well educated?* Boston: Beacon Press.

Lounsbury, J. (2004). Introduction: Policymakers, please think on these "things." In S. Thompson (Ed), *Reforming middle level education: Considerations for Policymakers* (pp. xiii-xvii). Greenwich, CT: Information Age Publishing.

National Forum to Accelerate Middle-Grades Reform. (1999). *Schools to Watch Criteria—Social Equity.* Retrieved April 25, 2005, from http://www.mgforum.org/improvingschools/STW/STWcriteria.asp

National Forum to Accelerate Middle-Grades Reform. (2002, July). *High Stakes Testing Policy Statement, Issue 3.* Retrieved on April 25, 2005, from http://www.mgforum.org/highstakes/page1.ht

National Forum to Accelerate Middle-Grades Reform. (1998). *Vision Statement.* Retrieved April 11, 2005, from www.mgforum.org/about/vision.asp

National Forum to Accelerate Middle-Grades Reform. (1994-2003b). *Policy on High Stakes Testing.* Retrieved April 11, 2005, from www.mgforum.org/highstakes/page1.htm

National Middle School Association. (1995). *This we believe: Developmentally responsive middle level schools.* Columbus, OH: Author.

National Middle School Association. (2003). *This we believe: Successful schools for young adolescents.* Westerville, OH: Author.

Pate, E. (2004). Middle school curriculum, instruction, and assessment through the 1970s, 1980s, and 1990s. *Middle School Journal, 35*(5). 70-74.

Paterson, J. (2004). Looking on the bright side? Considering the positives of increased assessment. *Middle Ground, 7*(3), 10-13.

Scales, P. C. (2003). Characteristics of young adolescents. In National Middle School Association, *This we believe: Successful schools for young adolescents* (pp. 43-51). Westerville, OH: National Middle School Association.

Smith, C., & Myers, C. (2001). Students take center stage in classroom assessment. *Middle Ground, 5*(2), 10-16.

Swaim, S. (2005). Perspective: Time for serious problem solving. *Middle Ground. 8*(4), 5.

Thompson, S. (2002). Reculturing middle schools to use cross-curricular portfolios. In V. Anfara & S. Stacki (Eds.), *Curriculum instruction and Assessment* (pp. 157-179). Greenwich, CT: Information Age Publishing.

Tomlinson, C. A. (1998). For integration and differentiation choose concepts over topics. *Middle School Journal, 30*(2), 3-8.

Vars, G. (2001). Assessment and evaluation that promote learning. In T. O. Erb (Ed.), *This we believe . . . And now we must act* (pp. 78-89). Westerville, OH: National Middle School Association.

Williams, C. (2002). We chose another road: Empowering students. In N. Doda & S. Thompson (Eds.), *Transforming ourselves, transforming schools: Middle school change* (pp. 57-73). Westerville, OH: National Middle School Association.

Organizational Structures that Support Meaningful Relationships and Learning

Deborah Kasak
Ericka Uskali

The operative word for middle grades education has long been flexibility. Young adolescent learning needs and characteristics defy rigidity. Successful schools for young adolescents are places that design their practice to reflect an understanding of young adolescent growth and development so that the odds of optimum results are increased. Organizational structures that facilitate learning and nurture relationships have to be flexible, small learning communities so the needs of students can be recognized and adjustments made in form and function to maximize learning. The best schools are ever-changing, learning organizations that carefully and thoughtfully address academic excellence through developmental responsiveness for all their students (National Forum to Accelerate Middle-Grades Reform, 1998).

The 21st century presents educators with shrinking resources and demands for increased accountability through No Child Left Behind (NCLB). The pressure of meeting adequate yearly progress has schools racing to make academic progress. Times dictate tough choices. Regrettably some schools and districts have taken the pathway that dismantles the very organizational structures that have the best chance to build meaningful relationships and learning (Juvonen, Le, Kaganoff, Augustine, & Constant, 2004; American Institute for Research, 2005). *This We Believe: Successful Schools for Young Adolescents* (NMSA, 2003) provides the beacon for making the social context and organization of schooling supportive of high performance.

Small learning communities or learning teams hold remarkable possibilities for student development when teams are high functioning and well implemented

The hallmark of an effective middle level school rests in its capacity to personalize learning. Small learning communities or learning teams hold remarkable possibilities for student development when teams are high functioning and well implemented. When schools are organized into small learning communities, close relationships between students and adults can be established and more individualized attention given to all learners (Arhar, 1990; Arhar & Kromrey, 1995). Team organizational structure alters and personalizes the working relationships between students and teachers, therefore enhancing the context wherein good instruction can thrive.

Over the past three decades middle level schools and their teams have experimented with many variations of interdisciplinary team organization. Teams, it has been found, have contributed to greater student contact and increased personalization. Teams establish shared responsibility for student learning that reduces the stress of isolation among students and teachers. Finally, teams are the platform for creating greater coordination, collaboration, and integration of learning opportunities (Alexander & George, 1981; Arhar, Johnston, & Markle, 1988, 1989; Carnegie Council on Adolescent Development, 1989; Erb & Doda, 1989; Felner et al., 1997; Flowers, Mertens, & Mulhall, 1999, 2000a, 2003; George & Alexander, 2003; George & Oldaker, 1985; Gruhn & Douglass, 1947; Johnston, Markle, & Arhar, 1988). Full and vigorous implementation is the expectation, and yet the level of implementation is a school-by-school reality, sometimes even a team-by-team situation. Depending on local fiscal and human resources, all manner of adaptations have been made when it comes to the actual implementation and function of small learning communities. Research does indicate that well-established interdisciplinary teams are beneficial, so the question becomes, *How do schools implement teams in ways that create high-performing learning communities for their students?*

Team Operation, Tasks, and Needs

> *The best thing to invest in right now is collegiality. The number one skill that teachers will need is to be team-based, collegial, sharing their knowledge and wisdom.*
>
> —Alan November (1998)

What constitutes an effective team? What resources must a team have if it is to improve students' academic outcomes? How can we create effective teams that share a commitment to improving student, team, and school performance? Research-based answers to these questions should guide practice and increase the chances for success.

The work of learning teams is significant and complex, but well worth the effort. Five characteristics of effective teams are (a) having a culture of discourse at their center, (b) having a clearly defined purpose that guides their work and specific measurable goals that they achieve, (c) being able to define and commit to norms that guide how the team operates, (d) being disciplined in maintaining their focus, and (e) communicating effectively within the team and with those outside the team (Center for Collaborative Education, 2001).

Teams in their early stages of implementation focus on coordinating class work, tests, student behaviors, parental contacts, and special team activities. Experienced teams progressively take on tasks that integrate and connect curriculum, concepts, essential questions, and instruction; experiment with blocks of time; develop service learning projects; hold individual student conferences; and plan strategies to increase parental involvement (McQuaide, 1994). During common planning time teams manage their time, establish performance goals, and engage in four broad sets of tasks: (a) curriculum coordination; (b) coordination of student assignments, assessments, and feedback; (c) parental contact and involvement; and (d) contact with other building resource staff (Shaw, 1993). Each of the four broad areas of team function is composed of different activities. The depth of team functioning is progressive. Teams cannot do everything at once, but as teams mature in their development and improve the quality of their practice they will perform the multitude of tasks with greater ease and frequency. Even "good functioning" teams cannot accomplish their objectives, tasks, and goals without sufficient time to plan and reasonable conditions within which to operate (Flowers, Mertens, & Mulhall, 2000a, 2000b, 2003; Warren & Muth, 1995).

Experienced teams progressively take on tasks that integrate and connect curriculum, concepts, essential questions, and instruction.

The presence of certain structural resources makes team effectiveness more likely and supports their contribution to the overall developmental responsiveness of a school. Information first released in 1997 from a longitudinal study of reforming middle level schools in Illinois identifies several necessary conditions for modifying instruction to improve student achievement (Erb & Stevenson, 1999; Felner et al., 1997; Flowers, Mertens, & Mulhall, 1999; 2000a). These studies have identified conditions needed for teams to make optimum changes and improve student performance:

1. **Common planning time in excess of four times per week for an equivalent of 40 or more minutes per day.** This common planning time is in addition to a teacher's individual preparation period. To successfully influence instruction and improve student performance, teams of teachers need sufficient time for team "work" and to accomplish team tasks.
2. **Team sizes of fewer than 120 students with smaller teacher-to-student ratios.** Small communities for learning must be just that—small. Teacher teams of two, three, and four members produce more positive outcomes for students. Homeroom class sizes on the smaller teams (25 or fewer students) increase results and overall team performance.
3. **The length of time a team has been together.** Stable team composition contributes to productivity since teams learn how to improve their performance and function as they improve their teaming practices. Higher order team operations occur when teams move beyond the beginning stages of learning to work together. Stable teams make discussions about instruction and assessment a major activity for team planning. (Flowers, Mertens, & Mulhall, 2000a)

All high-performing teams, whether in middle schools, business, or athletics, function best where there is time to collaborate, refine practice, reflect, invent, and work together.

The evidence for the benefits of collaboration is unmistakable. If teams operate under these conditions, the likelihood of the team's improving instruction and achievement is greatly enhanced. If teams function with less than these threshold conditions, their impact is ultimately diminished. All high-performing teams, whether in middle schools, business, or athletics, function best where there is time to collaborate, refine practice, reflect, invent, and work together. The clear relationship between collegiality and improvements for both teachers and students is evidenced in these ways: (a) remarkable gains in achievement; (b) higher quality of solutions to problems; (c) increased confidence among all school community members; (d) teachers' ability to support one another's strengths and to accommodate weaknesses; (e) the ability to examine and test new ideas, methods, and materials; (f) more systematic assistance to beginning teachers; and (g) an expanded pool of ideas, materials, and methods (Little, 1990). As studies continue to demonstrate that students in schools with teams that have dual planning time outperform students in schools without such planning time (Flowers, Mertens & Mulhall, 2003; Mertens & Flowers, 2003), policymakers and principals must take heed.

These are necessary conditions, however, but even in and of themselves not sufficient. There are schools that provide teams with adequate common planning time, desirable team size, and longevity, yet do not attain high levels of performance. Flexible organizational structures provide the *opportunity* for high performance to occur; but, the structure must be matched with high doses of vision, will, and creativity to make teams perform well.

Flexible organizational structures provide the opportunity for high performance to occur; but, the structure must be matched with high doses of vision, will, and creativity to make teams perform well.

Common planning time must be used well by every set of teachers in a building, and everyone must be held accountable for results. Just because teams have been created does not mean they perform well. Disappointing results may result when a school adopts the team or house structure and then fails to minimally implement it. In those situations, teams with common planning time are not expected to meet; or if they do meet, there is no organization or agenda to guide their meetings. Time is wasted on excessive conversation about matters that cannot be changed or have been discussed repeatedly with no resolution, or members violate the norms of acceptable team functioning by arriving late, grading papers, or missing the meeting altogether. Such teams, even with the best of organizational structures will under-perform, and the school will not meet adequate yearly progress (Anfara & Lipka, 2003; Brown, Roney, & Anfara, 2003).

Being a member of a great team entails far more and leads to highly satisfying results. In Chicago, during the era of the championship Bulls, a billboard read: *Players Play, Teams Win*. Interdisciplinary teams will make our schools win when they are done well, when they capitalize on opportunities to adjust time and student groupings to meet varied needs. Katzenbach and Smith (1993) described high-performing teams in these words:

> Groups become teams through disciplined action. They shape a common purpose, agree on performance goals, define a common working approach, develop high levels of complementary skills, and hold themselves mutually accountable for results. (p. 45)

To be successful at making the organizational structure serve its ultimate purpose, a school community needs to keep its vision of exemplary middle grades education clearly focused, examine all of its practices to align them with its vision, and hold each and every student and teacher accountable for the attainment of its vision and results.

When implementing flexible organizational structures, the key element is daily designated time to collaborate and work on instructional goals. Common planning time is pivotal. Without it, when in the course of a jam-packed day could teachers find the time to collaborate, engage in conversations about student work, or evaluate the quality of their assignments? Common planning time is the

When implementing flexible organizational structures, the key element is daily designated time to collaborate and work on instructional goals.

"placeholder." Without it, teachers have fewer chances for success. Of course, there are some schools that attempt to implement organizational structures with less than ideal conditions. Such schools may even report improvements in coordination, but their impact is severely limited. Schools and districts that seek to improve student achievement cannot escape the need to provide sufficient common planning time for teams.

High-performing teams spend two or more days a week in common planning time engaged in curriculum discussion, planning, and professional development.

High-performing teams spend two or more days a week in common planning time engaged in curriculum discussion, planning, and professional development. The use of instruments such as a weekly curriculum connections chart and "looking at student and teacher work" protocols add depth and dimension to discussions that may have once focused on misbehaving or challenged students but now focus on important curriculum and instructional issues. Formally looking at student work has proven to be a meaningful exercise.

> Looking at student work is a process. This highly meaningful strategy involves having teachers use their team time to examine a chosen piece of student work, talking about what the piece reveals about the student's learning, understanding, and possibly misconception of a particular skill, item, or assignment. (Association of Illinois Middle-Level Schools, 2005, p. 7)

Although teams may question the value of looking at student and teacher work in a concentrated process, most teachers admit that once tried, they would never return to their old formats for assignment discussions. The benefits are numerous. Gaining a greater understanding of what students know and are able to do, embedding professional development into a daily school schedule, and fostering a sense of community among the staff are just a few of those benefits. Looking at student and teacher work is perhaps the most effective form of professional development available to teachers today. Dennis Sparks (1998), executive director of the National Staff Development Council remarked, "The image of the future would be a group of teachers sitting around a table talking about their students' work, learning and asking, "What do we need to do differently to get the work we would like from kids?" (p. 19).

Many teams are now successfully using "Backward Design" models of curriculum development to focus their interdisciplinary units into more purposeful units of study for their students. These types of protocols and models for the effective use of common planning time directly relate to the quality of student work, a primary priority for having mutual team planning time.

Applying Team Tasks and Needs to Responsive School Structures

To establish teams in schools both large and small, the strengths of the teaching staff need to be assessed and considered. Many schools have teachers prioritize their strengths and liabilities, do inventories or learning styles ratings, and ask for confidential feedback as to whom they could effectively work with on a team. Diversity within a teaching team is valued because of the wide array of tasks a team must perform in order to be effective. A good team presents a balanced lineup with good role players held together by their common commitment to the education of their students (Erb & Doda, 1989).

The size of teams varies, ranging from two to five members. The implications of the NCLB definition of "highly qualified" have direct bearing on small teams, those learning environments that best foster relationships, and learning. There is no argument with the fact that middle grades teachers should be highly qualified, but they must be rich in content knowledge *and* skilled at teaching young adolescents. The research has shown that smaller teams get better results; so even with NCLB, schools must encourage dual content preparations to support smaller teams (Flowers, Mertens, & Mulhall, 2000a).

It has been common to establish teams composed of a teacher from each of the four core subject areas and sometimes a reading teacher. Teachers were more comfortable viewing team membership through their "discipline" lens. Before too long, it became common for schools to experiment with smaller teams of two or three members. Why was that? As teachers became adept at teaming and began to recognize the benefits associated with smaller more flexible teams, their view of teaching more than one discipline changed. Curriculum integration, a practice that matures with time, can be more easily accomplished on smaller teams where teachers have wider responsibility for multiple subjects. Some schools begin with smaller teams at the sixth grade and increase the size of teams toward the exit grade level.

Curriculum integration, can be more easily accomplished on smaller teams where teachers have wider responsibility for multiple subjects.

Staff teaching assignments on a team need not be rigidly prescribed. A team of teachers can review the curriculum they are accountable for in a given year and then determine who on the team will teach what topics with an eye on the requirements for highly qualified teachers. Teams may decide to remain with their students for more than one year to optimize student advancement and capitalize on long-term teacher-student relationships. Looping with students builds long-term relationships with students and families as well and strengthens a teacher's knowledge and awareness about the learning needs of individual students.

In addition, various staff members need to be regularly available to teams. Support staff such as special education teachers or gifted instructors are often assigned to work with teams in a collaborative fashion. These staff members, in consultation with the team, decide if a set of students will be pulled out for instruction or whether the special education teacher will co-teach in an inclusive model. Some schools include a unified arts or exploratory teacher on the teams either for a quarter, semester, or year (see Smith, Pitkin, & Rettig, 1998).

Deciding what and how many teachers are assigned to a team, as well as the relationship of the specialty staff are both done in collaboration with the building leadership team.

Deciding what and how many teachers are assigned to a team, as well as the relationship of the specialty staff are both done in collaboration with the building leadership team. Once school staffs decide to implement a team structure and provide adequate time and resources for teams to function, they need to provide "up-front" time prior to implementation for initial team development. This often occurs during professional development days or the summer prior to implementation. The teams progress through a series of stages beginning with the nuts and bolts of team operation. Team goals are set, roles and responsibilities are identified and assigned, operating procedures are established, and team process needs are addressed. All of these items are agreed upon by team members with the caveat that periodic adjustments may be necessary as each team begins to work. To successfully complete these initial steps, schools may hire a consultant, send staff members to conferences or institutes, engage in school visitations, provide relevant books and examples gathered from other schools, or join forces through a reform network.

Organizational options abound in successful middle schools. Looping promotes learning at Thurgood Marshall MS; ongoing professional development has strengthened the math department at Central MS; and young adolescents learn their own lessons by tutoring first graders at Scuola Vita Nuova, a K-8 school.

The school also needs to prepare its students and the community for teaming. Clear and concise messages about the benefits of this team or house structure and examples of successful implementation are instrumental in the adoption of this organizational structure. Parents need to be assured that their students will be better served through this structure. As a part of that assurance, visible evidence of the team in action through team newsletters, Web sites, open houses, team rules and expectations, team recognitions, and phone calls to parents are meaningful. This organizational structure creates a community of learners that parents and students can quickly identify with.

Flexible Use of Time to Enhance Instruction

In flexible organizational structures, teachers can see possibilities for further actions since instructional time is directly under the purview of the team. Since teams have a large block of time with their students, teachers are able to adjust and rearrange the instructional time as they see necessary in order to achieve the team's instructional goals (Hackmann & Valentine, 1998; Noland, 1998; Seed, 1998; Smith, Pitkin, & Rettig, 1998; Ulrich & Yeamen, 1999). The most flexible teams adjust the schedule on a week-by-week or even at times on a day-by-day basis depending on learning needs identified during common planning time. Academic priorities take precedence over regular, rigid period lengths and ringing bells.

This is not to say there is chaos in this flexible arrangement. On the contrary, teachers on the teaching team within the small learning community are attentive to where each student is at a given time and the reason for a student's placement. Since the team has a designated section of the building and the teachers meet regularly to discuss issues and make adjustments, the students are actually held to a higher level of accountability than in more rigid school structures with fixed periods, bells, and passing periods.

Even within an individual teacher's classroom, flexible grouping is the norm rather than the exception. Teachers differentiate instruction through the application of strategies such as collaborative learning, elaborated helping arrangements, progress-based grading, challenge activities, and graphic and learning organizers. The classroom teacher identifies individual learning strengths, needs, and styles then modifies instruction accordingly. Differentiating teaching for a broad range of abilities appears to occur more often as team functioning becomes more proficient. In schools that implement organizational structures well, teachers and students indicate that they are engaged more often in classroom instructional strategies that are interactive, hands-on, and challenging (Felner et al., 1997). In schools without flexible team structures or ones lacking time for planning, classroom practices are less likely to be altered, and teachers find it more difficult to implement strategies for heterogeneous classes.

Adequate team work or common planning time not only magnifies a team's operating potential, but also contributes to adoption of desirable teaching strategies. Common planning time within the school day serves as a vehicle for ongoing professional development through team dialogue and problem solving, a natural outgrowth of quality team functioning (Kain, 1995; Powell & Mills, 1994, 1995). In common planning time teachers share effective teaching strategies and support one another as they learn to expand their teaching repertoires. The learning culture established within high-performing teams includes outcomes for improvements in curriculum, instruction, and assessment.

Organizational Structure Is Critical

The organizational structure helps or hinders what can occur in a learning community. Savvy leaders seek out flexible, interdisciplinary team organization as a framework that gives life to a developmentally responsive middle school. The existence of such a team structure is not the end-all and be-all, but structural improvements greatly increase the chances that desired instructional changes will occur. The flexible use of time, staff, space, and instructional grouping sets up relationships whereby students learn and teachers teach in a more responsive, effective manner. Through the skillful guidance of committed teams of teachers acting in the best interests of their students, young adolescents have a better chance for a lifetime of possibilities and successes.

References

Alexander, W. M., & George, P. S. (1981). *The exemplary middle school*. New York: Holt, Rinehart and Winston.

Anfara, V. A., Jr., & Lipka, R. P. (2003). Relating the middle school concept to student achievement. *Middle School Journal, 35*(1), 24-32.

American Institutes for Research. (2005). *Works in progress: Key issues facing middle schools and high schools*. Washington, DC: Author.

Arhar, J. M. (1990). The effects of interdisciplinary teaming on social bonding of middle school students. *Research in Middle Level Education, 14*(1), 1-10.

Arhar, J. M., Johnston, J. H., & Markle, G. C. (1988). The effects of teaming and other collaborative arrangements. *Middle School Journal, 19*(4), 22-25.

Arhar, J. M., Johnston, J. H., & Markle, G. C. (1989). The effects of teaming on students. *Middle School Journal, 20*(3), 24-27.

Arhar, J. M., & Kromrey, J. (1995). Interdisciplinary teaming and demographics of membership: A comparison of students belonging in high SES and low SES middle-level schools. *Research in Middle Level Education, 18*(2), 71-88.

Association of Illinois Middle-Level Schools. (2005). *Looking at student and teacher work to improve students' learning*. Westerville, OH: National Middle School Association.

Brown, K.M., Roney, K., & Anfara, V.A. (2003). Organizational health directly influences student performance at the middle level. *Middle School Journal, 34*(5) 5-15.

Carnegie Council on Adolescent Development. (1989). *Turning points: Preparing American youth for the 21st century.* New York: The Carnegie Corporation.

Center for Collaborative Education. (2001). *Guide to collaborative culture and shared leadership*. Boston: Author.

Erb, T. O., & Doda, N. M. (1989). *Team organization: Promise—practices and possibilities*. Washington, DC: National Education Association.

Erb, T. O., & Stevenson, C. (1999). What difference does teaming make? *Middle School Journal, 30*(3), 47-50.

Felner, R. D., Jackson, A. W., Kasak, D., Mulhall, P, Brand, S., & Flowers, N. (1997). The impact of school reform for the middle years: A longitudinal study of a network engaged in Turning Points-based comprehensive school transformation. *Phi Delta Kappan, 78,* 528-532, 541-550.

Flowers, N., Mertens, S. B., & Mulhall, P. F. (1999). The impact of teaming: Five research-based outcomes. *Middle School Journal, 31*(2), 57-60.

Flowers, N., Mertens, S. B., & Mulhall, P. F. (2000a). What makes interdisciplinary teams effective? *Middle School Journal, 31*(4), 53-56.

Flowers, N., Mertens, S. B., & Mulhall, P. F. (2000b). How teaming influences classroom practices. *Middle School Journal, 32*(2), 52-59.

Flowers, N., Mertens, S. B., & Mulhall, P. F. (2003). Lessons learned from more than a decade of middle grades research, *Middle School Journal, 35*(2), 55-59.

George, P. S., & Alexander, W. M. (2003). *The exemplary middle school* (3rd ed.). Belmont, CA: Thomson/Wadsworth Learning.

George, P. S., & Oldaker, L. (1985). *Evidence for the middle school.* Columbus, OH: National Middle School Association.

Gruhn, W., & Douglass, H. (1947). *The modern junior high.* New York: Ronald Press.

Hackmann, D. G., & Valentine, J. W. (1998). Designing an effective middle level schedule. *Middle School Journal, 29*(5), 3-13.

Johnston, J. H., Markle, G. C., & Arhar, J. M. (1988). Cooperation, collaboration, and the professional development of teachers. *Middle School Journal, 19*(3), 28-32.

Juvonen, J., Le, V., Kaganoff, T., Augustine, C., & Constant, L. (2004). *Focus on the wonder years: Challenges facing the American middle school.* Arlington, VA: RAND Corporation.

Kain, D. L. (1995). Adding dialogue to a team's agenda. *Middle School Journal, 26*(4), 3-6.

Katzenbach, J. R., & Smith, D. K. (1993). *The wisdom of teams: Creating the high-performance organization.* New York: Harper Business.

Little, J. W. (1990). The persistence of privacy: Autonomy and initiative in teachers' professional relations. *Teachers College Record, 91*(4), 526-527.

McQuaide, J. (1994). Implementation of team planning time. *Research in Middle Level Education, 17*(2), 27-45.

Mertens, S. B., & Flowers, N. (2003). Middle school practices improve student achievement in high poverty schools. *Middle School Journal, 35*(1), 33-43.

National Forum to Accelerate Middle-Grades Reform. (1998). *Vision Statement*. Retrieved May 6, 2005, from www.mgforum.org/about/vision.asp

National Middle School Association (2003). *This we believe: Successful schools for young adolescents.* Westerville, OH: Author.

Noland, F. (1998). Ability grouping plus heterogeneous grouping: Win-win schedules. *Middle School Journal, 29*(5), 14-19.

Powell, R. R., & Mills, R. (1994). Five types of mentoring build knowledge on interdisciplinary teams. *Middle School Journal, 26*(2), 24-30.

Powell, R. R., & Mills, R. (1995). Professional knowledge sharing among interdisciplinary team teachers: A study of intra-team mentoring. *Research in Middle Level Education, 18*(3), 27-40.

Seed, A. (1998). Free at last: Making the most of the flexible block schedule. *Middle School Journal, 29*(5), 3-13.

Shaw, C. C. (1993). A content analysis of teacher talk during middle school team meetings. *Research in Middle Level Education, 17*(1), 27-45.

Smith, D. G., Pitkin, N. A., Rettig, M. D. (1998). Flexing the middle school block schedule by adding non-traditional core subjects and teachers to the interdisciplinary team. *Middle School Journal, 29*(5), 22-27.

Sparks, D. (1998). Professional development. *AEA Advocate, 24*(18, pp.18-21.

Ullrich, W. J., & Yeamen, J. T. (1999). Using the modified block schedule to create a positive learning environment. *Middle School Journal, 31*(1), 14-20.

Warren, L. L., & Muth, K. D. (1995). Common planning time in middle grades schools and its impact on students and teachers. *Research in Middle Level Education, 18*(3), 41-58.

14

School-Wide Efforts and Policies that Foster Health, Wellness, and Safety

Jean Schultz

National Middle School Association (NMSA) in *This We Believe: Successful Schools for Young Adolescents* (2003) describes the essential elements from which successful schooling of young adolescents is constructed. The position paper underscores the importance of health promotion for young adolescents when it states that in a developmentally responsive middle school "an emphasis on health, wellness, and safety permeates the entire school, with faculty members sharing responsibility for maintaining a positive school environment" (p. 31). This emphasis, when addressed systemically and systematically, can appreciably assist schools in meeting Adequate Yearly Progress (AYP) requirements of No Child Left Behind (NCLB).

How well has this essential element been made operational in your middle school?

- Can you map attention to student health across the curriculum, describe student outcomes, or demonstrate the assessment of health-related skills, concepts, attitudes, and behaviors?
- Are you able to identify those ports of safety within the school building where students may seek shelter from, and assistance with, the frequently rough waters of adolescence?
- Can you chart the connectedness of school and community services, instructional components, and planned reinforcement that create a coordinated, caring community of learners?

- Are your health promotion efforts policy-based and clearly articulated?

Acknowledging that health-promoting schools are essential to the academic and personal success of young adolescents assigns *fundamental* status to the placement of health in exploratory, related arts, or family and consumer life skills education. Responsive middle schools promote health not only among students, but also among faculty members through a wide range of school experiences. The support of health-related skills and concepts by all school personnel is consequently no longer relegated to accidental reinforcement, concomitant learning, or the occasional teachable moment.

Little attention has been given to health promotion as an essential element in middle schools.

A review of past practice reveals only cursory attention to health promotion as an essential element in middle level schools. Therefore, in order for health, wellness, and safety to permeate the entire school, all educators must accept and personalize the inclusion of a health focus in their work at the middle level. Though rarely mentioned in professional preparation programs or even at school sites, all educators have a part to play in promoting healthful behaviors while reducing risky behaviors among young adolescents.

Reasons to Promote Wellness

1. Poor health practices drain resources from education.

In the broadest sense, teachers and educational administrators must be alert to the financial impact poor health practices have on dollars earmarked for education in this country. Consider and ponder these points.

Medical care costs continue to rise:

- Poor diet and inadequate physical activity are the second leading cause of death in the United States and together account for at least 300,000 deaths (e.g., type 2 diabetes, hypertension, heart disease, cancer) and $100 billion in costs annually. Obesity and overweight are conditions of habit and expectation and have reached epidemic proportions in the United States. (U.S. Department of Health and Human Services, 2001)
- In 2002, the expenditures for Medicaid exceeded the expenditure for Elementary and Secondary Education in 17 states. If this trend continues to escalate, fewer dollars will be available for education. (National Association of State Budget Officers, 2003, p. 10)

Chosen behaviors impact personal health and subsequent costs:

- The elimination of tobacco use alone, either through the prevention of its initial use or through cessation of its current use, could prevent over 400,000 deaths annually from cancer, heart and lung diseases, and strokes. (U.S. Department of Health and Human Services, 2000)
- Less than a third of school children consume the recommended milk group servings on any given day. Hospitals report an increased number of fractures in adolescents. Osteoporosis is a looming concern. Teenagers drink twice as much carbonated soda as milk. (U.S. Department of Agriculture, n. d.)
- Today there are nearly twice as many overweight children and almost three times as many overweight adolescents as there were in 1980. (U.S. Department of Health and Human Services, 2001) Better dietary and exercise patterns can contribute significantly to reducing conditions like heart disease, stroke, diabetes, and cancer, and could prevent 300,000 deaths annually. (U.S. Department of Health and Human Services, 2000)
- The financial burden of heart disease and stroke amounts to about $135 billion a year. The annual health care and related costs attributable to alcohol abuse are $98.6 billion. The yearly costs of tobacco use amount to about $65 billion a year. (U.S. Department of Health and Human Services, 2000)

Today there are nearly twice as many overweight children and almost three times as many overweight adolescents as there were in 1980.

Shortfalls in state and federal health care dollars place education appropriations at risk. Because public education is contingent upon public funds, educators are wise to advocate for systemic community and school district action around health promotion. This effort is particularly critical at the middle level where young adolescents are most receptive to positive health messages and prevention strategies. With systemic support, educators can reinforce community and family efforts to modify risky behaviors and strengthen positive health practices among our youth, thereby increasing our society's quality of life and positively influencing the pool of public funds available for education.

2. **Behavioral, physical, and emotional problems interfere with learning.**

As educators, our primary job cannot be done unless we somehow address competing needs that students bring through the schoolhouse door each day. Students who need dental care, are undernourished, are affected by substance abuse, high mobility, or restricted opportunities, or who do not feel safe cannot focus their attention on learning. "School systems are not responsible for meeting every need of their students. But when the need directly affects learning, the school must meet the challenge" (Center for Mental Health in Schools, 2004, p. 1).

As educators we understand that

- Among fourth grade students, those having the lowest amount of protein in their diet had the lowest achievement scores. (Parker, 1989)
- Children with iron deficiency tend to do poorly on vocabulary, reading, and other tests. (Parker, 1989)
- Moderate under-nutrition can have lasting effects and compromise cognitive development and school performance. (Center on Hunger, Poverty, and Nutrition Policy, 1995)
- Morning fasting has a negative effect on cognitive performance, even among healthy, well-nourished children. (Pollitt, Leibel, & Greenfield, 1991)
- Academic achievement improves even when participation in physical education reduces the time for academics. (Blaydes, 2005; Kun, 2002)
- Participation in a breakfast program improves academic, behavioral, and emotional functioning and leads to increased math grades, lower absenteeism, and improved behavior. (U.S. Department of Health and Human Services, 1996)

Heightened academic achievement for all can be realized only when educators and the community invest in school-wide strategies to reduce behaviors that compromise student success.

Heightened academic achievement for all can be realized only when educators and the community invest in school-wide strategies to reduce behaviors that compromise student success. Our national economy and societal health depend, in part, upon accomplishing this task.

3. Youthful choices affect health.

In the past, health was largely compromised by an array of diseases (rubella, whooping cough, diphtheria, pneumonia, tuberculosis). Today, the quality and quantity of healthy life is primarily determined by what we choose to do. Through a national survey of adolescent behaviors called Youth Risk Behavior Survey (YRBS) (Kolbe, Kann, & Collins, 1993, p. 2), the Centers for Disease Control and Prevention has identified six behaviors that cause premature mortality and morbidity among American youth. The YRBS is an excellent resource to examine adolescent behaviors state by state and over time. From survey results, it is apparent that these widespread behaviors undermine health and the resulting capacity for personal success during adolescence and adulthood. These high priority risk behaviors, many of which may result in injuries both unintentional and intentional, are

- Tobacco use
- Acohol and other drug use
- Sexual behavior
- Dietary behavior
- Physical inactivity.

Risk-laden behaviors are complex; they develop through the interactions of persons and circumstances within and outside the school experience. Therefore, it is important to enlist persons, agencies, and organizations inside and outside of the school to challenge these confounding behaviors. Many existing prevention and management services designed to address these problems are funded categorically. The constrictive nature of this funding stream encourages symptomatic attention (separate programming for substance abuse, suicide prevention, tobacco use) rather than holistic, collaborative attention to the interrelated and precursor problems of youth at risk.

Two days a week during advisory period all students and faculty participate in physical exercise.
— DVD, Warsaw MS, "Morning Exercise"

During this time of shrinking resources and increasing need, the synthesis of new associations between existing and potential student support services is a necessity. New curricular alliances within schools are also needed. Only through holistic organizations that attend to underlying problems can schools and communities address health issues that compromise children's lives.

Each day teachers attempt to engage children whose ability to attend to instruction is diminished in some way. Unfortunately, this occurs during a time of shrinking district resources, increasing class size, and attacks on a public education system that is, despite its inadequacies, educating more youth to a higher degree than ever before. Health promotion that links school and non-school support systems and services assists teachers by providing an improved safety net for students in need, thus freeing students and teachers to focus on learning tasks. Our current loosely-coupled, differently-funded, and largely unfocused efforts miss too many children and burden teachers with too many health-related management concerns.

Can schools affect individual health as well as academic outcomes? How does a school incorporate "an emphasis on health, wellness, and safety that permeates the entire school?" The following discussion describes actions that will assist in moving toward an academically successful health-enhancing middle school.

Laying a Foundation for Health Promotion

Community response

Though overworked but underused, the African proverb, "It takes an entire village to raise a child" is the core of health promotion and disease prevention for young adolescents.

Although poor student health may negatively affect academic learning, the school need not tackle student health problems alone. Indeed, most often informed community groups successfully spearhead action on behalf of young adolescents. A community-based exploration of local concerns, county or city health-related statistics, and an assessment of student needs will reveal that there are many issues a community can choose to address on behalf of its children. School and community collaboration can result in healthful practices for young adolescents. Though overworked but underused, the African proverb, "It takes an entire village to raise a child" is the core of health promotion and disease prevention for young adolescents.

Many handbooks and guides are available to assist in the collaborative task-force process. *Health Is Academic: A Guide to Coordinated School Health Programs* (Marx, Wooley, & Northrop, 1998) is one of the many resources educators may enlist. Only by seeking the involvement and support of the community as a whole, will the "entire village" become part of the health promotion picture.

A school response

August 2004 saw the reauthorization of the Child Nutrition Act. Every school receiving funds for food service programs must adopt a wellness policy by the beginning of the 2006-2007 school year. Among other provisions, each school's wellness policy must include the following:

- Goals for nutrition education, physical activity, and other school-based activities designed to promote wellness
- Nutrition guidelines for all foods available on each school campus, with the objectives of promoting student health and reducing childhood obesity
- A plan for measuring implementation of the wellness policy, including the designation of one or more persons with operational responsibility

- Involvement of parents, students, representatives of the school food authority, school board, and school administration in the development of the school wellness policy
- State Departments of Health and Education will receive funds to establish team nutrition networks. These entities will encourage schools to *establish school health advisory councils* with the broad mission to address topics related to the health of students and staff members.

The establishment of a school health advisory council is a primary step in a school's effort to raise student achievement scores. As the advisory council focuses on its first charge (physical activity and nutrition issues) school and community-linked members learn of other success-sapping issues and, over time, the council may expand its focus.

The establishment of a school health advisory council is a primary step in a school's effort to raise student achievement scores.

In addition to creating links to the community, a school can identify and weave positive health practices and messages into its formal and informal curriculum (see MacLaury, 2000). A requisite to almost all other health-related initiatives is the establishment of a healthy school environment (Wisconsin Department of Public Instruction, 1997). Although considerations such as appropriate light and ventilation as well as regular building maintenance contribute to a healthy school environment, the definition is expanded to include the implementation of policies and practices that protect and promote student's emotional, social, and mental health.

How does a school assess its environment? A coordinated school health program assessment tool developed by the Wisconsin Department of Public Instruction (1997) assists school personnel in examining their environment. The assessment tool includes

Culture

1. Respect between and among students, staff, and parents is reflected in the hallway, classroom, cafeteria, and bus.
2. All adult school staff are role models or mentors who foster positive and healthy behaviors.
3. The school provides an environment conducive to parental involvement in the policies related to the health and safety of children.
4. Students, teachers, other school staff, administration, and parents feel safe on the school grounds, at school-sponsored events, and on school-sponsored transportation.

Physical

5. The physical environment inside and outside the school building is kept clean, safe, and well maintained.

6. The school buildings and activities are accessible to all students.
7. The school is equipped with adequate communications systems for quick accessibility and response in emergency situations.
8. Students have a clean, cheerful, and attractive serving and dining area.
9. Students and staff are given sufficient time for serving, eating, and cleaning up after meals.

Services

10. All food served or sold on campus (school cafeteria, vending machines, fund raising) supports healthy food choices.
11. The school has in place a plan to provide health and safety training and services (e.g., first aid, CPR, crisis management, and disaster preparedness).
12. An effective working relationship exists between school personnel and community health services regarding the health and well-being of children.

Policies

13. The school's policies regarding health and safety issues are regularly discussed with school staff.
14. The school has clear policies regarding the reporting of behavior problems and legal infractions.
15. Students and parents participate in the creation of school policies regarding health and safety issues.
16. A spirit of openness, honesty, and opportunity for expression of opinion exists among students, staff, and administration.
17. Students, parents, and school staff feel that all school policies regarding health and safety issues are implemented and enforced consistently and equitably.
18. Board policy clearly articulates and supports an intradistrict and school-to-community communication system that ensures confidentiality. (Wisconsin Department of Public Instruction, 1997, p. 4-6)

Each member of the school population deserves to feel and be welcomed and safe at school. School programs that foster responsibility, respect, and caretaking of emotional as well as physical health enable a school to become a welcoming and safe place for everyone. Such is the basis for a high performance learning environment.

An individual response

Beginning teachers are frequently amazed and appalled at the variety of student concerns that are before them each day. These concerns have little to do with academic content and everything to do with the lives of the children. Students who are in abusive relationships, involved with drugs, neglected, sexually abused, anorexic or bulimic, burdened with adult responsibility, depressed, pregnant, ill, poorly clothed, undernourished, afraid to go home, afraid to walk to school or pass in the halls, painfully shy, or sexually harassed cannot attend fully to academic achievement. Veteran teachers, no longer amazed, work to connect students with resources or provide a supportive environment. What else can an individual teacher do? Actually, quite a lot.

First, inquire regarding the status of the movement toward a comprehensive school health program in one's school or school district. Persons located within the state department of education or state department of health are familiar with the comprehensive and coordinated school health program model (Kolbe & Allensworth, 1987). In addition, various national organizations representing school boards, teachers, principals, superintendents, and other professionals are working to assist their members in this arena. Consult your state department of education, organization Web sites, or a Web search engine, and search using *coordinated school health* as keywords. Raising the issue and expressing an interest may get this ball rolling in one's school or district.

Second, inquire regarding the health-related skills that are taught in a variety of prevention curricula. In collaboration with the entire staff, choose one for school-wide emphasis. For example, many alcohol and drug prevention curricula include a decision-making strategy. Do all faculty members know this strategy? Is each language arts teacher well-grounded enough to use the strategy while discussing a short-story character? How might it be used by a social studies teacher in discussing a recent event? Does the health educator transfer this strategy to food choices? Does the physical educator use it to assist students in problem solving? Does the science teacher link it to the scientific method?

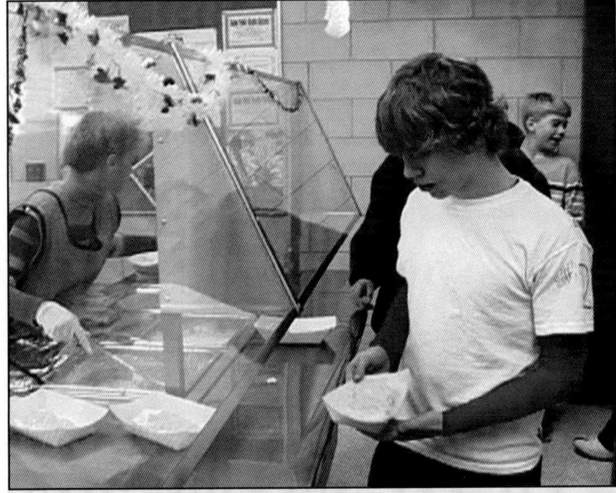

A mid-morning nutrition break improves learning and reduces discipline problems.
— DVD, William Thomas MS, "Nutrition Break"

Skill development is not skill inoculation. A skill development lesson in grade six does not transfer to new experiences in grade seven without guidance and practice. Negotiation, coping, decision making, and refusal skills must be revisited, reinforced, and reinterpreted through experience in order to be useful in the lives of young adolescents. All teachers, if they are familiar with a skill, can use their own academic content to teach and reinforce a skill chosen for school-wide emphasis.

Third, educators can help community people see what educators see, and know what educators know regarding the health-related problems that negatively affect academic achievement. Educators can advocate for *others* to bring student health-related problems to the school-community table.

Conclusion

For the students that are before us each day, there is no better time than now to develop a school that is safe, welcoming, and emphasizes wellness and health. The establishment of a school health advisory council and the systematic development of a health-promoting school provides a framework for addressing student health needs and will contribute significantly to NCLB Adequate Yearly Progress expectations. Fashioning a middle level school in which "an emphasis on health, wellness, and safety permeates the entire school" is no less important than the other characteristics of a developmentally responsive middle level school. Although there is much to do, there are also sources of information and guidance. Seek assistance, ask questions, and begin the process on behalf of young adolescents.

References

Blaydes, J. (2005). Advocacy: A case for daily quality physical education. Retrieved June 2, 2005, from http://www.actionbasedlearning.com/cgi-bin/article01.pl

Center for Mental Health in Schools. (2004, Fall). *Mental health in schools: Reflections on the past, present, and future from the perspective of the Center for Mental Health in Schools* (Executive Summary). Los Angeles: Center for Mental Health in Schools, Department of Psychology, University of California at Los Angeles. Retrieved April 26, 2004, from http://www.smhp.psych.ucla.edu

Center on Hunger, Poverty, and Nutrition Policy. (1995). *Statement on the link between nutrition and cognitive development in children.* Medford, MA: Tufts University School of Nutrition.

Kolbe, L., & Allensworth, D. (1987). The comprehensive school health program: Exploring an expanded concept. *Journal of School Health, 57*, 409-412.

Kolbe, L., Kann, L., & Collins, J. (1993). Overview of the Youth Risk Behavior Surveillance System. Public Health Reports. *Journal of the US Public Health Service, 108* (Suppl.1), 1-2.

Kun, P. K. (2002, December 10). *New study supports physically fit kids perform better academically.* Reston, VA: National Association for Sport and Physical Education. Retrieved April 27, 2005, from http://www.aahperd.org/naspe/template.cfm?template=pr_121002.html

MacLaury, S. (2000). Teaching prevention by infusing health education into the advisory program. *Middle School Journal, 31*(5) 51-56.

Marx, E., Wooley, S. F., & Northrop, D. (Eds.). (1998). *Health is academic: A guide to coordinated school health programs.* New York: Teachers College Press.

National Association of State Budget Officers. (2003). *State expenditures report 2002*. Washington, DC: Author. [Electronic Version]. Retrieved April 25, 2005, from http://www.nasbo.org/Publications/2002ExpendReport.pdf

National Middle School Association. (2003). *This we believe: Successful schools for young adolescents.* Westerville, OH: Author.

Parker, L. (1989). *The relationship between nutrition and learning: A school employee's guide to information and action.* Washington: National Education Association .

Pollitt, E., Leibel, R., Greenfield, D. (1991). Brief fasting, stress, and cognition in children. *American Journal of Clinical Nutrition, 34*, 1526-1533.

U. S. Department of Agriculture. (n.d.). *Healthy school nutrition environments: Promoting healthy eating behaviors.* Washington, DC: Author. Retrieved March 15, 2005, from http://www.fns.usda.gov/tn/Healthy/healthyeatingchallenge.html

U. S. Department of Health and Human Services. (1996, June 14). Guidelines for school health programs to promote lifelong healthy eating. *Morbidity and Mortality Weekly Report Recommendations and Report, 45*, RR-9.

U. S. Department of Health and Human Services. (2000). *Healthy people: 2000 midcourse review and 1995 revisions.* Washington, DC: Public Health Service.

U. S. Department of Health and Human Services. (2001). *The Surgeon General's call to action to prevent and decrease overweight and obesity.* Washington, DC: Author.

Wisconsin Department of Public Instruction. (1997). *Component quality: A comprehensive school health program assessment tool.* Madison, WI: Author.

Multifaceted Guidance and Support Services

Sherrel Bergmann

The Issues Surrounding Guidance Services in the Middle School

Spend a day with a middle school counselor and the guidance needs of young adolescents will be all too obvious. Society and the young adolescent culture have changed enough in the past few years to require middle level schools to seriously examine how they are, or are not, meeting the needs of their students. While many schools are attempting to change their climate and focus by providing proactive guidance programs, personnel, and services, others are struggling to maintain the few guidance personnel and services they have. The roles of counselors and social workers have changed significantly as they take on more students who need their help (Paterson, 2004). As societal ills creep into the school or are brought by the students themselves, a typical day for a counselor will include

- Four one-on-one conferences with students having peer relationship problems.
- A meeting with the sixth-grade team about an at-risk student.
- Eleven phone calls from parents or administrators of community agencies.
- Two meetings with probation officers.
- Miscellaneous counseling of students passing in the hall.
- Teaching one seventh grade class on substance abuse.
- Comforting a teacher who is ill and having a bad day.
- Teaching that teacher's class for one period so the teacher can rest.

- Attending two staffings on students recommended for special services.
- Meeting with the seventh grade team.
- Welcoming two new students to the school.
- Meeting with students in the Builders Club who are starting a community service project.
- Administering a standardized test to eighth graders.
- Meeting with two parents of chronically absent students.

On other days, the same counselor may be asked to do crisis intervention, explore new achievement tests, facilitate a divorce group, and update teachers on drugs found in the community.

While the guidance issues change every year, the need for social and emotional help at this age is not a new concept.

With all of the issues that students bring to school with them, the type of services provided must be carefully planned and evaluated for their effectiveness. While the guidance issues change every year, the need for social and emotional help at this age is not a new concept. Over 100 years ago, the social and emotional needs of the middle school student were being written about and discussed by educators. Brown (1902) stated

> This is a period of functional acquisition and re-adjustment. Mental change and physical activity appear in intellectual awakening, the storm and stress of doubt, the conversions, the intense emotional life, the fluctuating interests and enthusiasms, the general instability, and not infrequently the moral aberrations and perversities. (p. 411)

An extended, proactive guidance model must be evident in every middle school if our students are to survive their own culture, society's early demands on them, and the school as a social system.

For many years, the teacher was the one who dealt with all of the social and emotional interactions in the classroom. That is still true today, as some middle schools have adopted a cornerstone of the middle school philosophy that recommends that every student have an advocate in the building. This person knows the student as an individual and cares for him or her. This adult knows the student well enough to know whether or not the student needs further guidance or services (Alexander, 1969; Eichhorn, 1966; Cole, 1981; Galassi, Gulledge, & Cox, 1998; James & Spradling, 2001; National Middle School Association, 2003; Noar, 1961; VanTil, Vars, & Lounsbury, 1967).

An extended, proactive guidance model must be evident in every middle school if our students are to survive their own culture, society's early demands on them, and the school as a social system. The model described here is a compilation of the successful steps offered by middle schools that have completed the process. All agreed that a school must begin with an understanding of the questions affecting the lives of today's young adolescents. In 2002, Michigan Schools in the Middle set out to determine what middle school students really are concerned about. They asked thousands of middle school students to list the questions they had about the world, our country, themselves, their school, their community, their future, and their peers. A few of the often-repeated questions give insight into the guidance needs of young adolescents in this decade.

- Why do I feel so uncomfortable around people who are different?
- Do I have the right friends?
- Why am I picked on and called names?
- What do I do about someone who is bullying me?
- Will I be able to avoid doing drugs?
- What exactly is safe sex?
- When is the war going to stop?
- Why does there have to be war and fighting?
- Will the world always be so scary?
- Why are people so violent?
- Why am I so stressed all the time?

Every school must understand the compelling questions that affect the lives of young adolescents.

These examples describe what is on the minds of students who are also being asked to assimilate into large groups of peers for the first time, traverse the perils of puberty, transition from elementary to middle or middle to high school, and learn everything required in the curriculum.

Oftentimes the guidance concerns override the curriculum concerns from the student point of view so that the achievement of the student is impaired. To provide optimum guidance services requires that a middle school first understand the nature and developmental characteristics of students. In addition, an examination of the culture of the school will provide the degree to which specific services are needed. For example, is young adolescent alcohol use truly an issue in the community? How many students feel that they are bullied at school or on the bus? What do parents see as their role in the school? How many parents are raising their children alone? What are the major health issues of students in the school?

The Process of Developing Multifaceted Guidance and Support Services

Schools that have successfully adopted multifaceted guidance and support services have answered five guiding questions by first forming a guidance task force of counselors, administrators, teachers, parents, students, and community agency representatives. This task force is the fact finding, needs assessing, program designing, and researching group of the community. They must be committed to developing services based on the needs of their own students in their school.

Guiding question #1: Who are our students and what do they need?

Task forces that have completed this process began by determining a profile of their students. Many faculty comments are made about the changing needs of the students and the "baggage" being brought to school that affects learning. Current students appear to be less respectful, less responsible, and less eager to be involved in school activities. While researching the demographic data of their school community, task force members discovered that there were many extremes within just one grade level. One seventh grade teacher reported that of his 27 students

- One lived in a house with an indoor pool and bowling alley, while one came from the local homeless shelter.
- Nine lived with single parents, 13 lived with both parents, and five lived with relatives.
- Eight had never been out of the state, three had traveled to Europe, two had recently emigrated from China, and three had come from Mexico a year ago.
- Nine had older siblings, and seven were responsible for younger siblings before and after school.
- Four had been identified as gifted, and seven had learning disabilities.
- Seven distinct cultures were represented.
- Fifteen had a best friend, and five said they had no friends.
- Fourteen rode the bus, and 13 walked to school.
- Ten were involved in after-school activities; 17 were not.
- The range in height was 4' 6" to 6' 1".

All of this information had been relatively easy to gather by reading enrollment data, by observation, and by simply asking the students. Counselors were able to add other information about students' lives. With the help of social services, students dealt with abusive parents, alcoholic parents, the court system, divorced parents, physical illnesses, and eating disorders. While the caseload of the counselor was increasing for students with serious problems, the time to assist students with the normal day-to-day school concerns was decreasing. There was no time to offer the problem-solving minicourse that had been planned; contacts with parents of students who were having academic difficulties only happened after a crisis was referred.

As more and more students fell through the cracks, teams of teachers discussed those students and tried to provide as much help as they could with classroom issues. As the number of students with problems increased there was little time for prevention and limited resources for reaction. As school profiles of students were developed, members of the task force were then able to match those profiles with the answers to question #2.

The focus group is another place where kids can go and express their concerns and maybe have some of their social and academic needs met.
— John Campbell,
Math Teacher, Warsaw MS,
"Focus Group"

Guiding question # 2: How are guidance and support services currently handled in our school? Who does what, when, and for whom?

In most schools, the task force identified several programs already in the curriculum that dealt with specific guidance issues. For example, DARE was offered to sixth graders and SNOWFLAKE was available to all students who wished to participate. While these programs were successful from the students' point of view, there was nothing in place for eighth graders. Guidance issues were a part of the health curriculum, but they were only offered in a nine-week exploratory. All teachers and teams had developed time for remedial help for academic concerns, but there was no formal mentoring program for students with reading problems. Most of the teams had a recognition program, but there was little consistency in the types of recognition being given. Most of the teachers acknowledged the changes in student behavior, attitude, and achievement, but were not sure what to do except refer the student to the counselor. Because the role of the counselor was not clear to the teachers, they passed on many problems that could have been solved by simply talking with a student.

Brainstorming sessions at faculty meetings lead to impressive lists of services and guidance related lessons provided by teams and individual teachers within the school. These sharing sessions showed who was receiving services and who was being missed. Counselors provided a list of the numbers of students receiving each type of counseling or community service. The services offered by community agencies were explained to the entire staff and the roles of the counselor, social worker, and other specialists were clarified. With this information gathered, the task force could begin to work on question #3.

Guiding question #3: What are the basic components we must have in our school to meet the multifaceted guidance needs of our students?

Members of the Guidance Task Force used the basic tenets of the middle school concept outlined in *This We Believe: Developmentally Responsive Middle Schools* (National Middle School Association, 1995). One of the basic tenets useful to each task force was that all adults are advocates for young adolescents. One way to extend the guidance services of this school was to establish that every student would have an advocate. A study group was formed in each school to research how advocacy was implemented in other schools and how it could be implemented in their own. All agreed that one or two counselors could not be advocates for all students, but could assist the teachers by offering specific skills such as reflective listening, conflict resolution, and goal setting. The role of the advocate and the role of the counselor in each school were clearly defined. Essential activities such as communicating with parents, making referrals, and adding or deleting curriculum were outlined in the role description of advocates and the counseling staff.

With input from parents, teachers, students, and the community, many of the schools determined that a drug and alcohol program, Understanding Alcohol: Investigation into Biology and Behavior (Biological Sciences Curriculum Study, 2003), would become a part of the science and health curriculum in seventh and eighth grade. Use of a well-researched program would provide students with information to make wise decisions given the pressures found in their community. DARE would continue to be offered in the sixth grade. Other schools continued to use programs they had found successful, but articulated what was being taught by whom and when.

Proactive programs such as community service and advisory groups were in place in many of the schools and needed only communication among the grade levels to continue their success. Schools without proactive programs in place began looking at possibilities based on their school needs. With descriptions of potential programs in place, the task force members were able to move to the question of students with serious problems.

Guiding question #4: What services should be provided for students who are at risk and have serious social and emotional problems?

Each task force had to obtain from the counselors and social service agencies a realistic overview of the types of problems that had been brought to them. A local and state definition of at-risk was given. Trends and new issues were defined and discussed. Cultural expectations, media influences, online bullying, gang behavior, use of methamphetamines, and social activities within each community were related to middle school students and classroom achievement. Case management for special education and the laws surrounding students with special needs were explained in detail. With those details given, most schools found that teachers and parents needed to be educated and updated on trends in order to broaden the base of support for students. In most schools it was a matter of more communication among groups already servicing students and extending that communication to parents and school personnel. With so many of the services governed by law, the task force members could then determine what kinds of assistance to add or change in their school. It became obvious that the amount of time given to these students was necessary, but also kept the counselor from implementing proactive guidance for all students. As serious guidance issues continue to require the time of specially trained professionals, it is easy to find 90% of the time being spent on 10% of the students. Task force members then had to answer question #5.

Guiding question #5: How can we implement proactive guidance in our schools and offer essential guidance-related skills to 100% of our students?

With the implementation of No Child Left Behind, counselors and teachers are pressured to leave behind the social and emotional needs of students, concentrating instead on those core curricular areas that are always tested. Preparation for the testing process, increased data collection, and administrative paperwork take time that guidance personnel formerly spent teaching students how to make decisions, how to study, how to communicate, how to get along with others, how to transition to new schools, how to avoid drugs and alcohol, how to resolve conflicts, and how to develop their talents.

Each task force determined what guidance skills their students needed and then developed a purpose statement for each topic and a three-year comprehensive plan. The time spent on various topics and skills varied with the community and the age group. Homeroom, advisory time, block time, interdisciplinary team time, guidance-based units, community presentations, mentoring, parent volunteers, community service, and flexing the schedule were all ways these schools implemented extended guidance services. Some schools used guidance units that lasted only two days, while others implemented guidance issues into the content area curriculum and trained teachers to use them. Counselors connected teachers to community agencies that could provide information and experiences for the students. Each school defined the job of the advocate and trained teachers in advocacy skills. The plan of each task force included a clear job description of everyone involved, support for training teachers, and a description of the guidance services offered to each grade level. A representative group of students was asked to look at the plan and offer suggestions.

Each task force presented their plan to the faculty, parents, and school board for discussion and support. The need for ongoing assessment of guidance issues and services was apparent to all involved. The process allowed all participants to find the most appropriate services for their students and inspired middle schools to generate new programs and policies to meet their multifaceted needs.

References

Alexander, W., Williams, E. L., Compton, M., & Prescott, D. (1969). *The emergent middle school* (2nd ed.). New York: Holt, Rinehart, and Winston.

Brown, E. (1902). *The making of our middle schools.* New York: Longmans, Green and Co.

Biological Sciences Curriculum Study (BSCS). (2003). *Understanding alcohol: Investigations into biology and behavior.* Colorado Springs, CO: National Institutes of Health.

Cole, C. (1981). *Guidance in the middle school: Everyone's responsibility.* Fairborn, OH: National Middle School Association.

Eichhorn, D. (1966). *The middle school.* New York: Center of Applied Research in Education.

Galassi, J., Gulledge, S., & Cox, N. (1998). *Advisory: Definitions, descriptions, decisions, directions.* Westerville, Ohio: National Middle School Association.

James, M., and Spradling, N. (2001). *From advisory to advocacy: Meeting every student's needs.* Westerville, Ohio. National Middle School Association.

National Middle School Association. (1995). *This we believe: Developmentally responsive middle schools.* Westerville, OH: Author.

National Middle School Association. (2003). *This we believe: Successful schools for young adolescents.* Westerville, OH: Author.

Noar, G. (1961). *Junior high school: Today and tomorrow.* Englewood Cliffs, NJ: Prentice Hall.

Paterson, J. (2004). The changing role of school counselors. *Middle Ground, 8*(1), 42-43.

VanTil, W., Vars, G., & Lounsbury, J. H. (1967). *Modern education for the junior high school years.* (2nd ed.). Indianapolis, IN: The Bobbs-Merrill Co.

In Perspective–After 32 Years of Advocacy, What Have We Learned?

Edward N. Brazee
John H. Lounsbury

The Way It Is

Sally Diaz looked up as she entered the building, and the Grover Middle School sign caught her eye. She wondered how the school would be different from when she was a student at Grover Junior High School 30 years ago. She thought of those days fondly, remembering the ninth grade prom, playing on the basketball and volleyball teams, writing for the yearbook, and singing in the choir. Grover Junior High School had been good for her, but since she became an educator, she often wondered if it had been a good place for all students? Now in her role as educational consultant, she would be able to see what the school with its different name was like.

Having had only a few minutes on the phone with the new principal, Gary Evans, to get a quick rundown on the school, she was anxious to see it firsthand. Gary had received the school board's approval to bring in Sally to help his faculty assess the school. Was it meeting all its stated goals? Was the community satisfied with the quality of education the school provided? Were teachers preparing their students well for life after Grover Middle? Was the school offering the best possible educational experiences for all the young adolescents enrolled?

Six weeks later, having spent considerable time during several visits, Sally knew Grover Middle School inside and out. Like so many other schools since the 1970s, it was clear Grover had taken the name middle school, but little else had changed. Or to be fair, Grover had made some positive strides in the first years after becoming a middle school. Four-teacher interdisciplinary teams with common planning time had been instituted. Also, an advisory program, liked by most students and a few teachers, had been established to help meet the personal-social needs of students. These were heady changes in their time, and faculty members felt they were making changes needed, ones supported by the majority of their colleagues—at the time. But people moved on, and the institutional memory of what and why they were changing—the essentials of the middle school concept—faded, leaving some of the original innovations and their rationales behind.

Sally recognized she had a great deal of work to do, helping this entrenched faculty improve their practices across much of the school; she knew that the contentious part would occur when she asked them—including a few of her former teachers—to reconsider the middle school practices they had kicked around and discarded years ago, never having fully adopted them. How would she help these teachers adopt practices that have been proven to improve student learning, practices such as integrated curriculum, authentic assessment, and small group learning? How could they organize the school to achieve maximum benefit for students? How could Grover's faculty utilize fully the opportunities that teaming provides? Could they move to institute several smaller partner teams wherein students and teachers together plan learning activities?

One thing was clear; every teacher and administrator needed to study, reflect on, and in some cases, rediscover the basic concepts of middle level education. This faculty needed to explore in depth the philosophical questions that undergird the middle school concept. And Ms. Diaz knew that visits to excellent middle level schools should be arranged. The heavily tracked, subject-centered, teacher-directed school she saw in Grover, while supported by a small, but vocal group of teachers and some community members, was sadly out of touch with current research and the full range of the educational and growth needs of its young adolescents.

And while no one had asked students what they thought of the school, the numbers of discipline referrals, suspensions, class tardies, and absences told their own story. Another fact of life at Grover was that very few teachers, parents, or community members were really happy or satisfied with the school in its present form as a retro-junior high school. In fact, the opposite was true. "Keep-

ing the lid on" was an apt descriptor for life at Grover as students, faculty, and administration struggled daily, almost as adversaries. As Mr. Evans said to Ms. Diaz after the first round of the assessment, "There is nowhere to go but up."

The chapter authors in this book, all accomplished veterans, knowledgeable scholars, and strong teachers, have been among that still-growing host who have advocated for young adolescents and middle level education beginning in the 1960s—but not for the limited cosmetic changes made at Grover Middle School. These educators, as we, are convinced that the middle school concept, ***more than ever,*** holds the answer to fully educating 10- to 15-year-olds in a manner that helps them develop as high-achieving learners, and responsible, capable, and productive citizens. To achieve these goals, schools and faculties with the active support of parents and communities must commit to improving middle level schools in long-lasting and educationally sound ways. This task will require everyone with direct responsibility for the education of young adolescents to use what research and cumulative experience tell us as we develop schools that put into practice the vision of *This We Believe: Successful Schools for Young Adolescents* (National Middle School Association, 2003).

The now established research base that supports the validity of the middle school concept is substantial and clear (Backes, Ralston, & Ingwalson, 1999; Felner, Jackson, Kasak, Mulhall, Brand, & Flowers, 1997; Flowers, Mertens, & Mulhall, 2003; Lee & Smith, 1993; Mertens, Flowers, & Mulhall, 1998; Mertens & Flowers, 2003; Picucci, Brownson, Kahlert & Sobel, 2004). The research-based generalization that evolves, simply stated, is: *Those schools that implement the tenets of* This We Believe *faithfully over time report improvements in students' academic achievement and in their overall development as persons.*

Although we know that implementing sound middle school philosophy and practices does make a positive difference for young adolescents whether enrolled in a 6-8, 5-8, or K-8 building, too few schools have implemented the middle school concept consistently, thoughtfully, and yes, aggressively. Middle schools have been in existence for more than 30 years, and there are excellent examples of highly functioning middle schools in every state—schools willing to take risks, to buck the common tide of mediocrity, willing to stick to their beliefs and build academically and personally responsive schools for young adolescents. Schools that, as Joan Lipsitz (1984) said, are "disquieting," because in successful middle level schools it is clear how different these schools are from the rest. But regrettably, there are not nearly enough models. Why? Is the concept faulty?

Some critics have claimed the "middle school" has failed. Not so. The middle school concept has not been practiced and found wanting; rather it has been found difficult to implement fully and practiced then only partially. Because putting the whole concept into operation calls for a number of changes that run counter to long-standing, traditional school practices, ones that lie outside the experiences of all but a handful of educators, the full concept has had difficulty gaining an adequate foothold in most schools. The marked success in achieving the organizational aspects of the middle school, however, has led many to the false conclusion that the middle school concept itself was in force; therefore, lack of improvement in student performance was attributed incorrectly to the concept itself. Jackson and Davis (2000), authors of the widely acclaimed *Turning Points 2000,* refuted the notion of the failure of the middle school while recognizing that "gains in student achievement and other positive outcomes for students require comprehensive implementation of reforms over an extended period of time" (p. 16); they optimistically claimed, "Far from having failed, middle grades education is ripe for a great leap forward" (p. 17). Dickinson (2001), in his definitive book *Reinventing the Middle School* stated emphatically, "There is nothing wrong with the middle school concept. . . . The concept is as valid today as it was in either of its previous iterations at the turn of the 20th century or in the early 1960s." The problem, he says, is that the middle school itself is suffering from "arrested development" (pp. 3-4)—a point well taken.

The middle school concept has not been practiced and found wanting; rather it has been found difficult to implement fully and practiced then only partially.

What Have We Learned in 32 Years of Advocacy?

What lessons have emerged? What problems plague us? What barriers stand in our way? What successes have been recorded? Following are a number of sound generalizations that emerged as we put the development of middle level education in perspective. They provide lessons that will help educators plan for the future.

"The real difficulty in changing the course of any enterprise lies not in developing new ideas but in escaping from old ones."

This statement by John Maynard Keynes is particularly applicable to educational reform. Consider that 80 years ago, prominent educator Harold Rugg (1926) made these rather sobering observations, ones that would still be valid if voiced today:

> Not once in a century and a half of national history has the curriculum of the school caught up with the dynamic content of American life. . . . Partial, superficial, and timorous "revision" rather than general, fundamental, and courageous reconstruction characterizes curriculum-making in the public schools . . . the existing program is always taken as a point of departure. . . . Thus curriculum-making becomes a process of accretion and elimination. There is little, indeed almost no movement under way in public schools to initiate curriculum-making from the starting point either of child learning or of the institutions and problems of American life. For over fifty years, tinkering has characterized the attack on the curriculum. (p. 3)

And so the sound, new ideas advanced by the progressive education movement for the most part have lain dormant. Now in recent decades the middle school movement has revived many of these ideas, moved beyond tinkering, and, indeed, initiated curriculum-making "from the starting point of child learning or of the institutions and problems of American life." But those of us who are passionate middle school champions are, like Rugg, frustrated by not being able to put more of our advocacy into practice.

Why has it been so difficult to understand that fundamental changes, not merely surface level changes, must be made—and then tackle them? An overreliance on those commonly criticized but still entrenched textbooks, teacher-dominated classrooms, and that all-too-prevalent practice of "sorting and selecting"—rather than educating all students to their maximum—are among inappropriate practices that still dominate too many of our schools. Educators and their communities shouldn't "tinker toward utopia" as Cuban and Tyack (1995) said. We have the grand vision of *This We Believe* to guide us in changing the culture of schools, a process that entails exposing the outdated and seldom examined assumptions that underlie traditional practices.

Why has it been so difficult to understand that fundamental changes, not merely surface level changes, must be made—and then tackle them?

It boggles our minds when we realize what a hold on people's thinking the terms *subjects, periods, classes,* and *tests* have. The general public and even educators have trouble envisioning or articulating how formal education might be conducted except by using these containers or terms, and so cannot escape "from old ones." The Alpha team at Shelburne Community School, Vermont, is an excellent example, however, of what can happen when educators break out of these barriers (Kuntz, 2005). Eschewing the routine and the regular, members of that multiage team, which has been in operation for 33 years, tested nearly every "regularity" of school—from periods, to curriculum, to assessment, to what it means to be educated. These pioneer educators realized that the common routines and practices of school did not help young adolescents become real independent learners, whereas alternate ways of organizing for learning would. The Watershed Program (Springer, 1994) in Radnor, Pennsylvania, is another example of what is possible when educators—and students—are freed from the restrictions of classes, periods, and subjects. In such situations the role of the teacher undergoes a basic shift from being an instructor to becoming a facilitator of learning or coach. Reformers need to develop a sense of how effective middle level education can be when, as the popular cliché puts it, we "think outside the box." Today's reform and accountability efforts, however, continue to work in and on schools as they are *currently* organized, when what is needed are serious efforts to make schools *different*, to bring them more in harmony with what we know about learning and human development.

Today's reform efforts continue to work in and on schools as they are currently organized, when what is needed are serious efforts to make schools different.

There is little doubt that the focus in the first decade of the 21st century on student achievement as determined by standardized tests has had a deadening effect on middle level education. However, instead of abandoning efforts to implement the middle school concept because it is difficult and not "politically correct," we must stay the course. Ironically, just as we are fighting regression, middle school ideas such as teaming and advisory are now being adopted by high schools, elementary schools, and even universities, indications of their inherent validity. Schools enrolling the middle grades must continue to serve, without apology, the broad responsibilities that fall on middle level education. Ultimately, the public should come to recognize that success both in future schooling and in life itself will depend not so much on what content has been covered, but rather on what skills, dispositions, and habits of mind have been developed. When the widely accepted goal of academic excellence is examined thoughtfully it really comes down to being as much a matter of skills and attitudes as it is the possession of certain portions of knowledge. And the overemphasis on improving test scores works against developing some of the very attributes needed to succeed in today's society—initiative, teamwork, and the ability to solve problems, organize information, and articulate ideas.

"The whole is greater than the sum of its parts."

This adage, attributed to Aristotle, has become part of our common wisdom. It expresses a truth about the middle school concept, for that educational advocacy encompasses a spirit and a philosophy, which adds a dimension that makes it bigger than all of its organizational and instructional practices put together. All who seek to create a true middle school must be cognizant of this reality. The middle school concept cannot be implemented by initiating a series of separate elements in a non-supportive culture. Early advocates often chose selected middle school elements or characteristics but did little more. Hundreds of middle schools organized interdisciplinary teams and declared victory. Others implemented advisory programs, exploratory experiences, and activity programs, which while responsive to the needs of young adolescents were by themselves incomplete. Far too many schools stopped here, leaving the majority of each school day little changed. In school after school the heart and soul of the middle school concept that has to be played out in curriculum, instruction, and assessment has not been made operational. Nancy Doda (Doda & Thompson, 2002) has described well this incomplete implementation:

The heart and soul of the middle school concept is played out in curriculum, instruction, and assessment.

> Professional development initiatives have far too often been about enticing teachers to use models, means, and methods without inviting them into an examination of the critical philosophical beliefs and assumptions that give those practices educational leverage and value. As a result, some middle schools have remained merely junior high schools with flair. (p. 349)

The 14 *This We Believe* characteristics are not a checklist of items to be implemented one at a time. They constitute an interdependent web of beliefs about education, ones that have to be held by the faculty and staff in successful middle level schools.

"Good is the enemy of great."

This concept (Collins, 2001) can be applied to those many schools that put into practice some middle school characteristics, but stopped short of full and thoughtful implementation; they are good schools, better than they were before carrying out some middle school practices but still not all they could be and should be.

If middle schools are to become great, they must move beyond the easy to achieve structural and organizational aspects. While such changes may be typical in a good middle level school, great middle level schools recognize that such aspects are means not ends, first steps *only* in building a school culture that is responsive to every student and engages each one in learning that is high level, profound, and meaningful. Great middle level schools employ teaming and

If middle schools are to become great, they must move beyond the easy to achieve structural and organizational aspects.

other ways of collaborating—keys to making long-lasting changes, but they do not stop there; traditional four- or five-teacher teams may be replaced by two- or three-teacher teams that reduce significantly the number of different students teachers work with while increasing the time that these teachers spend with that smaller number of students and, therefore, are more able to know them and guide their learning and growing. Curriculum integration is also more likely to occur in smaller teams, some of which may stay together for two or three years through looping or multiage group arrangements.

In great middle level schools, professional development is ongoing, embedded, and meaningful. Teachers, administrators, and students are encouraged to take risks, make mistakes, and be as creative and innovative as possible, heartened by Margaret Mead's observation: "The most extraordinary thing about a really good teacher is that he or she transcends accepted educational methods."

The ultimate goal is always improved student learning. Such learning extends beyond a narrow test-determined goal of academic achievement and includes preparing young adolescents for a rich and fulfilling life. The vision of a committed staff is ever-present in such schools and is evident in their practice and policies—a yardstick used by everyone, every day.

"Middle schools too often counter Mother Nature."

Most organizational practices in education are bereft of any research to justify their continued existence.

The almost universally employed organizational practices of grouping by chronological age, having periods of 45 to 50 minutes, and class sizes of approximately 25 to 30 students, are bereft of any research to justify their continued existence. That condition is seldom recognized. And at the middle level these practices increasingly run counter to the nature of young adolescents who are rapidly changing and maturing physically, socially, emotionally, morally, and intellectually. Continuing to organize and operate as if 10- to 15-year-olds were still children, school practices regularly conflict with human development. Curricula are planned for groups rather than individuals; yet young adolescents are distinguished by the degree they differ, making one lesson for all seldom appropriate. While it may be justifiable at the elementary level to have largely teacher-directed classrooms in which a prescribed curriculum is covered, continuing such practices with middle grades youth further institutionalizes passive learning and hinders teachers in meeting young adolescents' *intellectual* needs.

Mother Nature provides, at this key transition time of life, a golden opportunity to take learning to a higher level, to move beyond rote learning, to challenge students intellectually, and to engage them actively in the teaching-learning enterprise. They are ripe at this age for being drawn into their education in new and more meaningful ways. Young adolescents are capable of learning and achieving at levels seldom realized. Although individual differences continue to be in evidence, we know that sometime during the middle level years students reach a level of mental maturity that permits them to be analytical, to question, to hypothesize. To bring this new mental prowess into bloom, teachers need to prod, entice, even cajole students, not simply "cover" content. As Ted Sizer has reminded us, "School isn't about old folks donating ideas to young folks. It is about young folks learning on their own and being provoked by old folks."

Mother Nature provides a golden opportunity to take learning to a higher level, to move beyond rote learning, to challenge students intellectually, and to engage them actively.

In addition, young adolescents seek increased independence and responsibilities, desirable traits the school should foster not thwart. Schools, however, continue to approach education as something done to students—when the innate, intrinsic desire to learn and students' heightened curiosity could readily be tapped. Yet the chance to exploit the possibilities for reflective thinking and engaged learning is not only ignored, it is directly countered all too often when schools underestimate the potential of young adolescents and follow tightly prescribed curricula.

"We learn what we live, and we learn it to the degree that we live it."

This maxim enunciated long ago by the famous progressive teacher and philosopher William Heard Kilpatrick is most appropriate for middle level education. In these days of politically initiated educational reform that focuses on prescribing a curriculum that will, presumably, yield higher test scores, we often overlook the fact that the school itself is a powerful teacher, presenting its lessons silently but surely. The middle school is not and cannot be just a physical place where teachers conduct classes; it is an environment in which youth come of age, acting out new roles as maturing social beings. The middle school is not a teaching factory, but a laboratory of living, not just a learning place, but a growing place.

The middle school is not a teaching factory, but a laboratory of living, not just a learning place, but a growing place.

Many of the accepted objectives of education, in fact, the ones most likely to be in play in one's daily life in the years ahead cannot be taught by direct instruction; they have to grow incrementally from multiple experiences. And more often than not those lessons that last a lifetime are by-products of a positive relationship between teacher and student. There is, then, real danger if we let the mission of the middle school become too small, too narrow. The middle school must not marginalize the development of those traits and dispositions required for a meaningful and productive life. While the academic achievement mission is central, the effective middle school has to be bigger than that. Its mission also calls for a school that deals openly and directly with character education, ethics, values, and self-concepts. It is particularly harmful if middle schools become too narrow in focus, since young adolescents are going through that period of life when they are deciding for themselves what they believe in, what they might aspire to be, and what attitudes and dispositions will guide their behavior. These are all facets of an education that students will encounter and make decisions about during the middle level years—with or without the help of schools and teachers. Character is neither inherited nor learned in the usual sense of the word; rather it is acquired gradually by the cumulative effect of many thoughts, actions, and experiences. Middle level teachers, next to parents, are often the significant others whose modeling makes the biggest difference. Somehow we must help the public grasp a bigger and better vision of what constitutes an "education" and recognize the importance of the teacher as a person and as a model. Conventional wisdom about young adolescents and the critical lifelong influence of the educational experiences they encounter still lag.

An education in its fullest sense has to involve heart as well as head, attitude as well as information, spirit as well as scholarship, and conscience as well as competence.

Our nation's problems, when one thinks about it, are, with rare exceptions, the result of consciously chosen behaviors of individuals. And all education ultimately, is directed toward changing behavior. Middle schools must exert the influence on behavior that, by the nature of young adolescents, they are uniquely suited to yield. Inescapably, middle school teaching is a moral enterprise, and an education in its fullest sense has to involve heart as well as head, attitude as well as information, spirit as well as scholarship, and conscience as well as competence.

If middle schools do not fulfill their rightful role in developing ethical, responsible, self-motivated, thinking individuals, they will have failed at what ultimately is their most important responsibility. Middle schools simply must be concerned about what students are becoming not just about what test scores they are making. We should all consider carefully the serious point made by Mark Twain when he joked, "I never let my schooling interfere with my education"; for it appears schools are so emphasizing the limited informational aspects of an education that they are neglecting the critical behavioral ones.

We need middle schools with missions big enough to help youngsters decide what to read as well as simply how to read. Big enough to ensure that their mastery of mathematics will not be applied in an embezzlement scheme. Big enough to recognize their history lessons apply to their futures as well as to the past. John

Ruskin put it thus: "Education does not mean teaching people to know what they do not know. It means teaching them to behave as they do not behave." And Teddy Roosevelt warned: "To educate a person in mind and not in morals is to educate a menace to society."

Looking Ahead

In 1982, the original *This We Believe* set forth a vision of middle level education that became the foundation for the ideas expressed in later editions and in this volume. The successful practices you see in the accompanying DVD are outgrowths of that vision. In 1989, the Carnegie Corporation's influential report, *Turning Points: Preparing American Youth for the 21st Century,* called middle level education "the last best chance" for young adolescents and recommended changes that were very much in line with the vision of *This We Believe*. Guided by such visions we have made marked progress in the intervening years, but we still have a very long way to go before common practices reflect this vision of how young adolescents can be well served during these challenging middle years of schooling.

Not long after we have moved beyond the current narrow definition of educational excellence and the related testing mania has abated, we will look back with disbelief and wonder why we continued practices so out of line with what we know about young adolescents and the principles of learning. We are confident that the middle school concept will be the standard as schools strive to provide the full and meaningful education every 10- to 15-year-old deserves. We believe the middle school concept is, indeed, the conscience of American education and will prevail.

As you read, re-read, and reflect on the chapters in *This We Believe in Action,* and as you watch examples from these successful schools, begin to visualize how your school would look if you took the initiative to implement such a vision. Imagine what your school would be like

- If each student were held to high expectations and passionately engaged in learning.
- If each student had opportunities to pose and answer in-depth questions about world and personal issues.
- If each student had an active adult advocate who knew that student well.
- If technology were effectively used by both teachers and students to support learning.
- If all parents felt supported and they in turn supported the work of the school.

- If students evaluated their own work and there were no competitive grades.
- If the curriculum were intellectually stimulating and viewed by students as worth learning.
- If democracy were not just studied but practiced.
- If learning activities were focused on the skills and dispositions needed for a productive life as much as on the content.
- If the school were truly responsive to the educational and developmental needs of each and every student.

We believe the middle school concept will become more widely accepted in the hearts and minds of untold numbers of educators who come to grasp the good sense and the research-based validity of the vision set forth in *This We Believe*. As the limitations and negative effects of educational reform by tests and sanctions become ever more apparent, and as further examples of marked success by middle grades schools that pursue vigorously this vision become known, the middle level movement will experience dramatic new acceptance.

The Way It Could Be

Maria hoisted her backpack as she walked up the steps of Worthington Middle School. The new 8:45 a.m. start was a great relief and she now actually came to school feeling rested on most days. Last year in sixth grade, her school day started at 7:35 a.m., and she began every day feeling tired.

Today she was 15 minutes early because she and two of her classmates, Jessica and Manuel, needed one last tryout of a presentation they were to make later in the morning. They had worked for over a month on a feasibility study for a new senior citizens' center, collecting information about the economic, environmental, and cultural impacts of such a center on their small town.

As a part of this rigorous service learning project which drew on all the major subject areas as well as the arts and humanities, they met with two builders, the town manager and town council, and many citizens of various ages. Much of their work was done electronically on laptop computers which were used all day as they took notes, wrote their initial and subsequent drafts of position papers, and logged into several databases to track the data they collected. Using the Internet to find other towns that had built similar senior citizens' centers in Arizona, Florida, and Ohio, was invaluable. Middle school students in each of those states contributed to the project by collecting and sending essential information to Maria and her research group that was later incorporated into the final report.

As she mentally clicked down the list of key points for the presentation, Maria was excited but more nervous when she discovered that the review board hearing their presentation would include the town manager from a neighboring town, the director of the gerontology program at the university, a contractor for the project, and a vice-president of the local bank. Yet, she was proud of the work her group had done and was anxious to hear the board's response.

Jessica and Manuel were waiting for Maria. Several other students were also in the room working quietly, reading, or logging into their laptops to check e-mail or to join one of several continuing discussions about various school projects. This large, open room had been the home for the team and two teachers for the last two years. It was carpeted, comfortable, warm, and inviting, with tables and chairs, a couch and several lounge chairs, books everywhere, and student work prominently displayed. Two students were talking on cell phones, collecting information for their own projects.

In fact it was difficult for someone new to this school to recognize the official beginning of the school day. With the late start, all teachers had this common planning time every day where they meet to talk about projects underway, conduct parent conferences, or work with individuals or small groups of students. A recent visitor to the school noted that the atmosphere of every room in the building was purposeful, unhurried, focused, and intent. It looked and sounded like a well-run laboratory with highly qualified people enjoying both their work and each other.

As their final task, the three students checked their well-worn copies of the state standards to make sure they had included the English-language arts performance indicators on "stylistic and rhetorical aspects of reading and writing" in their handouts. Their report would present a detailed plan for creating a senior citizens' center with specific timelines and areas of responsibility. This report would clearly illustrate how they had used a variety of skills by drawing content from various academic areas—all of which built a positive attitude about what they had learned doing this project.

Pleased with their work and plan, but still anxious about the upcoming public presentation, they placed their laptops, notebooks, and papers on their own desks and moved to the center of the room where they joined their 38 classmates and two teachers for opening ceremonies.

Another day of good learning and growing begins at Worthington Middle School.

References

Backes, J., Ralston, A., & Ingwalson, G. (1999). Middle level reform: The impact on student achievement. *Research in Middle Level Education Quarterly, 22*(3), 43-57.

Carnegie Council on Adolescent Development. (1989). *Turning points: Preparing American youth for the 21st century.* New York: Carnegie Corporation.

Collins, J. (2001). *Good to great*. New York: Harper Collins Publishers.

Cuban, L., & Tyack, D. (1995). *Tinkering toward utopia*. Cambridge, MA: Howard University Press.

Dickinson, T. (2001). *Reinventing the middle school*. New York: RoutledgeFalmer.

Doda, N., & Thompson, S. (Eds.). (2002). *Transforming ourselves, transforming schools: Middle school change*. Westerville, OH: National Middle School Association.

Jackson, A., & Davis, G. (2000). *Turning points 2000: Educating adolescents for the 21st century.* New York: Teachers College Press and Westerville, OH: National Middle School Association.

Felner, R., Jackson, A., Kasak, D., Mulhall, P., Brand, S., & Flowers, N. (1997). The impact of school reform for the middle grades. In R. Takanishi & D. A. Hamburg (Eds.), *Preparing adolescents for the twenty-first century: Challenges facing Europe and the United States* (pp. 38-69). Cambridge, UK: Cambridge University Press.

Flowers, N., Mertens, S., & Mulhall, P. (2003). Lessons learned from more than a decade of middle grades research. *Middle School Journal, 35*(2), 55-59.

Kuntz. S. (2005). *The story of Alpha: A multiage, student-centered team—33 years and counting*. Westerville, OH: National Middle School Association.

Lee, V.E., & Smith, J.B. (1993). Effects of school restructuring on the achievement and engagement of middle-grade students. *Sociology of Education, 66*(3), 164-187.

Lipsitz, J. (1984). Successful schools for young adolescents. New Brunswick, NJ: Transaction Publishers.

Mertens, S.B., & Flowers, N. (2003). Middle school practices improve student achievement in high poverty schools. *Middle School Journal, 35*(1), 33-43.

Mertens, S. B., Flowers, N., & Mulhall, P. (1998). *The middle start initiative, phase I: A longitudinal analysis of Michigan middle-level schools.* (A report to the W. K. Kellogg Foundation). Urbana, IL: University of Illinois. Retrieved April 30, 2005,, from http://222.cprd.uiuc.edu

National Middle School Association. (2003). *This we believe: Successful schools for young adolescents*. Westerville, OH: Author.

Picucci, A.C., Brownson, A., Kahlert, R., & Sober, A. (2004). Middle school concept helps high-poverty schools become high-performing schools. *Middle School Journal, 36*(1), 4-11.

Rugg, H. (1926). *Curriculum-making: Past and present, twenty-sixth yearbook of N.S.S.E.* Chicago: National Society for the Study of Education.

Springer, M. (1994). *Watershed: A successful voyage into integrative learning*. Columbus, OH: National Middle School Association.

Authors

by order of appearance in this publication

Thomas O. Erb, professor emeritus at the University of Kansas, is Elizabeth P. Allen Distinguished University Professor of Education Studies at DePauw University, Greencastle, Indiana, and editor of *Middle School Journal.*

C. Kenneth McEwin, a Lounsbury Award winner, is professor of education at Appalachian State University, Boone, North Carolina.

Thomas S. Dickinson, former editor of *Middle School Journal*, is professor of education studies at DePauw University, Greencastle, Indiana.

Patti Kinney is principal of Talent Middle School, Talent, Oregon, and president of National Middle School Association in 2005-2006.

Linda Robinson, educational consultant, is past president of National Middle School Association and recently retired as principal of Alvin Junior High School, Lee, Texas.

Sue Swaim is executive director of National Middle School Association, Westerville, Ohio.

Marion Johnson Payne, educational consultant with The Principals' Partnership, is a former principal and resides in Hilton Head Island, South Carolina.

Candy Beal is associate professor of education at North Carolina State University, Raleigh.

John Arnold is professor emeritus of education at North Carolina State University, now residing in Pinehurst, North Carolina.

Gert Nesin is clinical instructor in education at the University of Maine, Orono.

Ross M. Burkhardt, a former teacher at Shoreham-Wading River Middle School (New York) and a past president of National Middle School Association, is an educational consultant in Las Cruces, New Mexico.

J. Thomas Kane, educational consultant, is the retired principal of Holdrum Middle School in River Vale, New Jersey.

Joyce L. Epstein is the director of the Center on School, Family, and Community Partnerships and the National Network of Partnership Schools and a research professor of sociology at Johns Hopkins University, Baltimore, Maryland.

Chris Stevenson is professor emeritus of education at the University of Vermont, now residing in Pinehurst, North Carolina.

Penny A. Bishop is assistant professor of education at the University of Vermont, Burlington.

Barbara L. Brodhagen is learning coordinator and a teacher at Sherman Middle School, Madison, Wisconsin.

Susan Gorud is a teacher at Sherman Middle School, Madison, Wisconsin.

Sue C. Thompson, a former middle school principal and director of middle grades education, is associate professor of education at the University of Missouri, Kansas City.

Dan French is executive director of the Center for Collaborative Education, Boston, Massachusetts.

Deborah Kasak is executive director of the National Forum to Accelerate Middle-Grades Reform, residing in Champaign, Illinois.

Ericka Uskali is assistant executive director of the Association of Illinois Middle Level Schools, Champaign, Illinois.

Jean Schultz is coordinated school health specialist at National Middle School Association, residing in Sacramento, California.

Sherrel Bergmann, a Lounsbury Award Winner, is a middle school consultant retired from National Louis University, now residing in Charlevoix, Michigan.

Edward N. Brazee is professor of education at the University of Maine, Orono, and professional publications editor for National Middle School Association.

John H. Lounsbury, the first Lounsbury Award winner and former editor of *Middle School Journal* is a former dean of education and professor emeritus at Georgia College & State University, Milledgeville, as well as consulting editor for National Middle School Association.